THE WORLD NATURALIST

The Natural History of Trees

THE WORLD NATURALIST
Editor: L. Harrison Matthews

The Natural History of Trees

Herbert L. Edlin

Weidenfeld and Nicolson
London

Weidenfeld and Nicolson
11 St John's Hill London SW11

ISBN 0 297 77129 9

Printed in Great Britain by
Cox & Wyman Ltd
London, Fakenham and Reading

For
David and Joanne

Contents

Plates

Acknowledgements
The author provided photographs for the plates, with exceptions noted below: Plate 4 by Robert Beard; Plate 5 reproduced by permission of the Director, Royal Botanic Gardens, Kew; Plate 30 by George Dey; Plate 39 by Dr Graham Edlin.

Figures

Acknowledgements

Most of the figures in the text were drawn by Christine Darter from sketches provided by the author. Source material was kindly made available by: Mr L. W. Newman, Figure 1; The Forestry Commission of Great Britain, Figures 5, 6 and 7; University of Michigan Press, Figure 16; Messrs Collins, London, Figure 17.

Introduction

AT THE dawn of this twentieth century men suddenly realized that their relationship with the trees around them is a finite one. Traditional beliefs in limitless natural forests, holding inexhaustible reserves of commercial timber, yet ready to renew themselves unaided once the logger had laid his axe to the virgin stands, took a rude jolt. Developments in machinery and communications meant that man could now overcut world timber reserves, just as he could overkill the world's limited resources of fish or game. Economists assure us that nothing has value so long as it is available, like fresh air, in unlimited amounts at no cost. Wood, and the trees that produce it, acquired fresh worth as soon as they represented a limited source of supply.

Along with this practical assessment of wood as an industrial resource came a re-appraisal of what can be broadly called the cultural value of living trees and woods. People enjoy having trees around them. Trees give shelter from wind, rain, snow and burning sunshine. Their grace of form, and seasonal renewal of fresh green foliage, often enlivened by gay flowers, provide welcome scenery, and offset the hard lines of man-made buildings. On the larger scale, forests create majestic landscapes, especially where they surround lakes or spread over mountainsides. They also provide habitats for remarkable wild flowers, beasts and birds that would perish if the woods disappeared.

Woods appeal to our wanderlust. Any forest track demands exploration. Recreations of many kinds, from hunting and cross-country running to painting, photography or watching wildlife, add an appreciation of life that we can never gain from a treeless countryside.

The key-word in the new approach to trees and forests is *conservation*. Man now regards himself as the custodian of living individual trees that have a life-span comparable with his own – though some far exceed it. Forests, of which these trees form a part, may have taken thousands of years to develop their present character and grandeur, though some are recent creations, owing everything to human planning, foresight, and skill. Both kinds demand a long forward look if they are to survive as a heritage from the past for our successors to enjoy.

The critical date in this change of outlook is the year 1905 when, under the sponsorship of President Theodore Roosevelt, the American Forest Service was created, under Gifford Pinchot, to take charge of national forests, now extending to 180 million acres. In the same year the teaching of forestry in Britain gained an academic standing, at both Edinburgh and Oxford Universities. This started a train of events which led on to the formation of a national Forestry Commission in 1919, and the planting of two million acres of bare land over the next sixty-seven years. This exceptional achievement was promoted by an Australian forester, Roy Lister Robinson, and was rightly recognized by his eventual elevation to the peerage as Lord Robinson of Kielder Forest and Adelaide.

Both the American and the British pioneers owed a great deal to earlier teaching in France and Germany, where a respect for the forest as an element of the environment, as well as a source of commercial timber, had survived the cut-throat economics of the nineteenth century and its Industrial Revolution. Sir William Schlich, a German forester who carried Continental conservation practices into the Indian Forest Service, and later became the first forestry professor at Oxford, was a leading figure in the spread of this tradition through the English-speaking world.

I have constructed this book in the pattern of the classic Continental teachers, who insisted that every student knew how a tree grew up before they let him cut one down. The concept of a botanist with a bulldozer, besides his accustomed microscope, may seem bizarre, but it fits the modern forester. The microscope will tell him what to plant, the bulldozer and its allies, the plough and the grab, will build his roads, cultivate his land, and harvest his timber. If his plans are well conceived on a sound scientific basis, his forests will flourish and remain profitable. But if he proceeds without such guidance they will quickly dwindle under the impact of modern high-speed, high-powered technology.

In our first section, entitled 'Life Pattern, Structure and Function', we look through the botanist's eye at a tree as an organism that deserves study in its own right. Like all plants, it is nourished by soil, water, and the carbon dioxide carried by the air, aided by oxygen and the energy of sunlight. It differs from lesser plants in the remarkable provisions it shows for growth that continues, through annual and seasonal rhythms, for long spans of years, till it attains great size. Every development from the small seed onwards prepares the way for this continued expansion. Lavish provision for the individual's eventual replacement is made by complex processes of flowering and fruiting, repeated annually.

But as a forester by profession, I always feel that the trees I tend are different from those I studied in the botanical textbooks or examined beneath the microscope in the university laboratory. Mine are alive! They thrust shoots into the moving air and roots into the deep moist soil. They have flexible trunks and slender branches that sway in the wind as they resist its wildest gusts. They are sometimes hot and sometimes frozen, but always thirsty. Their buds open with bewildering speed to release shoots, leaves or flowers that quickly mature into seed-bearing fruits. Even their inner timber is continually maturing to heartwood, different in character from the sapwood around it, while their bark shows fascinating changes as it ages.

The academic botanist can, and on occasion must, examine the tree and its structure in isolation from its environment. To me, as an actual grower, his precise findings have no reality once they become divorced from their surroundings. A bent stem spells out the work of the wind, an expanding leaf becomes green only in response to sunlight, and the magnificent flower spike of the horse chestnut has no significance – except as a thing of beauty – unless it attracts the buzzing, pollen-bearing bee that promotes the development of its seed.

This approach leads on to the book's second part, called 'Ecology and Environmental Relationships'. Here the trees are first considered as members of communities of their own and allied kinds. The increasing size and long life-span of each individual tree causes interactions with its neighbours that are rarely encountered so forcefully among smaller, shorter-lived plants. Soil, climate and weather influence the growth of forests. But each is, in turn, modified by its association with the forest complex.

In the book's third part, 'The World's Forests', we review the subject geographically. In response to varied climates, forests of different characters have developed in the cold north and south, the hot and humid equatorial lands, and even over the sun-baked territories that lie between these extremes. In many regions these tree-clad lands are vital for the conservation of soil and water resources, and as refuges for wildlife. But they are everywhere under threat. Improved communications have opened them up for exploitation that may be followed by the destruction of the fertility of whole countrysides. Intensive ecological studies are needed before any natural forests are sacrificed to short-term needs, however pressing the immediate demands for timber, cash, or fresh agricultural land may be. Yet wise management for sustained yields of all that the forest can provide –

timber, water, shelter and recreation, may enable them to remain perpetual assets to the nations that own them.

Men work with trees in many ways and these are outlined in Part IV, 'Trees in the Service of Man'. Some – the nurserymen – raise them from seed or cuttings for others to tend later on. Others, the arboriculturists, grow them as things of beauty to ornament a garden, park or highway. Orchardists tend them as sources of fruit and nuts, in crops repeated annually over long spans of years. The timber merchant and the paper-maker see them primarily as raw material for their factories, though nowadays both have an eye to sustained supplies from perpetual forests, to match the large scale and substantial capital value of their factories.

This brings us round again to the individual tree. An ancient proverb assures us that 'The creation of a thousand forests is one acorn'. Every effective forester, fruit-grower, nurseryman and arboriculturist works in terms of hundreds, thousands, and even millions of trees. The sawmiller calculates his effort by daily throughputs of thousands of cubic metres or board-feet of lumber, while the paper-maker does his sums in millions of tons. But the basis of every plan, affecting the livelihood and standard of living of scores of thousands of men, is the single tree, anchored to the ground by a solitary roothold, and leading its intricate life by virtue of its place in the sun, its claim on the refreshing rain. From my window, perched on a hilltop overlooking a broad basin in the Surrey hills, I can survey ten thousand trees. Each has its own fascinating natural history, its particular relationship with the men who own and tend it. So it goes for all the seedlings, saplings and tall timber trees in all the forests, orchards, streets and gardens of the world.

Note: All conversions from metric to Imperial measure units are approximate to the nearest appropriate round figure

Part 1

Life Pattern, Structure and Function

Chapter 1

A Tree's Life Pattern

A TREE is a land plant that develops a woody perennial stem and also, wherever circumstances permit, a single erect main stem called the tree trunk. These properties, providing strength, long life and a purposeful direction of growth, enable a tree to grow larger than other land plants, such as herbs and shrubs. Plates 3, 41 and 61 illustrate woody stems in this context. There are no other definitive characteristics. Curiously, the tree habit is found in many botanical families that also include non-woody plants, though certain families consist exclusively of trees and shrubs.

Because of their variety, long life span and enormous increase in *size* from seed to maturity, any study of trees calls for a different approach to that of smaller and shorter-lived plants. We must consider the occupation of increasing space, with the physical problems it brings, and changes in character over a term of at least a century.

The Seed

As a starting point I select a tree that I observe as I write, a European ash, *Fraxinus excelsior*, flourishing above a hedge that divides two gardens. Fifty years ago it started its independent existence as a seed blown from a parent tree on a farm in a valley half a mile away. It consisted of a brown oval grain about 10 millimetres long attached to a brown papery wing extending to about 20 millimetres. It weighed only 10 milligrammes. As it flew through the air its chance of survival to tree size was about one in a million. The vast majority of its associated seeds fell on farm land where if they sprouted at all the resultant seedlings were ploughed into the soil or else eaten by grazing sheep. This fortunate seed, aided by its wing, was carried by a fierce autumn gale to a new housing estate where it alighted at the base of a newly-planted hawthorn hedge. Nobody noticed it so nobody later on pulled up the resultant seedling as a weed. Trees can only establish themselves naturally where there is continuing

5

protection from cultivation, grazing and the diligent attention of tidy gardeners! Plate 1 shows a mature ash tree, Plate 7 its seed.

For eighteen months nothing happened. Ash seed, in common with that of many other trees, has the strange property of *dormancy*. It will not sprout until it has passed through the cold of two winters.

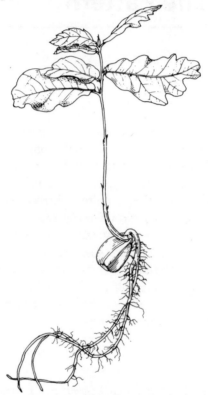

Figure 1   Seedling of pedunculate oak, *Quercus robur*, after six months growth. In this species the two seed-leaves (cotyledons) remain in the seed (hypogeal germination). Note root, root-hairs, leaves and terminal bud. Shoot is 15 centimetres (6 inches) long, root 12·5 centimetres (5 inches) long.

The Seedling

Under the warmth of the second spring after it ripened on the parent tree, the seed drew in moisture from the soil through its absorbent husk. Growth then began with the appearance of a root from the embryo tree hidden within the seed. Actively dividing organic cells at the pointed root tip moved this tip out through a crack in the husk and it promptly turned downwards under the influence of gravity to enter the soil. This contact with the ground, achieved within about three weeks of first germination, is destined to remain fixed for the tree's lifetime of a hundred years or more, with the remnants of the first seedling root below the centre of the tree's stout trunk. Already the root had begun to carry out one of its primary functions, the anchorage of the future tree firmly to the ground.

Within a few days the tiny root sent out fine root hairs. These are short-lived structures that penetrate for a season or two the tiny gaps between the grains of soil. They draw in moisture and so begin the second major function of every tree root system, namely, the supply of water – essential for all life – to the organism as a whole. This flow of water in the form of ascending root sap will continue throughout the whole of the tree's life, moving rapidly in spring and summer but falling to a minimal rate during the cold winter resting season. Each root hair endures only for a matter of months, then it dies and is replaced by others.

The upward current of water from the soil is never pure but carries with it in solution minute amounts of mineral salts. This is a handy term for soluble compounds of elements essential for plant life. The full list is a long one. Nitrogen, phosphorus and potassium are the best known because they are the ones most often supplied in fertilizers to aid tree growth. Equally vital though usually naturally present in adequate quantities are silicon, calcium, iron, magnesium, sulphur, sodium, copper, manganese, chlorine, zinc and boron.

The very small amount of minerals needed to sustain a tree's life becomes evident when you look at the little pile of ash left after a big log is burnt. All the soil nutrients except water and volatile nitrogen are represented there. Yet the whole weight of the mineral ash is less than 1 % of that of the log. Nevertheless no tree can grow on pure water. Minerals must be available both as catalysts and as ingredients of its living substance.

To stress the essential functions of the root, which continue throughout the life of the tree, let us consider what happens if they fail. If the root no longer supplies water the tree dies of drought. If it cannot secure enough mineral salts the tree remains a stunted bush for all its life. If root-hold fails the tree falls. This is a common occurrence when a great gale sweeps the land, as roots are more likely than tree trunks to break under exceptional strain.

The ash seedling, now firmly anchored and supplied with water and mineral elements by its small root, next began to develop its shoot. The soft white stem became turgid with moisture and started to bend at the critical point where it entered the soil. Within a few days it turned under the influence of gravity, which guides cell internal growth directionally against the pull of the earth, and sunlight, which attracts it from a flat

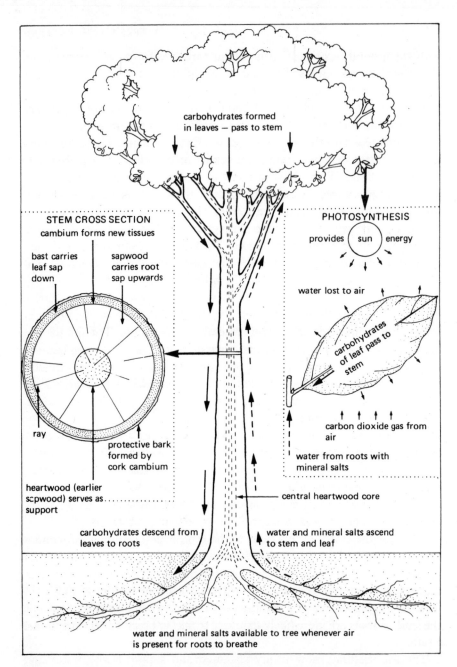

STEM CROSS SECTION
cambium forms new tissues

bast carries leaf sap down

sapwood carries root sap upwards

ray

protective bark formed by cork cambium

heartwood (earlier sapwood) serves as.............. support

carbohydrates descend from leaves to roots

carbohydrates formed in leaves — pass to stem

PHOTOSYNTHESIS

provides (sun) energy

water lost to air

carbohydrates of leaf pass to stem

carbon dioxide gas from air

water from roots with mineral salts

central heartwood core

water and mineral salts ascend to stem and leaf

water and mineral salts available to tree whenever air is present for roots to breathe

Figure 2   Nutrition and sap circulation. Water, carrying mineral salts from soil, ascends sapwood of tree trunk, where most is transpired to the atmosphere. Sunlight energy enables moist leaves to win carbon compounds from surrounding air. These travel in soluble form through the bast, just below the bark, to all parts of the tree. Rays carry nutrients horizontally through the wood and also store them.

8

position to an upright one. As a rule the stem lifts the seed coat with it but this is already split and it soon falls away. From within the husk two seed-leaves, or cotyledons, now expanded. These seed-leaves were unlike any that the ash would bear later. They were oblong in shape with smooth edges. During the seed's resting phase or dormancy they were white in colour and held most of the future seedling's store of nourishment. They now turned green and began the leaf's main function of winning carbon compounds from the atmosphere.

Basic Life Processes

The green colour of the seed-leaves is due to chlorophyll. The name tells us little as it is simply Greek for 'green of the leaf', but chlorophyll is the key chemical on which all the earth's life, both plant and animal, ultimately depends. It is a highly complex compound of carbon, oxygen, nitrogen, iron and magnesium, and all these elements are essential for plant life. Under the right conditions the chlorophyll present in the cells of every living leaf can 'fix' carbon, always present as carbon dioxide gas in the air, as solid carbon compounds that the tree can use for energy and growth. The process is called *photosynthesis*, meaning 'building-up by light'.

A basic requirement for photosynthesis is an adequate supply of *sunlight* which alone gives the input of energy that the process needs. Photosynthesis can only take place in daylight and ceases each night. Throughout the tree's career its light supply will affect the whole pattern of its growth. Every leaf will be positioned to receive sunlight. When as a result of outward growth a leaf-bearing shoot becomes overshaded it will die and fall away. If the whole tree becomes overshaded by competitors the whole tree will die. Foresters class ash as a 'light-demander', which means that by comparison with 'shade-bearers' such as beech and spruce, it can tolerate very little overshading.

Another requirement for photosynthesis is the presence of abundant water. This, we have seen, is provided by the tree's root system. Because the cells of the leaf blade must have channels available for the free passage of air, the water supplied by the root system is constantly evaporating from the leaves. In the botanical scheme of things this process is given the name of *transpiration*. The stream of root sap brings with it another essential, the dissolved mineral salts mentioned above.

A large volume of water must pass through a thin leaf like that of ash but provided the soil is both moist and warm enough the roots can supply it. In winter when the ground becomes too cold for the process of root absorption, and may be actually frozen, the supply to the leaves is insufficient. Therefore each autumn the leaves of ash fade and fall. Otherwise the tree would die from drought through losing moisture that it could not replace. Evergreen trees, which retain their leaves, either grow in constantly hot, wet climates such as the tropical rain forests or else bear foliage that is specially modified to retain water and resist its loss to the air: holly leaves and pine needles are good examples of the latter.

A further essential for photosynthesis is the availability of carbon dioxide gas, CO_2. This is always present in the air as a minute proportion averaging 0·03% of the whole. As a steady flow of air passes through the leaf the carbon dioxide is made to combine with an equivalent amount of water to produce glucose sugar, a soluble *carbohydrate* compound. Though the actual process performed by the chlorophyll is complex it may be expressed in simplified form by the equation:

$$6\ CO_2 + 12\ H_2O + light \longrightarrow C_6H_{12}O_6 + 6\ O_2 + 6\ H_2O$$

carbon   water   glucose   oxygen water
dioxide

The seedling ash tree now had a continuing supply of soluble and therefore mobile carbon compounds which it could use in two ways, for growth and to provide energy for life. It was no longer dependent on the food reserves locked in the seed but could develop its own almost unlimited supply by converting the glucose it derived from air and water with the aid of light energy. These carbon compounds are built up by elaborate chemistry into all the varied tissues of a living tree – wood, bark, leaves, roots, flowers and to complete the life cycle the seeds that will one day enable successor trees to repeat the process.

All this creation of new materials requires the presence of water and the materials created incorporate varying proportions of the 'mineral' elements in the water supplied by the soil, particularly nitrogen.

The creation, or synthesis, of the carbon compounds also involves the consumption of energy. In fact all the tree's life processes other than the photosynthesis of the glucose itself, consume energy that the tree must supply from its own resources. One constant and considerable need is fuel for the transport of large volumes of root sap up the stem, which is offset to only a small degree by the counter current of leaf sap downwards. This energy is provided by *breathing*, a process carried out in all parts of the tree, both in sunlight and darkness. It is chemically similar to the breathing of animals but proceeds at a lower temperature. Trees, however, need no lungs for breathing is spread through all their tissues. It follows that if any part of a tree is deprived of air and therefore of oxygen it can no longer function and must perish. A common example is the death of a tall tree after the land on which it has grown up has become waterlogged.

The basic equation for breathing is:

$$C \;+\; O_2 \;=\; CO_2 \;+\; \text{energy}$$
$$\text{carbon} \quad \text{oxygen} \quad \text{carbon dioxide}$$

or in words, carbon plus oxygen becomes carbon dioxide gas with the liberation of energy. The amount of carbon dioxide returned by the tree to the air overall must of course be less than that taken in for photosynthesis or growth will cease.

The next stage in the development of the ash seedling in the hedge was the growth of a short upright shoot which sprang from a bud between the seed-leaves. After a few weeks of growth it expanded two 'juvenile leaves', each with an oval outline and a pointed tip. They bore no close resemblance to the familiar compound ash leaf, composed of many leaflets along a central stalk. Such a-typical or juvenile leaves are found on many trees and are held to represent an earlier stage in their evolutionary pattern. Later on the young ash bore leaves with three leaflets, then five, working up gradually to the normal quota of nine or so.

A common feature of all these ash leaves is that they are set in opposite pairs, whereas those of a beech are borne singly. Leaf arrangement is a valuable aid to tree identification.

As the days grew shorter and the weather got colder, the few leaves on the seedling ash prepared for winter. They ceased to expand and sent down their last minute supply of carbon compounds into the little stem and root, where they were stored through the colder months. The green chlorophyll broke down and the leaves faded to drab brown. At the base of each leaf-stalk a protective waterproof layer of cork, called the abscission or cutting-off layer, developed. The faded leaves fell in autumn, either torn off at this point by the wind, or else forced off by frost expanding the moisture held outside the abscission layer. This explains the rapid fall of leaves in an autumn thaw; the frost holds the stalk through the night and next morning the sun melts the icy layer and releases the stalk.

In each successive autumn the leaves fell to the ground and slowly decomposed to form humus. Ash leaves, though not their stalks, are often eaten by earthworms. Minute mites and fungi also play a part in leaf breakdown. Whatever the channel of decay the minerals held in the leaf are eventually returned to the soil to be recovered in due course by the roots. This cycle of mineral nutrients is important for the continued life of the tree. It fertilizes its own land by returning essential elements for re-use.

A deciduous tree like an ash does this annually. Evergreen trees do the same though more gradually over a spell of several years.

Developing Structure

When the leaves fell at the end of the ash tree's first season of life an important new feature was revealed. At the tip of the seedling's shoot a small hard black bud had developed. This is called the *terminal bud* and is one of a number of *winter resting buds* that recommence growth next spring. Terminal buds on leading shoots are very important for tree growth. They exert what is called *apical dominance* over other buds and cause the tree to grow strongly upwards and so produce the vigorous *leading shoot* or *leader* which results in a tree *trunk* and hence in true tree form. In brief they make the first call on available nutrients. Every forester judges the rate of a young tree's growth and hence the rate of timber production in a plantation by the length and vigour of these leaders.

Below the terminal bud, side buds had developed. Two of these were just below it, others further down. On the ash side buds are paired, with successive pairs set at right angles to each other. All are hard and black. Some hold future leaves, others future shoots that will in turn bear leaves. These structures are already fully formed within the buds when the winter resting phase begins.

In spring as the days lengthen and warmth increases, the protective, hard, waterproof bud-scales break apart and fall away. They are pushed open by the rapidly expanding leaves and shoots beneath, which emerge as soft, pale green tissues. Nourished by the roots which are now actively absorbing moisture and by the small food reserve held in the stem, the leaves soon reach full size, harden and become functional.

The little tree now had a fresh and larger supply of carbon compounds to keep it going through spring and summer. Its shoots extended rapidly, completing their development of length and thickness in a few weeks. They then became firm and their outer surface hardened.

The lower length of the stem which grew in the previous year now underwent the remarkable transformation that is the basis of all woody plant growth. It started its *secondary thickening* – a misleading term because it accounts for nearly all the thickness of most tree trunks. The process is so called to distinguish it from the *primary thickening* of the first year's shoot growth. In a young first-year shoot the conductive channels for sap resemble those of a leaf stalk or leaf vein. Each channel holds two groups of cells. One called the *xylem* carries root-sap upwards. The other called the *phloem* carries leaf-sap downwards.

When secondary thickening begins these channels become united into two circular zones surrounding the stem. The outer ring always consists of *phloem* or *bast* tissues carrying leaf-sap downwards. The inner ring consists of *xylem* or *wood* tissue and carries root-sap upwards. In addition during the spring months the wood transports the mobile food reserves of sugar stored in the tree's stem.

Inside the *xylem* a small cylinder of *pith* remains, which was the heart of the first year's growth. This pith plays no further part in the tree's life processes, though it sometimes appears as a minor defect on a sawn plank of timber scores of years later.

Cambial Activity

An extremely thin, circular zone of actively dividing cells developed between the little ash tree's narrow zones of wood and bast. This is called the *cambium*, and it is the essential tissue for the formation of wood and the growth in thickness of the stem. It is never more than three cells thick, and it forms a continuous sheath – which has been likened to a dunce's cap or a hollow cone – around every growing woody stem. During the active seasons, the cambium, by repeated cell division, produces fresh *bast* tissues on its outer surface, just below the bark. At the same time, it also produces fresh *wood* tissues on its inner side.

In the process of forming this wood on its inner surface, the cambium inevitably pushes itself outwards. Therefore it automatically expands in radius to match the growing thickness of the stem. It is able to grow so fast because it is supplied on its inner face with root-sap and also on its outer face with leaf-sap. The raw materials for making fresh cells reach it in these two opposite, steady sap flows all through the growing season. In a large tree, the rate of cambial activity is adjusted to the size of each part of the trunk or branch. Woody stems grow thicker in proportion to the strains they must bear, and this results in the marvellous and beautiful symmetry and fitting proportions of every undamaged, free-standing tree.

The rate of activity of the cambium varies with the season of the year. During spring when there is an immediate need for root-sap to swell the expanding shoots and leaves above and promote active transpiration, the tree needs in its wood the maximum amount of conductive space. The cambium therefore makes thin-walled tissue with large through spaces, forming a ring of light *springwood*. In the ash, though not in every tree, this springwood holds a circle of vessels large enough to be seen with a hand lens, or even the naked eye. Ash is therefore called a *ring porous* timber.

As summer advanced, the ash stem needed stronger tissues to support the increasing weight of the developing shoots that it carried. The cambium responded by adding a fresh ring of stronger, denser tissues with less space for the movement of sap. This is called the *summerwood* and in the ash it may clearly be seen, on a cross-section of any stem, as a denser and darker zone, without obvious pores.

The cambium ceased growth in autumn and remained inactive through winter. The combined result of its spring and summer activity is called an *annual ring* of timber, though there are actually two rings, an inner one of springwood and an outer one of summerwood. This production of circular zones of timber will continue yearly throughout the active life of every stem and branch of the ash, though its rate may vary greatly with the tree's vigour.

At this point it is helpful to look about ten years ahead to a stage when the stem of our seedling ash had grown really stout and woody. The cross-sectional area of the stem, which represents its sap-carrying capacity, had now become too large for the tree's nutritional needs. The tree must, however, continue to expand outwards, as only newly-formed sapwood can carry its vital water stream. When this occurred, a remarkable chemical and physical change began at the centre of the stem. The *sapwood*, which had so far carried sap, changed to *heartwood*, which no longer did so. Its cavities were blocked off from the moving stream, and were filled with tannins or similar organic chemical compounds. In consequence the heartwood became darker and somewhat stronger than it was before. In many trees, though not in ash, it also becomes more durable, particularly when the tree is felled and its timber put to practical use. All timber starts life as sapwood, and heartwood is always a *transformation product*.

The finer detail of wood will be described in the next chapter. Briefly, the *hardwood* timber of ash and other *broadleaved trees* consists of three sorts of structures arranged throughout the concentric annual rings. These are structural *fibres* for support, slender hollow *tracheids* for upward sap transport, and larger hollow *vessels*, or *pores*, for more rapid sap movement. The *softwood* timber of *coniferous trees* is simpler and lacks vessels.

In both these tree groups there are also tissues, called *rays*, that are radially disposed and cross the rings at right angles. Rays, which can be seen with the naked eye on certain timbers such as oak, serve the essential purpose of transporting sap, and therefore nutrients, horizontally through the stem at right angles to the main vertical sap flows, both up and down. Rays also serve as storage tissues, holding nutrients won in summer through the winter resting season, ready to promote active growth next spring.

The cambium layer, though apparently simple and certainly extremely thin, is able to produce cells for all these complex tissues as the needs of the growing stem require. There is no rigid geometrical pattern, but every stem of every tree conforms to a master plan for its own particular kind. This wood production process goes on in every side branch, too, and there is a corresponding process of thickening in the main roots below ground.

As the ash trunk expanded year by year, its successive fresh layers of wood gradually enclosed the bases of the side branches. These buried branches are known as *knots*. They persist in the timber and are revealed when the tree is eventually felled and sawn up.

Growth Towards Maturity

Our ash seedling, now equipped for continued growth, increased in height until it reached the top of the young hawthorn hedge where its seed had first alighted. Next year its leading shoot rose above the level at which the hedge was regularly trimmed, and now it was lucky. The gardener who trimmed that hedge each summer, an old countryman, remembered the tradition of the estate where his father had worked, and spared the sapling tree. Many estates followed this rule to ensure a future supply of 'hedgerow timber' at no cost, and these protected trees remain an enormous asset to the English landscape, providing shelter and shade for crops and cattle, magnificent scenery, as well as a useful timber supply.

The young ash, now enjoying full sunlight after the half-shade of the hedge, now grew rapidly. Its lower side branches, shaded by the haw-thorns, died and eventually broke away. The bark on its slender trunk thickened and became wrinkled.

Bark, a specialized tissue found only on woody plants, serves mainly to stop water loss from the saturated conductive tissues, the bast and the wood, that lie beneath it. Its waterproof properties are well shown by ordinary bottle corks which are cut from the thick bark of cork oaks. Bark is such a good seal that it needs special pores to allow air through so that the living trunk beneath can breathe; on some trees, such as cherry, these pores, called *lenticels*, are quite conspicuous. Bark also shields the tree from casual injury and from temporary extremes of heat and cold.

Bark is formed by the *bark cambium*, a layer of cells placed outside the bast and the main, or 'wood', cambium. As the latter adds more thickness to the stem, the bark cambium adds further cells to the surrounding bark. But on most trees the outermost bark layer, formed first, cannot expand. So it splits, in a variety of patterns, each peculiar to one kind of tree. Their remarkable range is a great aid to identification. In the ash the aging bark develops an open network of ribs, interveined with hollows.

Flowering and Fruiting

Unlike the smaller plants and shrubs around it, this ash tree showed no signs of flowering or seed-bearing until it was twenty years old; some trees flower sooner, others still later. This ability of the organism to postpone reproduction yet still perpetuate its kind is a remarkable and constant feature of tree life cycles.

When flowering began, a few shoots near branch tips began their spring expansion ahead of the usual foliage. Each shoot opened a cluster of simple greenish-yellow blossoms, designed for wind pollination. An individual flower, if 'complete', consisted of two, short-stalked oblong male *stamens* and a central flask-shaped female *pistil*, ending in a two-pointed oval *stigma*. But certain flowers were not 'perfect' or 'complete'; they held stamens but no pistil. Other ash trees, at the same time, were opening flowers that showed the reverse situation, with a female pistil in each but no male stamens. Such variable arrangements of the essential sex organs are found in many trees. The commonest pattern, found in oak, is for a tree to have male catkins and female catkins on the same tree. But certain trees like willows and poplars always bear the catkins of the two sexes on separate trees. Others, like the cherries, normally have complete flowers, with both stamens and pistil present. In most trees, flowering takes place in spring, and is dependent on nutrients stored in the trunk from the previous summer.

Pollen carried by the wind from male stamens reached the receptive stigmas on the ash tree's pistils. It had an easy passage since the flowers were not yet shielded by leaves around them. After a pollen grain had travelled down the pistil's *style* or stalk to the *ovary* at its base, fertilization was effected. An ovule in the ovary began to develop into a seed. Its growth during the summer months was now aided by the active foliage that supplied nutrients. By autumn the flower clusters had become bunches of winged, single-seeded fruits, which are called ash 'keys' from their resemblance to the simple keys used in medieval locks. When the leaves faded and fell away these fruits were revealed hanging from the bare twigs. Gradually the wind blew one seed after another from its hold on the twigs. A slender stalk snapped and each in turn began its independent existence, with a one-in-a-million chance of survival to tree size and form.

Flowering and fruiting will continue throughout the active lifetime of the ash tree, but not with equal vigour in every year. These energy-consuming functions are dependent on food reserves that must be rebuilt

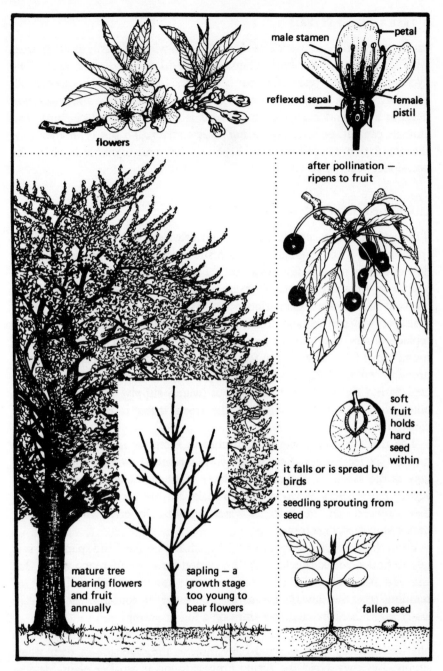

Figure 3 Life cycle of a cherry tree, *Prunus avium*. The seedling advances through a sapling stage, bearing no flowers, to a fertile stage, when flowers appear, with male and female elements. After pollination, in this case by insects, ovules ripen to seeds. These are dispersed by birds, sprout, and give rise to fresh seedlings.

each summer for next year's seed crop. Years when the ash, or other trees with large seeds, bear them abundantly, are known as *mast* years. The cycle of good seed years and poor seed years, or years with no seed at all, probably begins by chance. But indirectly it aids the tree's reproduction because in a good mast year more seed is shed than the local birds and animals can eat, or seed-destroying insects attack. To put it another way, the population of seed-eaters is kept to a low and tolerable level by the occasional years of scarcity.

Limits of Life and Growth

Throughout a long reproductive life our ash trees will continue to release thousands of seeds, enough to start a substantial forest. Despite this outflow of energy towards flowering and fruiting, it will continue to grow taller and larger for scores of years. Eventually, at an age of, say, 100 years, the outward and upward expansion of its crown will slow down and cease. The tree will still expand fresh shoots each spring but they will simply replace others that die off and fall away. The tallest ash that can be found today is 45 metres (150 feet) high, and the greatest spread of crown probably no more than 20 metres (65 feet) across. There is no simple explanation for such size limits, but water supply through the thin outer ring of active sapwood in the tree's trunk is probably a major constraint.

The tree's trunk, however, continues to increase in diameter, up to 2 metres (six feet), long after the crown has reached its maximum size. So long as the ash lives, the cambium layer will become active every spring, adding fresh layers of wood cells to make further annual rings, for only new sapwood can transport its water supplies. In brief, the tree trunk *cannot* stop growing stouter.

From the character of its growth, the ash has no fixed life span. Yet it is rare to find a tree of this kind that has stood for more than 200 years. Oak and yew often exceed that figure, but they too eventually fall. Ages of standing trees are always estimates, but those of sound *felled* trees are easily ascertained by counting rings on a log or stump.

Trees seldom, if ever, die 'naturally'. Their end may be due to some physical calamity such as wind-blow, fire, or the diversion of their water supply. But they avoid the ageing process found in smaller plants, and in animals, by creating fresh young growth zones and growth points every year. Though the centre of an ash trunk may have originated 200 years ago, its outer wood zone and youngest shoots are never more than one year old!

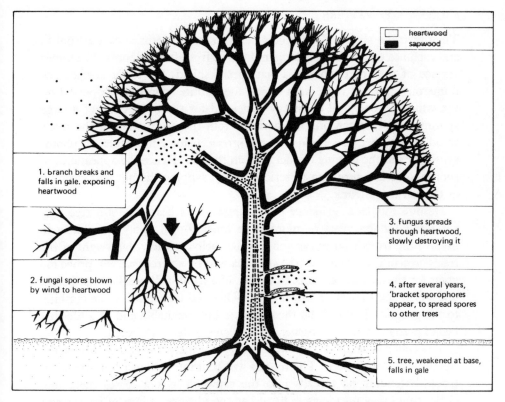

heartwood

sapwood

1. branch breaks and falls in gale. exposing heartwood

2. fungal spores blown by wind to heartwood

3. fungus spreads through heartwood, slowly destroying it

4. after several years, 'bracket sporophores appear, to spread spores to other trees

5. tree, weakened at base, falls in gale

Figure 4   Decay in the woody stem. Spores of a wood-rotting fungus alight on an exposed wood surface. The fungus progresses steadily through the tree trunk, destroying heartwood. Eventually it produces toadstool-like sporophores, which release fresh spores. Ultimately the weakened tree falls.

The usual reason for an old tree's downfall is the physical collapse of its main trunk, caused by fungal decay, or more simply, *heart rot*. The spores of the fungi concerned are always present in the air, but they cannot gain entry to suitable tree trunk host material so long as it is protected by healthy bark and living sapwood. Eventually, however, the chance breakage of a side branch, or a pruning injury, will provide a practical point of entry for a wood-rotting fungus, or else it may gain access through a root. Once it has gained a foothold, the fungus will send its thin, invisible threads, or hyphae, spreading slowly through the ash tree's heartwood, both up and down the trunks and out into the branches and main roots.

For many years there will be no outward sign of this hidden attack, for the sapwood, bast, and young shoots are not affected. But the fungus, like the tree, must reproduce its kind if it is to survive, and eventually it will develop large and obvious *sporophores* that emerge from the tree trunk. These are often situated close to ground level, but may arise higher up.

19

They take the shape of toadstools or brackets, sometimes called 'conks', and each is a device for shedding millions of fresh fungal spores. The upper surface of the sporophore is a waterproof shield; the lower surface has numerous pores or rays, from which the minute spores are dispersed on the wind. A good deal of energy is needed for the production of a large sporophore. This can only be derived from the destruction of the tree's wood tissue, because fungi are non-green plants, incapable of photosynthesis and the gaining of energy from the sun. Hence the appearance of sporophores is a sure sign of serious decay, sapping the physical strength of the ash tree's trunk.

Despite this clear evidence of weakness at its heart, the ash tree may yet stand for ten years or more. The inner fungal decay is unlikely to involve the trunk's outer sapwood, which helps to carry the weight of the tree's crown. But eventually the stress caused by a fierce gale will prove too great for the weakened trunk to resist. The trunk will break at the height of a storm and the whole crown of branches and foliage will come crashing to the ground. This will be the dramatic but inevitable end of a life that began perhaps 200 years earlier. Plate 4 shows decay in beech.

The collapse of the tree, however, does not mean the end of life for the fungus that destroyed it. The fungus will continue to flourish in the fallen trunk, extending its threads into the sapwood as life ceases there too. Other fungi may invade as well, and as rot advances a host of insects and other invertebrate creatures will colonize the mass of dead wood, shoots, and roots. After a few years the whole tree will have become broken down into mould. The nutrients that it had won from the soil will return there, to nourish, eventually, other trees or plants that spring up at the same place.

To a forester, the 'natural' decline and death of a timber tree can only represent the needless loss of an asset. If he could have intervened at the first sign of invasion by the fungus, he would have felled the tree and sold its valuable trunk for sawmill timber before decay made it worthless. He would have taken the branches for firewood logs. But he too would have allowed the finer twigs, foliage and roots to remain where the tree had stood. Even if the twigs were burnt, their ash content, rich in mineral nutrients, would have been left at the site. The 'harvesting' of a tree removes surprisingly little nourishment from the soil, and this explains how a perpetual yield can be secured from a forest, with no real risk of its eventual decline.

A tree, then, is mainly a huge plant built up by marvellous life processes from the air around it, by the winds that bring the rain and the carbon dioxide that comprise it, and the shining sun that supplies energy for the amazing transformation that its growth implies. It has a long and fascinating life span, but ultimately vanishes with its substance scattered again on the winds, or returned to the soil that supported it.

In theory there are no limits to the growth of trees. In practice they do not exceed well-known figures, due probably to problems of moving water supplies and nutrients over increasing distances. Ash, for example, rarely if ever exceeds 45 metres in height, or two metres in diameter of trunk. These figures are linked to maximum ages of 200 years. World records, found among the sequoias of California, are 117 metres in height for the coast redwood, *Sequoia sempervirens*, and 7.6 metres in diameter for the giant sequoia, *Sequoiadendron giganteum*. Such huge dimensions are only achieved by exceptionally long-lived trees, over 3,000 years old. The most amazing feature of such long-sustained growth is the way in which the outputs and requirements of crown and roots remain in balance throughout.

Endurance of the Elements

I have lived on the same hill as this ash tree for twenty years – a third of my life span so far but possibly only one-tenth of the tree's potential life. During this period I have watched it survive, unharmed, the stresses of severe climatic extremes. In winter it is often clad in snow, hoar frost, or thick white rime, and it came unscathed through a terrible month of continuous freezing with temperatures down to −20°C and deep snow. It is unchecked by long droughts in summer, on a dry hillside, with temperatures touching 30°C. Gales that sweep round our bluff, 120 metres (400 feet) up in full exposure, lash its branches in summer and winter alike until its whole crown is bent into strange distorted shapes. Yet everything promptly returns to normal. Having absorbed the great kinetic energy of the gusts like some great spring, the branches resume their natural, stately disposition as soon as each blow of the wind passes on.

In any textbook account it is easy to present a tree as though it grew in still air in a 'temperate' climate of nicely-matched, evenly-spread rain and sunshine. In real life it has to cope with irregular extremes of the elements, and to do so successfully for centuries.

Chapter 2

The Woody Stem and its Work

HAVING traced a tree's life history in the previous chapter, we next examine the structure and purpose of its separate elements in greater detail. Trees, despite their occurrence in many natural botanical families, are exceptional plants in many ways. Their peculiar features, in which they differ from smaller, shorter-lived herbs and grasses, naturally claim most attention here.

Elements of Wood

An outstanding feature of the woody stem or trunk of a typical tree is its great complexity, combined with a relatively short active life for the tissues that are built up on such an elaborate plan. Taking an oak as a representative broadleaved tree – and conceding that conifers have a somewhat simpler structure – we find that every sizeable fragment of its timber holds four kinds of cells, or cellular structures.

Three of these run vertically and their functions are to give support and transport sap upwards. The most numerous type are the *tracheids*, which are slender hollow cells, each around one millimetre long by 0·1 millimetre across, that discharge both these main functions.

In the conifers, which have narrow needle-shaped leaves, only tracheids are present. But a broadleaved tree like an oak needs, in addition, larger channels of sap supply to meet the transpiration needs of its larger, more active, foliage. These channels, created by groups of united cells, are called *vessels* or *pores*. In the oak they are so large that they can be clearly seen by a low-powered lens, or even with the naked eye. Individual vessels may be quite long, up to 25 millimetres, though they are only about one millimetre across.

The presence of so much space in the wood's structure might tend to weaken it. But it is reinforced by cells of another type, the *fibres*, which add strength but do not transport sap.

Rings

All these vertical elements are formed, surprisingly, by the action of the very thin, and apparently simple, circular sheath of cambium cells. All through the growing season this cambium sheath throws off fresh cells on its inner surface, but the proportions of each kind vary. In spring, more conductive space is produced, in the form of hollow vessels and thin-walled tracheids. This *springwood* is adapted to the rapid upward transport of root sap. In summer, the cambium produces a higher proportion of fibres, fewer and smaller vessels, and tracheids having thicker walls and less conductive space. The resultant *summerwood* is better adapted to give the trunk strength. The two zones together make one annual ring. Plate 42.

The cambium ceases growth in autumn, before the leaves fall, and remains inactive until next spring. Then the cycle is repeated over long spans of successive years.

The width of the ring is a good indication of the vigour of the tree, and is accepted as such by foresters everywhere. A tree that receives its optimum quota of water, sunlight and soil nutrients produces wide rings. Conversely, a tree deprived of one or more of these essentials grows narrow rings.

Yet the rings do not have a consistent width and character throughout the whole tree. At some points the sheath of new wood formed each year is nearly always thicker than at others. In effect its dimensions are moulded to suit both physical and physiological needs, which vary throughout the tree's woody structure. Its character may also vary. Portions of the stem that come under exceptional strain may have a higher-than-normal proportion of fibres and thick-walled cells. This results in areas of abnormal timber, called *tension wood* in broadleaved trees like the oak, or *compression wood* in conifers. These zones can prove troublesome later on to the timber merchant who converts the logs in which they lie into sawn timber because they warp or twist when stresses are removed.

As a rule, slow-grown timber may be expected to prove stronger than fast-grown material. But oak reverses this simple rule. An oak tree struggling on poor soil produces springwood with large vessels on the usual plan, but fails to add a fair proportion of strong summerwood later. Its timber, overall, is therefore light and brittle. Conversely, oak growing fast on good soil builds up strong summerwood zones and becomes heavier and tougher. These are examples of the remarkable variability of timber produced as a living tissue in response to the tree's physiological needs, which change with time and place.

Rays

The fourth essential element of the living wood consists of *rays* which, as we noted in the first chapter, are best regarded as 'horizontal' tissues running through the stem, at right angles to the rings, from the radius towards the centre. They were once called 'medullary rays', because some of them end centrally in the medulla or pith that remains from the stem's first year of growth. But this connection is accidental. Rays are part of the true wood, essential to its life processes, and their important connection lies with the outer bast, not the inner pith.

In the oak these rays are clearly seen as narrow bands or lines radiating from the centre of each log on any cross-cut surface. If the log is cleft or sawn radially they appear as broad plates with shiny surfaces; this feature is often used for decorative effect as the 'silver grain' of the oak. The vital rays occur in *all* hardwood and softwood timbers; though they are rarely so obvious as in the oak.

Rays have two main functions. They are channels for the horizontal movement of sap and nutrients, and they act as storage tissues during the resting season. Both these purposes are aptly shown by the well-known sugar maple, *Acer saccharum*, of eastern Canada and the north-eastern United States, which is tapped in spring for sugar. This sugar can only be manufactured, originally, in the leaves of the tree's crown, but these leaves fall in autumn. Before they drop, the sugar has been sent down into the trunk through the bast tissues which lie just below the bark. It then moves horizontally at various levels into the rays and is stored in their cells. Next spring it takes an upward course, to nourish the foliage and flowers that are rapidly developing from the newly-opened buds. This upward course is effected through the sapwood tissues of the wood, and not through the bast, which is a downward means of transport. The farmer who taps the maple tree drives his spout into the wood to intercept and draw off part of this upward current. It flows out steadily under low pressures.

The rays are also the means whereby the wood cells receive the fuel they need to give impetus to the upward movements of root sap, which only takes place through living, and therefore breathing, sapwood.

Finally, by their radial structure of strong-walled cells, rays add to the strength and rigidity of the tree trunk.

Sapwood: The Riddle of Sap Transport

Living wood is always saturated, or nearly so, with water. The idea that sap 'goes down' in autumn, 'stays down' through the winter and 'comes up' in the spring is pure fiction, though deeply entrenched in country folklore.

Logs felled in winter actually hold rather more water in relation to their dry matter than do logs felled in summer, because the latter are constantly losing moisture to meet the transpiration needs of the foliage; hence they are not quite saturated when cut down.

The difference between the winter and summer conditions of the living tree trunk is simply that, in winter, the water held in the trunk is static, whereas in spring and summer it is moving steadily upward from the tree's roots into its crown.

The dynamic forces needed to convey large volumes, which mean heavy weights, of water from soil level to the top of a tall tree, possibly 100 metres (330 feet) above the ground, have attracted the attention of plant physiologists for many decades. The usual physical theories of capillary attraction, osmosis and vacuum suction cannot, even when considered in combination, account for the sap's upward flow. This involves a huge consumption of energy and it is maintained night and day all through the growing season. It is now becoming increasingly accepted that it is a biological process carried out only by living wood elements that are supplied with fuel from the bast tissues near at hand, which convey sugar down from the crown of the tree.

There are many pointers to this explanation. Dead trunks carry no sap. Neither does the inner heartwood in a large stem. Though it gives important support to the sapwood around it, it is physiologically inert. Only the outer stout tube of sapwood is functional, and this receives its sugar supply from the bast tube that surrounds it.

If a tree is *ring-barked*, which is a simple operation involving the removal of bark and bast, right round the stem, it dies from that point up, although the sapwood remains undamaged. This suggests that upward movement of root-sap can only occur through wood cells in immediate connection with downward flow and pressure of leaf-sap. The upward sap flow cannot cross a gap, only a few centimetres (inches) wide, at the level of ring-barking. Partial ring-barking does not kill the tree; it only slows down its growth until the break heals over.

The mechanism of propulsion of sap upwards is believed to lie in strands of protoplasm that run through the *bordered pits*, which are curious holes, surrounded by a band of thicker tissue, found in the walls of all wood elements that carry sap. These tiny propulsion units escaped discovery until recent years because they break down when wood is prepared for microscopic examination. The purpose of the bordered pits as links between cell and cell was understood, but their mode of function baffled enquirers.

Reviewing the structure and purpose of the woody stem as a whole, in a large tree like an oak it holds a thick heartwood core that no longer carries sap but simply supports the tree's crown. Built up around it comes the active sapwood zone, which moves sap up all through the growing season and acts also as a vital storage organ during the resting season. The sapwood is enlarged each year on its outer surface by the all-important cambium. But at the same time, in any large stem it loses an inner layer through conversion to heartwood. Around it on the other side of the cambium lies the bast zone that brings carbohydrate fuel, and therefore energy, to the living sapwood. Then comes the protective bark, which prevents water loss but allows air to penetrate.

This last fact is most important. Sapwood is a living tissue that must *breathe*. A simple example underlines this often-forgotten fact. A few years ago a well-meaning highway authority in Hampshire reconstructed a road that ran through a grove of magnificent, healthy oaks. The carriage-way level had to be raised, so to get the right effect good soil was piled round the oak trunks. Deprived of adequate air at this level, the trunks ceased to function and the trees promptly died, even though their roots extended to unaffected surface soil elsewhere.

Heartwood: Alive or Dead?

The transformation of active, functioning sapwood to inactive heartwood is one of the most remarkable features of the course of life in a tree's woody stem. The facts associated with it are widely misunderstood, even among academically-trained botanists. There are many, often conflicting, factors to remember. See Plate 42.

First, heartwood is *never* found in young stems, nor in the younger portions of old ones. There is no heartwood near the tips of growing shoots nor in the outer zones of old ones. Young trees hold no heartwood whatsoever.

Second, heartwood occurs only in the inner and lower zones of older and larger woody stems. No tree trunk is composed solely of heartwood. Heartwood is incapable of growth, and can only be derived from living, growing sapwood.

Third, all heartwood is formed by conversion, through chemical changes, from previously formed sapwood. The circular layer at which this conversion occurs is not a tidy geometrical figure. It follows the general trend of the annual rings but does not coincide with them overall. All the varied tissues of the sapwood – the tracheids, the vessels, the fibres and the rays – are converted at the same time into heartwood.

Fourth, in some trees these chemical changes result in a clear colour distinction between heartwood and sapwood. Heartwood is typically darker, as in sweet chestnuts, *Castanea sativa* and *C. dentata*, yew trees, *Taxus baccata* and *T. brevifolia*. But in other trees, notably the spruces, *Picea* species, *no* colour change occurs. In others, such as ash, *Fraxinus* species, it may be slight, varying from one individual tree to another. As a general rule, those heartwoods that become darker become more durable. Colour changes are occasionally masked by temporary superficial effects; for example, oak sapwood when attacked by mould fungi becomes darker than heartwood, which resists those organisms.

Fifth, the chemical changes that occur in heartwood formation *may* or *may not* increase the *durability* of the timber concerned. As examples most oaks, *Quercus* species, and all larches, *Larix* species, hold heartwood that is remarkably durable; that is, resistant to invasion by the fungi that cause decay, although their sapwood is perishable. But pines, *Pinus*, and beech, *Fagus*, hold heartwood that shows little greater resistance to rot than does their sapwood.

Sixth, the foregoing is true only as regards the *timber cut from a felled tree*. During a tree's lifetime its living sapwood is, by contrast, more resistant to decay than its inert heartwood. An odd result of this is that an old oak with all its heartwood decayed may stand for a century or more supported only by an outer cylinder of living sapwood. Such trees are freaks, although they are common enough in the English countryside. Most are pollard trees, which were lopped in former days to yield firewood and small fence timbers. This repeated lopping every ten years or so had the odd effect of rejuvenating the tree, prolonging its life by centuries! All the same, these trees remain freaks and normally the loss of heartwood through decay leads to the early death of the tree through its collapse.

We come then to the crucial question, is heartwood alive or dead? To the academic plant physiologist it is a dead tissue. There is no life in its protoplasm. But to a practical forester, it is very much a part of a living tree. If it rots, his tree usually falls and dies. The maintenance of sound heartwood is essential to the profitable life of his plantations and to the profitability of his whole enterprise.

Flexibility

The trunk as a whole is almost saturated with water during its active life. This is clearly shown by its loss in weight, after felling and seasoning, which averages about 50% of the 'green' or 'fresh-felled' weight. One important effect of this saturation is the flexibility of the living timber elements. On a small scale this is well known to craftsmen such as hurdle-makers, who can twist and interweave thin rods and split-sections of hazels, *Corylus avellana* or *C. americana*, so long as they are newly-felled and 'green'. Once they dry, they become brittle.

The sturdy bole or trunk of a stout oak appears very rigid and lacking in flexibility. But the main stem of a taller tree is sure to exhibit some degree of bending during a high wind, and so are its side branches. The ability to bend readily, and to recover original shape unharmed, is well shown by a plantation of a tall conifer, such as a larch, *Larix* species. The upper crowns of high trees, 30 metres or more tall, may thrash about in a gale, waving in great arcs. In this way they absorb much of the momentum, or kinetic energy, of the wind, and in fact slow it down at the levels where they occur.

The physical properties of the living tree should never be wholly judged – though they often are – by those of a dead, felled, and probably fully-seasoned log!

Bark and Bast

The protective layer of bark which surrounds every woody stem appears at first sight to be a minor element in the tree's structure, no more than the wrapping around the parcel. In fact it is essential to the functioning of the whole organism, and no tree nor part of a tree can live without satisfactory bark cover.

It is important to remember that in common usage the term 'bark' includes two quite distinct sheaths of cells. Just outside the main cambium comes the thin layer of *phloem* tissue, also called 'inner bark' or bast, which conveys the sugar sap from the leaves down towards the roots. This is extended annually by cell division *in the main cambium* and inevitably grows in diameter in line with the growth of wood below.

Around this bast zone comes the true or 'outer' bark which is purely protective. Its essential purpose is to give a waterproof cover to the sap-saturated tissues within. In its absence the bast, the cambium and the sapwood would dry out, leading to the death of the woody stem at a time of water stress. The layers of corky cells that comprise the outer bark are in fact almost air-proof as well as waterproof. Breathing pores, called 'lenticels' are therefore provided to allow the ingress of air needed to supply oxygen for the living trunk to breathe. These can be clearly seen on the common cherry, *Prunus avium*, and related species.

Subsidiary functions of the bark are the protection of the living tissues beneath it against physical damage of various kinds. It is a thin but possibly effective shield against temporary extremes of heat and cold. One example is found in the beeches, *Fagus sylvatica* and *F. grandifolia*, which have rather thin bark and can suffer from sun scorch if trees that have stood in the shade of the forest suddenly get their trunks exposed to direct sun when their neighbours are cut down. Thicker-barked trees such as oaks show no such damage. The remarkable thick fibrous bark of the Californian giant sequoia, *Sequoiadendron giganteum*, gives protection against scorching by forest fires. These trees stand for over 3,000 years, and it appears unlikely that the groves concerned escape casual ground fires entirely over so long a span of time. In Scotland, thick-barked old stems of Scots pine, *Pinus sylvestris*, often survive ground cover fires in the surrounding heather, but thin-barked young stems die from the scorching of their inner tissues.

Bark may also lessen the effects of sudden short-lived cold spells such as night frosts in the spring growing season, though it cannot, of course, resist *continued* freezing temperatures. It is also a good 'buffer' to protect the tree from casual impacts which occur even where man has no part in the proceedings. It shields the stem when, for example, a large branch falls from a taller tree and strikes it, or when a squirrel or woodpecker digs its claws into the surface. As a rule the bark checks the gnawing and nibbling of the stem by mammals, though hungry horses often bite the trunks of elms, *Ulmus* species, and both deer and squirrels damage thin branches of beeches, *Fagus* species, and the maples, *Acer* species.

Bark is produced, renewed and extended by a vital though often over-looked tissue called the *bark cambium*. This lies outside the bast, which separates it from the *main* or *wood cambium* that lies closer to the heart of the stem. The bark cambium is nourished by the downward flow of leaf-sap from the crown. One of the essential functions of the bast is, therefore, to support the growth of bark, as well as that of wood.

The production of fresh bark cells takes place only on the inner face of the sheath of bark. It occurs annually during the active growing season because the bark must expand to match the growing thickness of the stem. Bark formed in previous years is inevitably pushed outwards. Its cells, pushed away from the bast's current of living sap, die, but remain intact on most trees as a continuing protective layer for an indefinite term of years.

The very oldest tissues of an aged tree are the central heartwood at its core and fragments of its outermost bark. All the intervening tissues have arisen through growth in the intervening period, and must be younger than the inside and the outside.

On most kinds of tree, the outer layers of bark split as they are forced outwards and the circumference of the tree increases. The pattern of breakage is peculiar to each kind, and is in practice a very useful aid to woodsmen when they have to identify trees in the forest. Although the pattern changes with advancing age, it does not vary with the season, and it is always available at a convenient height above ground. Bark patterns tend to follow the general family relationships of the trees concerned, but there are notable exceptions. Among the pines, of the genus *Pinus*, the lodgepole pine, *P. contorta*, bears bark like a bird cherry, *Prunus padus*, and the lace-bark pine, *P. bungeana*, has bark like a plane tree, *Platanus*, though the general pine pattern is one of thick fibrous plates.

Deciduous bark, which flakes off after some years of growth, is found on the planes or American sycamores of the genus *Platanus*, European sycamore, *Acer pseudoplatanus*, and the Alaskan Sitka spruce, *Picea sitchensis*, but is exceptional. 'Deciduous' here means 'falling away', and does not refer to the foliage characteristic of the tree – the sycamores are deciduous (foliage) trees, but the spruce is evergreen.

As a rule, the removal of bark from a living stem causes its death because the bast tissues come away too. But with the cork oak, *Quercus suber*, found in southern Spain and neighbouring countries, the separation occurs at the bark cambium layer. The bast below remains unharmed, and obligingly produces a fresh coat of valuable corky bark.

Bark in the broad sense is remarkably rich in the carbohydrate substances called tannins, which have the valuable property of converting hides and skins into leather. Its harvesting for this purpose was, until recent times, a valuable source of revenue for the forest. Commercial tanbarks occur on a wide range of trees. Oaks are rich in tannin and so are spruces of the genus *Picea*, hemlocks of the genus *Tsuga* and wattles of the genus *Acacia*. A common feature of all tannins is their ready solubility. In practice, bark was always stored with its waterproof outer surface upwards, to protect the tannin-rich inner layers below. Removal of tanbark invariably killed the stem concerned, so it was restricted to the time of felling for timber. But the tree stumps could survive, and oak in particular produced repeated crops of poles as coppice growth (see Chapter 9), which bore successive supplies of bark and firewood.

Knots

The basal portions of side shoots normally become overgrown by fresh annual rings that develop around the main stem that supports them. They persist there throughout the life of the tree, and usually become an integral part of its timber. The woodworker who reveals this hidden shoot later on when he saws through a plank calls it a *knot*. Quite simply, a knot is a 'buried branch'. If the portion of the branch concerned was living when it was overwhelmed, it becomes and remains a so-called *live knot*, firmly

united to the surrounding wood. But if it had died before becoming surrounded, it makes a *dead knot* which never unites with the wood around it.
Dead knots are apt to fall out, leaving a round *knot hole* as a defect in the
timber. Sometimes they become decayed or else very hard and resinous.

Timber merchants today regard live knots as a minor fault in ordinary
commercial timber, but dead knots remain a major defect. Because they
deflect the 'run' of the grain or vertical cells, knots lessen the strength
properties of planks, and very knotty timber may have to be discarded.

The outer zones of large timber stems hold no buried branches, as all
side shoots had fallen off before these particular annual rings were laid down.
Such timber is called knot-free or clear. In the past it was fairly easy to
harvest such high-quality – and high-priced – timber from great virgin
forests undergoing exploitation for the first time. But nowadays clear
timber is getting increasingly scarce. The central core of *any* tree is always
knotty.

The World's biggest Woody Stems

Tallest tree: Coast redwood, *Sequoia sempervirens*, 117 metres (384 feet).
Stoutest tree: giant sequoia, *Sequoiadendron giganteum*, 7·6 metres (25 feet)
in diameter. Both in California.

Chapter 3

Buds, Shoots, Leaves and Roots

THERE is great variation in shape and size between the buds, shoots, leaves and roots of different kinds of trees and these variations prove of great value for the identification of species. But each organ serves the same basic purpose. The enormous compound leaf of the tree of heaven, *Ailanthus altissima*, which may be one metre (three feet) long, carries out photosynthesis in just the same way as the minute narrow leaf of the tamarisk, *Tamarix pentandra*, which measures only 2·5 millimetres (0·1 inch) in length. The former is 400 times as long as the latter, and has a surface area at least 4,000 times as great, but its function is the same. The huge roots of a great mature Californian redwood, *Sequoia sempervirens*, tap the soil for moisture in just the same way as do those of a dwarf juniper, *Juniperus communis*. Buds may be minute, as in the black locust tree, *Robinia pseudoacacia*, or large as in the horse chestnut, *Aesculus hippocastanum*, but each result in shoot extension of a similar type.

Buds and Shoots

The extension of a tree's woody stem is effected by shoots that spring from buds. Although these shoots are the basis on which the woody stem is later built up, they are, during their first months, quite different in character. They have as yet no cambium and no wood. The conduction of sap upwards and downwards is effected through composite channels, like the veins of the leaves, that hold both xylem elements for upward transit, and phloem elements for downwards movement. In brief, the outward and upward growth of the woody tree is carried out by soft, rapidly growing elements like those found in a smaller, soft-stemmed plant. The tips of the woody stem are essentially *non-woody*.

The mechanism of growth is found in the *apical meristem* at the tip, or growing point, of each shoot. This rapidly-dividing tissue produces cells of various kinds behind it, and in consequence pushes itself farther upwards or outwards. Its rate of growth can be fantastic. It is far greater than that of the cambium layer which produces wood in the woody stem below. This cambium rarely advances more than a centimetre outwards in a year, increasing the stem's total thickness by no more than two centimetres, though growth occurs all round the stem.

Starting from a single bud, a shoot of a hybrid poplar, genus *Populus*, on a good site in Somerset may grow two metres, that is 200 centimetres, taller in one year. As its active growth period comprises only the months of May, June, July and early August, no more than 100 days in all, its average rate of elongation is two centimetres *per day*. In Imperial units, the shoot grows longer by four-fifths of an inch each day, or six feet in one growing season.

Shoots of sub-tropical pines, such as the Californian Monterey pine, *Pinus radiata*, when grown in South Africa, will grow two metres (six feet) longer in the course of only a month of active extension, equivalent to a *daily* extension of about $6\frac{1}{2}$ centimetres, or $2\frac{1}{2}$ inches.

As a rough comparison, on an annual basis, trees can grow taller two hundred times faster than their stems grow outward. Their upward growth, and outward crown extension is carried out at a number of *points* that increases rapidly with the growing size of the tree. By contrast, expansion in stem thickness occurs over a *surface area* that likewise increases with both the spread of the branches and their increase in individual diameter. The actual measure of stem thickness growth capacity is the cambium surface area of trunk and branches combined.

The shoot that extends so rapidly arises from a *resting bud*. This is so called because it is formed during a previous season of active growth, and 'rests' during an inactive season. In temperate climates this is naturally the winter, but in the tropics it may be, instead, a dry season when moisture is insufficient for active growth. Each resting bud holds the structures for a whole season's growth, including the 'embryonic' leaves and/or flowers that the shoot will bear.

These delicate contents are usually protected from water loss and casual damage by an intricate series of overlapping bud scales which are quickly shed when the bud bursts in spring. The horse chestnut, *Aesculus hippocastanum*, with its 'sticky buds' that probably resist insect attack as well as drought, is a good example of this winter protection. A few exceptional trees, like the English wayfaring tree, *Viburnum lantana*, of the chalk downs, lack bud scales. Such trees are said to have 'naked buds', and it is possible to see their structure of shoot, leaf, and flower elements already laid down, neatly enfolded and ready for growth. Protection against water loss is in this instance afforded by a dense coating of downy hairs.

33

In effect, a growing tree directs a high proportion of the energy acquired in one season's growth to preparations for the next. The rhythm of extension, preparation for further extension, rest and then a fresh cycle of further extension continues through the life of the tree. In the life cycle as a whole, it starts with the first growth of the shoot and ends when the fertilized flower, ripening its fruit, packs food into its seed to prepare each seed for its first bout of active growth as a seedling.

In the context of alternating cold and warm, or dry and wet, seasons, this 'stop-go' rhythm is easily understood. But it is found also, to some degree, in the rain forests of the tropics where both heat and rainfall are adequate for growth the whole year round. Few trees there grow steadily. Most have periods of rest succeeded by sudden spurts of growth. These are not simultaneous for all the varied sorts of tree found in the forest. While some are resting, others will be putting forth rapidly growing shoots of young growth with fresh leaves.

The resting periods may be quite short, far less than the six months found in temperate Europe and North America. In Malaysia, for instance, the Para rubber tree, *Hevea brasiliensis*, which has been introduced from Brazil and very extensively planted, shows a regular resting period of only six weeks. This coincides with a spell of drier-than-usual weather, during which this otherwise evergreen tree sheds most of its leaves. Growth is then resumed with exceptional vigour, slowing down gradually over the ensuing forty-six weeks of the year.

Attempts to make temperate zone trees grow continuously under artificial conditions never succeed. In one representative experiment, the Forestry Commission of Great Britain grew seedlings of a western American tree, the Sitka spruce, *Picea sitchensis*, which normally become about 10 centimetres tall in their first growing season, under optimum conditions in all respects. Within a greenhouse they were given continuous heat and light, with optimum air humidity and ample nutrients. Instead of ceasing growth in autumn, they grew rapidly right through winter until, in the next spring, they stood one metre tall, ten times their customary size. But they then went into a state of dormancy. All further growth ceased and it proved impossible to stimulate them into renewed normal life. A resting spell, even though a short one, appears essential to the annual rhythm of growth of every tree.

The huge number of fresh shoots produced by a growing tree have various destinies. Only a small proportion can possibly continue growth to become woody stems, so forming elements in the framework of the tree's crown. The majority function for a few years and then wither and fall.

A common cause of this decline is overshading. Once a shoot is outgrown and shaded by its neighbours, its effectiveness as a unit for carbon fixation by photosynthesis declines. Eventually it is reduced to a state known as the *compensation point*, when the energy it needs for its life processes matches the energy it can produce by fixing fresh carbon compounds from the air. Beyond this point it becomes a liability to the tree, a passenger to be carried by the efforts of other shoots better placed to make use of sunlight. It is therefore discarded. It receives no more sap from the stem and it dies, withers and eventually falls. There is a constant rain of such dead shoots from the canopy of every living forest on to the forest floor. In fact the total dry weight of shoot debris approaches that of the spent leaves over the same span of years.

In many kinds of trees only a small proportion of the shoots are adapted, from the outset, to prolong the outward growth of the tree's crown by becoming branches. These are called *long shoots*. Others, known as *short shoots* or *spurs*, never elongate substantially. Usually their purpose is to bear flowers and fruit. This pattern is well shown by the orchard apple trees, derived from the wild crab apple, *Malus pumila*. See Plate 6. Here the orchard pruner plans the best framework of the crown by preserving well-placed long shoots. He leaves the spurs intact knowing that they are the only source of blossom and apples. Another kind of shoot modification is found in many spiny trees, such as the hawthorns, *Crataegus* species, in which a proportion of the shoots are modified to form protective spines.

Overall, shoots must be regarded as temporary, expendable organs of the tree's structure. Most of them function for a short spell and are then discarded. To replace them, fresh buds are continually created at or near the well-illuminated extremities of each shoot.

The progression of each individual shoot is marked by the scars left by bud scales that fall every spring. For the space of a few years its annual extension can be seen and measured. In many kinds of conifers, each annual stage of extension is also marked by a whorl of side branches. The point where this occurs is called a *node*, and the intervening length of stem between two nodes is called an *internode*.

Leaves

The green leaf, the essential organ wherein the tree receives its nutrition by photosynthesis, is at once a marvellous biological structure and an intricate physical and chemical laboratory. Trees produce leaves in lavish quantities only to discard them after a few months, or at best a few years, of active life. All through each growing season the tree must therefore lay down fresh leaf buds, to renew these vital organs that are perpetually being wasted.

35

The expansion of the leaf in the spring warmth takes place with remarkable speed. Fed by sap from the roots which for a brief spell transports stored nutrients from the wood, it expands from a compact leaf element in the resting bud to a blade that may be fifteen to thirty centimetres long or, in coppice shoots of royal paulownia, *Paulownia tomentosa*, a whole metre across. All this occurs within a few weeks.

At this time the leaf's tissues are soft and weak, and its colour is, in most species, a bright pale green. Exceptions occur in certain poplars, including the Euro-American hybrid *Populus* 'Serotina', in which the young leaves are bronze-coloured, while in the tree-of-heaven, *Ailanthus altissima*, and the catalpa, *Catalpa bignonioides*, they are reddish-brown to crimson. Within a month of their first appearance the leaf tissues harden and the colour changes in most species to a darker shade of green.

Leaves become functional from the outset, beginning their essential work of photosynthesis as soon as their green colour shows that the chlorophyll, that vital catalyst, has become active within. In evergreens they remain functional until the leaf eventually turns brown and withers, possibly several years later. In the deciduous, or 'one-season' trees, they cease work at the approach of the cold, or the dry, season. The breakdown of the chlorophyll is accompanied by the marvellous display of autumn colours due to pigments called carotins in the yellow-orange-red range and anthocyanins in the blue-mauve-red range. After the last nutrients have travelled down the veins into the stem, the conductive channel of the leaf is severed at the base of its stalk. It then remains loosely attached to the twig until a winter wind whips it away, or frost, by forming ice at the junction, forces it outwards, leaving it to fall when the thin ice layer melts.

In its present form, the substance of the leaf is lost to the growing tree. But after it reaches the ground it slowly decays into leaf mould or humus, and the remaining nutrients that it held become available to the tree's roots. This nutrient cycle, though far from perfect, is a major element in the continuation of tree growth, especially in forests. Once established, the trees re-fertilize their soil indefinitely. The return of the element phosphorus, in this way, is particularly important.

Types of Leaf

Every active, functioning green leaf is the meeting place of two elements, water and air. The water is fed in as a constant current by the stem. If this current slows down the leaf wilts until the sap supply is restored at adequate strength. If it ceases, the leaf dies. Air enters through pores called stomata, mostly on the underside of the leaf's surface. If air is to leave behind its contribution of carbon dioxide, a constant current must pass through. The departing air inevitably takes with it additional water vapour. Every leaf is therefore constantly exposed to the risk of drying out, or desiccation, by its own inevitable transpiration stream.

The intake of air to the interior of the leaf takes place through minute pores located on the leaf's lower surface or else grouped, in some species, in sunken channels. Each pore is called a *stoma*, plural *stomata*. These pores are opened and closed by a pair of *guard cells* on either side of each stoma, and this variation controls the flow of air through the leaf. In hot, dry weather the apertures are restricted to prevent undue water loss that would dry out the leaf tissues. This action inevitably reduces the possible intake of carbon dioxide gas and so restricts growth. Under cooler conditions when air humidity is higher, the pores open wider and more air can flow through.

Within the leafy crown of a single tree, at one and the same time some leaves may be strongly illuminated in relatively dry air while others may be deeply shaded in a lower air zone of higher humidity. The stomata of each leaf provide appropriate, though varied, controls. The best conditions for rapid growth occur where high atmospheric humidities occur along with high growing season temperatures. This is found in the tropical rain forests, in the temperate rain forest along the Pacific seaboard of North America, and also along the western coasts of the British Isles.

The 'one-season' leaves of familiar broadleaved trees such as oak and beech are described as *mesophyllous*, meaning 'middle of the road' leaves. This is in contrast to *xerophyllous* leaves adapted to constant dry conditions, and *hygrophyllous* ones that are suited to constant high air humidity, as in rain forests. The commoner mesophyllous leaves have no special adaptations to check water loss. When winter cold approaches they are discarded because the roots cease to supply adequate moisture when the general temperature falls below 6°C, or the soil becomes frozen. A similar situation arises in countries where, although temperatures remain high the whole year round, there is a long dry season. In both situations the leaves must be discarded because if they remained their transpiration would desiccate all the tissues of the tree and kill it.

In contrast many other trees called evergreens, or *sclerophyllous* trees, meaning 'hard-leaved', are able to check water loss. Characteristic features of their leaves are greater thickness, a leathery texture or 'feel', a dark green, smooth and glossy upper surface and also, in the broadleaved kinds, a paler under-side.

There are other remarkable modifications to check, under conditions of water stress, the ingress of air into the leaf. The under-side of the leaf,

37

where most of the stomata lie, may be clad in felty hairs to slow down air movement, as in the Mediterranean evergreen oak, *Quercus ilex*. In conifers the stomata are often located in narrow bands along grooves in the needles. Altogether the restriction of water loss is a complex requirement for which varied solutions are found.

One common feature is the presence of waxes or resins in the outer layers of the leaf. These remarkable compounds have the property of resisting the passage of water without halting completely the movement of air. This is seen in practical everyday use in shoe polish, usually based on the leaf wax of the Brazilian carnauba wax palm, *Copernicia cerifera*.

Because there are waxes in the leaves of evergreen broadleaved trees and resins in the needles of evergreen conifers, their foliage is highly inflammable. I do not think it has been recorded elsewhere that such foliage holds a positive heat energy balance. This implies that the energy released on combustion exceeds that needed to change their incombustible water content into steam. It is, however, well known to every forester and bush fire fighter, who regards such foliage as potential dynamite! In contrast, the soft-textured foliage of summer-green broadleaved trees will never burn during the growing season when they are functional and full of sap. Such foliage has a negative balance of heat energy, and can only be destroyed by fire if extra fuel is continually supplied, as for example by a flame gun.

Evergreen leaves have active lives that extend for varying spells of time, but always exceed one calendar year. On overshaded branches of quick-growing pines, *Pinus* species, they may wither after only three years of active life. On the monkey puzzle or Chile pine, *Araucaria araucana*, they remain functional on sunlit branches for a dozen years or more.

Unlike the one-season foliage of summer-green trees, evergreen foliage does not fall all together in an autumn season. Its decline and departure is more gradually spread round the year, though some trees, such as cypresses of the *Cupressus* genus, have a marked midsummer peak. Overall there is a steady rain of spent leaves from the crown of every evergreen tree. The enterprising park planner who said that the only trees he would plant would be evergreens, since their leaves 'never fall off', was doomed to disappointment. Trees are untidy things!

Leaf Stalks and Leaf Movement

The great majority of leaves on broadleaved trees have distinct stalks to carry their blades. The sessile leaf, springing directly from the twig, is exceptional. It is found, however, as 'juvenile' foliage on Australian eucalyptus trees of the large genus *Eucalyptus*. After about five years of juvenile growth with round, stem-clasping leaves, a eucalyptus tree starts to bear 'adult' foliage. The adult leaf has a long, narrow oval blade set on a distinct stalk. The stalk adjusts the position of the leaf blade so that it is set edge-on to the sun. This restricts transpiration loss because it keeps the leaf cooler than it would be if its surface faced the sun's rays. But in consequence the eucalyptus tree gives only a minimum of shade to the sun-scorched traveller.

At the other extreme come the poplars, species of the genus *Populus*, growing for preference where water is available in unrestricted amounts. These usually grow and thrive best in alluvial soils beside lakes or rivers. Their slender leaf stalks allow the blades to flutter incessantly in the slightest breeze. This motion apparently stimulates transpiration loss in much the same way as a handkerchief waved in the wind dries quicker than one left in still air. Poplar timber has exceptionally large vessels to supply the large quantities of moisture that its foliage needs in the active growing season. Its timber in consequence is exceptionally light when seasoned, though as heavy as most kinds when it is actually transporting sap. The actual mechanism that enables a poplar leaf to flutter so easily is found in its long leaf stalk, which is flattened from side to side, enabling it to twist readily.

Conifer needles have very short stalks, but even here there is some degree of positioning, or *autotropism*, to secure the best amount of illumination. Exceptions occur among conifers with stem-clasping needles, such as cypresses in the genera *Cupressus* and *Chamaecyparis*, where the leaf position is rigidly fixed.

Leaves function best under conditions of low water stress. The world's tallest and fastest growing trees are all found in rain forests, either in the tropics or in high rainfall areas of the temperate zones, notably along the Pacific seaboard of North America, home of the coast redwood, *Sequoia sempervirens*, the world's tallest tree.

Roots

The root system on which a tree depends for its anchorage, water supply and mineral nutrients, is always in relative terms amazingly shallow. A tree 30 metres (100 feet) tall is unlikely to have a root system more than three metres (ten feet) deep. Plates 5, 44.

Forest folk-lore insists on a strong tap root that descends into the soil to some unplumbed depth matching the tree's height or even to hell itself. Tap roots are frequent but such long ones unknown!

39

Whenever a tree blows down and reveals its real root system the wise-acres say it failed because it was an exceptional, unfortunate individual that remained 'shallow-rooted', unlike survivors that endured the gale. Nobody embarks on the very hard labour of investigating the supposed 'deep roots' of these surrounding trees!

The reason why trees fail to root deeply are simple. It is both physically difficult and unrewarding. The physical problems lie in penetrating the consolidated material found in the lower layers or sub-soil of most geological formations, and in getting a sufficient supply of oxygen at depths where this material allows no free flow of air.

There are two requirements which are scarce at these depths: water and mineral nutrients. The rain that falls on a tree's surroundings must pass through the surface soil and can be intercepted there; only exceptionally does a useful reservoir arise at deeper levels and this can only be tapped to a depth where the soil is not waterlogged. Nearly all the nutrients that exist in forms available to plants occur in the upper soil layers, and largely in the humus layer of decaying plant remains. Little is found in available form at greater depths.

Tree roots therefore extend mainly outwards at relatively shallow levels. There are no fixed limits to their spread. As working rules the roots below a broad-crowned, open-grown tree extend outwards at least as far as the spread of its branches. With narrow-crowned, and forest-grown trees, the root spread is often equal, in all directions, to the tree's height. Thus a tree 20 metres (65 feet) tall will have a root system with a diameter of 40 metres (130 feet). Its radius of root penetration may increase by as much as one foot a year.

In any plantation or forest stand of trees, the roots of the many trees present criss-cross one another repeatedly. There are no exclusive areas, but each tree sends its searching roots far into the territories of its neighbours.

The main roots of a tree resemble branches in having strong woody tissues and in their steady increase in thickness as time goes on. Those portions of each main root that lie close to the base of the trunk have an essential support function, holding it firm against the stresses imposed by the wind. In some kinds of tree they are joined to buttresses that by their angular positions act as struts to resist any force from any direction that would tend to overturn the tree. In temperate forests small buttresses develop on mature trees of beeches, *Fagus* genus, and spruces in the *Picea* genus of conifers. In the tropics buttresses may become enormous. On the Honduras mahogany tree, *Swietenia mahogoni* for example, they may extend six metres (20 feet) up the trunk, and extend outwards for two metres (six feet) at the base. Tree fellers are obliged to set platforms on the trunks above the buttresses in order to fell such trees.

Yet relative to the total area explored by a tree's root system, the 'support zone' is small. This is shown by many examples of trees in urban areas where the level of surrounding soil has been lowered during building developments. Provided a firm cylinder of concrete or masonry is provided, a pillar of earth only three metres (ten feet) across will support a broad-crowned tree 20 metres (65 feet) tall.

The rest of a tree's root system has no support function and does not need to be exceptionally strong. At only a short distance from the trunk the roots become thin and flexible: being themselves supported by the soil through which they run, they are thinner and weaker than the corresponding twigs of the tree's crown. The trend of these long exploring roots is mainly horizontal. They run through shallow layers, just below the surface of turf or leaf litter where there is ample air, moisture and the optimum supply of nutrients arising from decaying humus. Branching repeatedly, they form an intricate network of criss-cross strands.

The actual work of water and mineral salt assimilation is done through smaller branch roots that are only short-lived. Each arises from a permanent root and extends, outwards or downwards, to tap a fresh volume of soil. After exploring and exploiting this for a year or two, they wither and decay, leaving slender channels where they ran. Fresh rootlets arise at neighbouring points along the major ones. A tree is therefore constantly exerting an influence on the soil in which its roots run. It is not a static being, but a dynamic force.

The branch rootlets themselves bear much finer *root hairs*, which are again short-lived organs. These fine filaments penetrate between the grains of soil to absorb the moisture and minerals that the tree needs. The larger root elements serve for transport, not for absorption.

The unseen world of a tree's roots is thus a place of constant change. One can speak of a constant root system, but this term can only cover the larger elements. The smaller ones are deciduous, being dropped when and where they no longer contribute to the tree's welfare. Fresh roots then explore new ground. Where nutrients are plentiful, those roots that tap them swell rapidly to enlarge their conductive channels. In contrast, roots that encounter poor soil remain slender.

Root growth is seasonal, but less strictly so than the growth of shoots. Active extension begins in spring and continues through the summer, then slows down only gradually through the autumn. Any freezing of the soil brings it to a standstill.

In regions that have mild winters foresters take advantage of the autumn continuation of root growth by planting out young trees at that season. So long as the soil stays warm enough roots are able to make that firm contact with the soil on which the tree's moisture supply, and hence its life, depends. Elsewhere it is usual, in temperate countries, to plant in the spring, so that the stimulus of warmth secures the same contact. In countries that have wet and dry seasons planting is usually done at the onset of the rains.

The essential contact between root and soil, which ensures a constant flow of moisture into the tree's system, must be a very firm one. A common device to ensure this at planting time is to stamp the earth firmly around the tree's roots. The commonest cause of failure in tree planting is to treat the tree too gently, by sprinkling loose soil around the roots to avoid any risk of harming them.

Chapter 4

Reproduction

TREES like other forms of plant life show a lavish and extravagant production of the flowers and seeds that ensure both their survival and dispersal. It is quite usual for a single tree during its long life span to bear a million fertile seeds, only one of which is needed for its replacement when it eventually dies and falls. The flowering and fruiting patterns of trees are broadly similar to those of other higher flowering plants, but certain features peculiar to trees as a group claim attention.

Flower Structures and Sex Arrangements

First, trees show a very wide range of flowering structures and arrangements of their fertile male and female organs. Many trees bear the familiar 'perfect' flowers that we are accustomed to see on garden plants. 'Perfect' here implies the possession of functional organs of both sexes, with associated sepals, petals and nectaries. A laburnum tree, *Laburnum anagyroides*, in the large sweet-pea family or Leguminosae, bears blossoms that are the same in structure as those of the common garden pea, *Pisum sativum*. They have similar green sepals to protect the whole interior structure whilst it is still in the bud. Within these comes a whorl of yellow petals to attract pollinating bees and other insects, which are also lured to the flower by its sweet perfume and the provision of nutritious nectar which is secreted by nectaries within the base of the flower. As they seek the nectar the bees brush past the male stamens, which bear anthers that scatter yellow pollen. This pollen is transferred in the course of the bee's wanderings to the receptive pistil, the female reproductive organ, on the flower of another laburnum tree. A pollen grain caught on the stigma at the tip of the pistil develops a tube through which it travels down the slender style to the ovary at the pistil's base. There it fertilizes a single ovule, the future seed. This seed ripens within the hard pod that develops from the previously soft green ovary. It is scattered

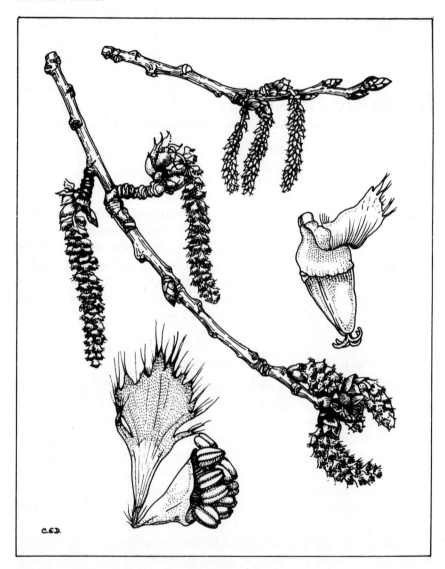

Figure 5   Male and female catkins of grey poplar, *Populus canescens*, borne on separate trees. Shown at natural size. Also individual flowers, magnified twelve times. Each male flower, *left and bottom*, has a leafy bract and a green cup holding many stamens. Each female flower, *right and top*, has a similar bract and cup, holding an ovary tipped with four stigmas.

when the ripe pod bursts in autumn to begin life as a seedling the following spring. 'Perfect' flowers appear in Fig. 3, p. 17 and Plate 10.

But side by side with the laburnum grow oaks, genus *Quercus*, and many other kinds of tall forest trees that bear flowers of another character altogether. They rely on the wind to carry their pollen and so they bear no bright petals, nectaries or scent to attract insects. Each flower consists of nothing more than essential reproductive organs, either male stamens or female pistils, together with the little leaf-like bracts that protect the sex organs in the bud.

These simplified flowers are commonly borne in groups loosely called 'catkins'. The word has no precise botanical significance, and means in fact nothing more than a 'kitten' or 'little cat', apparently suggested by the furry aspect of the catkins of 'pussy' willows, *Salix* species. Its German equivalent, *Kätzchen*, and its French one, *chaton*, denote feline kittens as well as tree flowers and fruits. A wide range of tree flower groups are nowadays called 'catkins', for want of any handier term.

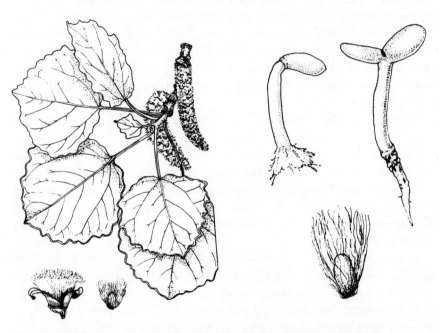

Figure 6   Foliage and seed catkins of aspen poplar, *Populus tremula*. Each separate pod (*below, left*) releases scores of hair-tufted seeds. It ripens and splits open in May.

Figure 7   Germination in aspen poplar, *Populus tremula*. After 10 days, the seed (*foot*) has produced a root, and raised its husk on an upright stem (*left*). After 20 days two seed-leaves have emerged and started photosynthesis (*right*).

The flowers found in catkins seldom bear nectar, but the willows are an exception: their pollen is carried by visiting bees, who eat a lot of it, as well as by spring breezes. In most catkins all the flowers are either male *or* female, but again exceptions occur. The sweet chestnuts, *Castanea* species, bear their female flowers at the base of otherwise male catkins. These catkins also bear nectar to encourage bees to cross-pollinate them, as well as scattering pollen on the wind.

In the majority of catkin-bearing trees, the individual catkins are entirely male or entirely female, but catkins of both the two sexes grow on the same tree. This is technically called *monoecious*, meaning 'living in one home'. But certain trees, notably willows and poplars, *Salix* and *Populus* genera, are *dioecious*, implying 'two separate homes', so that on a male tree you can only find male flowers, while only a female tree can bear female flowers, fruits and seeds. It is, however, perfectly feasible to graft, say, a male *branch* on to a female tree, and so obtain flowers of both sexes on one tree trunk. There does not appear to be any natural advantage in this restriction of each sex to particular individuals. Tree breeders and seed collectors find it a nuisance since a particularly fine individual tree may yield no seeds at all, or alternatively bear no pollen for a desirable cross. Horticulturists occasionally find it an advantage, as when they plant all-male poplars to avoid the female's fluffy seeds, or all-female sumac trees, *Rhus typhina*, to get showy red female fruit clusters instead of dull green male blossoms.

Other strange variations in tree sex patterns are found in certain major flowering structures, generally called inflorescences, such as those of the European sycamore or maple, *Acer pseudoplatanus*. The same inflorescence may hold, at the same time, functionally female flowers, functionally male flowers, hermaphrodite ones with active organs of both sexes, and sterile blossoms too. Apparently the potentials to produce both male and female flowers are present in each flower bud, but only one sex, or none at all, achieves fulfilment.

In the great natural order of conifers, the flowers are invariably borne in catkins of one sex only. But with rare exceptions both sexes occur on the same tree. Conifers are always wind-pollinated so the attractive colours seen for example on larches, *Larix* genus, and Korean silver fir, *Abies koreana*, serve no useful biological purpose that we know of.

Even after fertilization has been successfully achieved, the ripening of the seed is far from assured. A proportion of fertilized ovules commonly fails to develop and becomes aborted. The premature fall of unripe fruits such as apples, *Malus* species, is a constant feature of fruit growing. In most conifers the ovules near the tip and occasionally those near the base

46

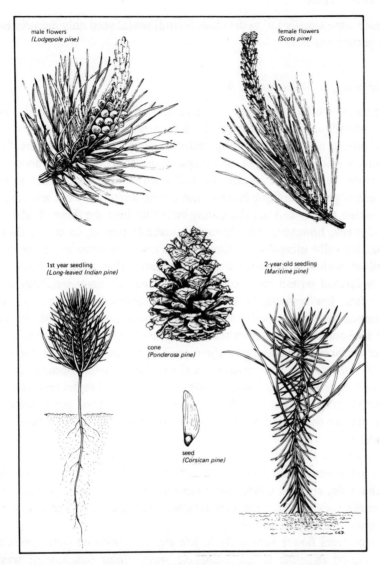

Figure 8 Reproduction in conifers, illustrated by pines, genus *Pinus*.
Top left: Male flowers of Alaskan Lodgepole pine, *P. contorta*, midway along
shoot.
Top right: Two female flowers of Scots pine, *P. sylvestris*, at shoot tip.
Centre: Cone of Californian ponderosa pine, *P. ponderosa*, with scales open
after release of seeds. *Below:* Winged seed of Corsican pine, *Pinus nigra*
variety *maritima*.
Bottom left: first-year seedling of long-leaved Indian pine, *P. roxburghii*, with
whorl of long seed-leaves beneath solitary juvenile needles.
Bottom right: second-year seedling of maritime pine, *P. pinaster*, showing
paired adult needles succeeding solitary juvenile needles.

of each cone usually fail to develop. Sound, useful seed only matures below the central scales.

Flowering in Relation to Age

The age at which trees flower is the subject of widespread misunderstanding. Actually there are no firm rules. Some trees flower when only five years old, others postpone flowering until they are fifty, and others flower regularly when aged 500, or even 4,000 years! It is pointless to draw parallels from the human or animal world. One must remember all the time that the *active* part of any tree is never more than a few years old anyway. It is the young tissues and not the ageing ones that bear the flower buds.

All trees, however, pass through a juvenile period, in which they are physiologically incapable of flowering. This is obvious in the sprouting seedling which only displays the seed-leaves that have previously lain ready-formed within the seed. It is also clear in many seedlings during their first few seasons, because they bear characteristic *juvenile foliage*. Examples are simple leaves instead of compound ones in the ash, *Fraxinus*, and free-standing needles instead of adpressed ones, that is needles with inner surfaces pressed against their neighbours, in the western red cedar, *Thuja plicata*. It is less apparent in the orchard apples, *Malus*, but every fruit propagator knows that if he grafts juvenile wood on to a rootstock, the resulting graft will not bear flowers and fruits for several years. Instead he uses mature wood for his scions and so secures fruit within a year or two of grafting.

In general the perpetually juvenile varieties of trees that are popular with gardeners do not flower or bear fertile seed. But there are exceptions to this rule, such as *Cryptomeria japonica*, variety *elegans*, a form of the Japanese cedar or *sugi* tree that retains immature leaves but occasionally develops mature sex organs.

Some trees flower very early in life and are therefore called *precocious*. A common example is the lodgepole pine, *Pinus contorta*, of western North America, which frequently bears female cones when only five years old. Male flowers, which would appear to make lesser demands on the tree's resources, do not appear until it is a few years older.

But most trees postpone flowering until their first active spell of rapid upward and outward growth is over. All their nutrients are directed towards physical enlargement rather than towards the reproduction of their kind. This is what one would expect on logical grounds. The tree should first achieve dominance over its competitors and then divert its energies towards securing the survival of its race. Its natural longevity makes this possible.

An annual plant must bear seed in its single year of life or its species may perish. But a tree can postpone seeding for a century without risking its eventual replacement by one or more of its offspring.

The postponement of flowering until a fairly late stage in life is most marked in dense stands or close plantations of both broadleaved and coniferous trees. If a high proportion of each tree's crown of foliage is shaded by its neighbours it does not develop flower buds. Instead it diverts its resources into upward vegetative growth in order to keep its place in the rising leafy canopy. If a forester wishes to secure seed from such a plantation, his remedy is simple. He thins the trees out so that those he retains are no longer unduly shaded but can expand broader crowns into unrestricted sunlight. Within a few years he is rewarded by ample flowering and seeding, though the height growth of his trees may slacken off.

The same procedure is followed in *seed orchards*, established for the production of high grade seed, in which all the trees are widely spaced. In the fruit-growing field, the provision of adequate space around each fertile tree is an absolute essential. Whether you are growing oranges, coconuts or cherries, you must allow each individual tree its full quota of all-round sunshine so that it will develop a deep crown and use the maximum available sunlight energy to build up a rewarding crop of fruit.

Periodic Seeding by Mature Trees

Even when a tree has reached maturity it may not bear seed every year. A few trees, notably the birches, *Betula* species, can be relied on to develop heavy annual seed crops year after year. But others have varying years of plenty, scarcity or complete absence of fertile fruits and seeds. Often a rhythm or cycle of abundant or sparse seeding becomes established and is maintained for scores of years. Several factors contribute to this sequence of events.

A heavy seed crop requires and exhausts a substantial reserve of nutrients. In practice this must be built up in the year *preceding* the heavy crop, for it is then that the flower buds are formed. If all goes well with the processes of flowering and seed formation, the tree will tend to put so much nourishment into them that it has nothing to spare for the year following. So in this next year few or no flowers are borne whilst the tree is restoring its reserves. The third year of the series may see a moderate seed crop and the building up of fresh reserves, so that a heavy crop becomes possible in the fourth year.

If, however, a sharp late frost damages flowers in that fourth year, little seed may mature. In that event the bumper crop will be postponed until the fifth year. Cycles like this are frequent among large-seeded broadleaved trees, particularly oaks, *Quercus*, and beeches, *Fagus*. The traditional name for the heavy crop year is *mast* year, from the Scandinavian root word *mat*, meaning food. In the past the oak and beech mast or seed provided a welcome food for fattening swine. The Domesday Book of the English King William I, circa 1084 AD, values village woodlands in terms of the swine they could feed.

Seasons of abundance and scarcity are well known to fruit growers for they have an immediate impact on their prices and profits. They occur also among conifers, but foresters have developed an effective method for smoothing out their effects. In good seed years they collect more seed than they need for their next year's sowing and store it in cold stores at temperatures just above freezing point. Most though not all kinds of conifer seeds retain their viability for several years, so if a poor seed year occurs the forester simply draws seed from his store to fill the gap.

It is believed that years of abundant seeding, or mast years, can prove of great value for tree survival. Normally there is a certain level of predation by insects, beasts and birds on ripening or mature seed which allows only a small proportion to escape unharmed. In a mast year the amount of seed available exceeds the capacity of the seed eaters to destroy it, so a higher proportion survives to become new trees. In the ensuing year of seed scarcity, so the argument goes, many predators die of starvation, or else seek other feeding grounds. Whatever the reason, foresters have long realized that abundant natural regeneration is only likely to spring up after a season of abundant mast.

A charming if utterly unfounded folktale tells how 'kind Mother Nature' provides heavy crops of holly or hawthorn berries to nourish her little dicky-birds during exceptionally hard, snowbound winters. This kindly spirit, we are assured, has foreseen trouble ahead and made provision for it. In truth, heavy seed crops bear no relation at all to cold winters in the future, but are the outcome of hot summers in the past. The summer immediately preceding the bumper seed crop plays some part in this exceptionally heavy seeding, but it is mainly the *summer before that* which enables the tree to build up higher-than-average reserves for flower bud formation.

As an example, if the summer of 1981 proves exceptionally warm and sunny, we may expect heavy seed crops in the autumn of *1982*. This prophecy could, however, be upset by adverse weather such as a frosty spring or a poor summer during the process of flowering and fruit formation in 1982. In that event, the heavy crop could be postponed till 1983.

Delayed Ripening, Late Dispersal and Dormancy

In the great majority of trees the ovules that are fertilized in spring, or other appropriate season, ripen through the summer and become dispersed in the following autumn. They sprout next spring, so the time interval between fertilization and germination is only one year. Certain genera and species, however, take two or even three years to ripen seeds. Two years is usual for most pines, of the genus *Pinus*, cedars of the *Cedrus* genus, and the American red oak *Quercus rubra*. At any one time, a fertile tree commonly bears two seed crops, each destined for a different year of ripening.

Even after the seed is fully ripened it is not always released by the tree. Certain pines, notably the Canadian jack pine, *Pinus banksiana*, the Californian bishop pine, *P. muricata*, and the Californian Monterey pine, *P. radiata*, have what are called *serotinous* or 'late opening' cones. These hang on the branches with their scales tight shut for many years, but the seed still retains its viability within them. Normally there is a trickle of seed falling from ageing cones during each dry summer. But if a catastrophe strikes the forest, for example a hurricane that uproots trees or a fire that – strange to relate – can destroy trees and foliage yet not kill all cone-held seeds, then a sudden bounty of seed becomes available. This promotes the quick natural regeneration of the destroyed forest and becomes evident a few years later in a crop of even-aged trees.

Dormancy is another curious feature encountered in the seeds of several quite unrelated kinds of broadleaved trees. In its commonest form, seed that ripens in autumn refuses to germinate in the following spring but sprouts readily a year later. It remains dormant but alive in the ground for eighteen months, but can only survive if conditions are right. Foresters, who have known this for centuries, get over the problem by *pitting*, also called *stratification*. They collect holly (*Ilex*) berries, hawthorn (*Crataegus*) berries, and ash seeds, *Fraxinus*, to name three commonly-grown sorts, mix them with sand, and sink them in moist earth. These pits are protected against marauding squirrels and mice by small mesh wire netting. After their long sleep, the seeds are sown and sprout normally.

It is hard to see what advantage this strange habit has for any tree's survival. Curiously, if ash seeds are sown immediately before full ripening they do not go dormant but sprout at once. This suggests that dormancy is an induced state linked to the final ripening process.

Seed Size

Tree seeds vary in size from the minute to the massive. In terms of weight you must gather 400,000 grains of the seed of European silver birch, *Betula pendula*, to make up one kilogram. But you need pluck only four coconuts, the seed of *Cocos nucifera*, to get the same measure. The coconut therefore weighs 100,000 times as much as the birch seed.

The difference of seed size obviously affects the *number* of seeds that a tree may bear during a single season. To take average figures, the coconut may bear 100 seeds and the birch tree 100,000. At first sight the birch might appear to have a thousand times more chances of securing a replacement, that is a successfully rooted seedling, than does the coconut. If both crops of seed received equal care in a tree nursery, this could indeed be true, but in the wild things do not work out so simply. The little birch seed has minimal food reserves and unless it alights on a spot of bare earth, moist in the spring, it cannot germinate effectively. The big coconut has a far greater store of nutrients, and its huge seedling can easily compete with other vegetation. In broad terms, the larger the seed, the greater the prospects of individual seedling survival.

One might expect the tiny birch seed, equipped with a little wing, to travel farther than the heavy coconut. A strong wind for example might carry it a kilometre or so from its parent tree. But the coconut is better fitted for long distance dispersal. It grows within a huge fibrous husk which can float it on ocean currents for 3,000 kilometres or more. After becoming stranded on a distant tropical beach, it can still sprout successfully.

There is no link at all between the size of the seed and the ultimate size of the tree that grows from it. The world's largest trees, the Californian giant sequoias, *Sequoiadendron giganteum*, sprout from some of the smallest seeds. You need 100,000 of these seeds to make one kilogram, but the biggest sequoia is estimated to weigh around 100 tonnes. That is around 10,000 *million* times as big!

Dispersal of Seed

Trees employ most of the devices found in other plants for the dispersal of their abundant seed crops. Winged seeds designed for wind dispersal are perhaps more commonly found on trees than on plants of lower stature. The greater height of trees gives them a better start on their travels. Membranous wings are found on many broadleaved tree seeds such as those of maples, and also on the great majority of conifer seeds. Other trees such as willows, poplars and planes have seeds tufted with many minute hairs that effectively support them on air currents. Large floats are found on sea-borne coconuts, and small ones on the seeds of alders, which are spread by flowing rivers.

Thanks to their large size and abundant food resources, trees can produce relatively large nut seeds, such as walnuts, chestnuts, acorns and beech nuts. These attract many marauders but a proportion always escapes to germinate later. Certain trees such as apples, plums, cherries and the mangoes of the tropics ripen seeds in large, juicy fruits that also attract hungry birds and beasts, including man. The juicy pulp rewards the fruit eaters, who 'spit out' the hard seeds within the fruit and so ensure their effective spread. Birds in particular will carry seeds over great distances in the course of their wanderings and migrations. Tree seed may even be carried internally by a bird that swallows a berry, fails to digest its seed and later voids it undamaged. Elder saplings, *Sambucus* species, will spring up freely below roosts of starlings, *Sturnus vulgaris*, far distant from any flowering elder trees.

Certain tree seeds show no particular adaptation to secure their spread. For example the black locust tree, *Robinia pseudoacacia*, holds in its pods many hard, black seeds that bear no wings and carry no attractive sweet pulp. Though small to the human eye they attract small creatures such as wood mice and song-birds that consider them tasty morsels.

Vegetative Reproduction

The ability of a plant to reproduce its kind vegetatively by offshoots of one kind or another can be important for its survival in the wild and of immense value in agriculture and horticulture. Most trees can be increased in this way, which is indeed the standard practice in fruit growing. But it is only locally important in natural forests, or even in commercial timber production. All plants that have been reproduced by vegetative means have of course the same genetic constitution as their solitary parent. The resultant unvarying strain is called a *clone*, or a *cultivar*.

Natural vegetative reproduction of trees without the deliberate aid of man takes five forms. Certain trees are able to produce *suckers*, that is shoots arising from their roots which ultimately become individual trees. Many plums such as *Prunus spinosa* can sucker vigorously and become a nuisance in a tidy garden. In the wild one bush may develop into a dense thicket. White and aspen poplars, *Populus alba*, *tremula* and *tremuloides* do likewise, Plate 60. Suckering appears with them to be a more effective method of reproduction than is seeding. Certain elms such as the English elm, *Ulmus procera*, sucker far more often than they set seeds.

Natural *sprouting* or *coppicing* can be a significant form of regrowth for certain species. The verb 'to coppice' originates from Norman French *couper*, to cut, though modern French foresters use the verb *taillir* with the same meaning. It arose through deliberate cutting back of trees to gain repeated crops of small poles from a long-lived stump. In nature the only similar stimuli arise from the death of a tree in a forest fire, which is often followed by the coppicing of birch, for example, or from the fall of a mature specimen. The power of sprouting does not exist in all trees and many lose it with advancing age: a young beech will sprout vigorously; an old one not at all. Few conifers will sprout after their first active spell of young growth.

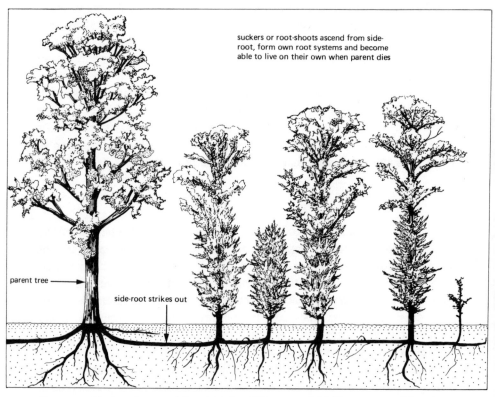

suckers or root-shoots ascend from side-root, form own root systems and become able to live on their own when parent dies

parent tree

side-root strikes out

Figure 9   Sucker shoots of Cornish elm, *Ulmus carpini folia*, var. *cornubiens is*, springing from roots, eventually develop into individual trees, which succeed their parents.

Californian redwood, *Sequoia sempervirens*, sprouts vigorously regardless of the age at which it falls or is cut back. A distinguished palaeobotanist, the late Professor John Walton of Glasgow University, visiting a grove of the oldest redwoods in California, noticed that some of the oldest and largest individuals grew in close circular groups. To him the implication was clear. These 3,000-year-old trees were the outcome of sprouts from a vanished parent that first began life as a seedling far earlier, possibly 6,000 years ago!

Natural *layering* of trees, whereby a branch that touches the ground takes root and eventually becomes an independent tree, is common in certain species but unknown in others. In the Indian banyan, *Ficus bengalensis*, it is a major means of increase and it is quite common for a single tree to become a small grove by sending down branches that strike root on touching the ground. This implies a reversal of the major growth direction from downwards to upwards! The two-way system of nutrient circulation found in a woody stem – wood upwards, bast downwards – is well suited to effect this. Each tissue, wood and bast, is a system of cells that can move nutrient solutions either way, from source of supply to point of need.

Kew Gardens near London has a remarkable 'walking beech' which is advancing outwards because its branches have rooted down and become a ring of young trees where they struck the ground. The western red cedar, *Thuja plicata*, of America's west coast will also root readily wherever branches contact the leaf mould of the forest floor. Factors that prevent natural layering are the death by overshading of low side branches in the dense forest, browsing of low branches by deer or cattle in parklands and pruning by tidy gardeners. Otherwise it would be a far more common event.

The stilt-rooted mangrove trees such as *Rhizophora mangle*, of tropical estuaries, spread over tidal mudbanks by a process akin to layering. The same tree is also remarkable for its so-called 'viviparous' or 'live-birth' seeds, which begin to sprout even before they fall from the parent tree on to soft warm mud.

Trees are occasionally reproduced by *natural cuttings*, a process that is properly called *vivipary*, or 'live birth' in smaller plants. For example fragments of willow branches torn off their parent tree by high winds may be carried downstream by a river and eventually become stranded on mud banks. There they take root. Such relatively large woody plants have a better chance of survival through alternating flooding and drought than any tiny seedling. They may play a significant part in building up new land.

Natural grafting, though scarcely a method of reproduction since it does not create new individual plants, is an interesting expression of tree vitality rarely found in non-woody plants. It can only occur among closely related individuals and only happens when their branches come into close physical contact without active movement. I have seen it in European beech and Norway spruce, but only under the sheltered surroundings of overgrown hedges. The Persian ironwood, *Parrotia persica*, which readily forms natural grafts under cultivation, will also do so in the wild. In the mountains of the Caucasus it forms dense thickets, reputedly impenetrable, where the branches of neighbouring trees touch and interlock.

Another curious method of perpetuating life is *root-grafting*. This occurs quite commonly in stands of trees where roots interlace below ground. It becomes evident where the stump of a felled tree starts to heal over, being nourished by the photosynthesis of standing trees of the same species nearby. Unfortunately certain tree diseases such as the white rot of conifers due to the fungus *Fomes annosus*, and Dutch elm disease, *Ceratocystis ulmi*, are readily transmitted through root grafts.

The mechanism of all forms of grafting is the contact of live cambial layers belonging to two separate individual trees, so that they form a link. In nature the outer bark prevents this unless and until it is worn away by slight movement of crossing stems or broken by the expansion of stems or underground roots.

Part 2

Ecology and Environmental Relationships

Chapter 5

Trees Growing Together

IN nature the solitary tree is the exception rather than the rule. The gardeners and landscapists who plan tree planting in gardens, parks and roadside avenues usually place trees in isolation from their fellows, aiming at individual effect. By contrast, the forester and the student of ecology are nearly always concerned with trees growing in close association with others, either belonging to their own kind or to other species.

Various terms have been coined to describe such groupings. Foresters speak of a *stand*, a *crop* or a *plantation*, particularly where the group has been established artificially. Biologists refer to a tree *association*, such as a *pinetum*, or grouping of pine trees, though their terms usually embrace related vegetation such as heather among the pines. Though the forester is able to 'manage' his stands and the ecologist writes studies of his associations at great length, tree groupings remain complex subjects constantly changing and difficult to evaluate. As in all tree studies, we are dealing with extensive dimensions of space and time. The trees in each group will rarely be all of the same age, and never of identical size and shape. Usually one has to contemplate interactions between individuals at different stages in their respective careers. The situations encountered are very different from those found among annual crops such as wheat or cabbages.

Seedling Thickets

One of the commonest and simplest tree groupings to study is the thicket of natural tree seedlings that springs up now and again and here and there when a gap arises in a full-grown forest. It is the 'classical' way whereby the loss of one leading, dominant tree is made good without human intervention. The forester describes it as a form of 'natural regeneration', though he is usually ready to manipulate events by artificial means to encourage its growth and development. Plate 12.

A simple example occurs in a tall beechwood where the dense overhead shade of mature trees prevents the growth of green plants of any kind on the forest floor. During a great summer gale a single giant tree blows down and is promptly removed by the forester for sale as timber. The succeeding autumn proves to be a 'mast' year in which all the surviving beeches ripen a heavy crop of seed. This falls to the forest floor and attracts flocks of pigeons and parties of hungry squirrels, wood mice and badgers. But the seed is so abundant that even after these marauders have taken their toll many seeds remain hidden in the forest litter. On every square metre (square yard) there may be, say, around 100 grains, weighing together around half a kilogram (one pound). Next spring they sprout. The great majority fail to progress because there is insufficient light on the beech-wood floor. Those that fell in the gap where the beech tree blew down are more fortunate than their fellows. Here there is ample light for growth and they quickly become established. A seedling thicket results. Its member trees grow vigorously in the centre of the gap where light is most abundant but less vigorously around the shaded edges.

During their first summer the beech seedlings, growing at random spacings about one centimetre apart from each other, do not compete with one another to any serious degree. Moreover their numbers are reduced by casualties, for a proportion get gobbled up by birds or even gnawed away by snails. But in their second year their searching roots meet below ground and their young shoots bear leaves that start to shade those of their fellows. Mutual competition for soil nutrients and moisture, growing space and sunlight has begun.

Over the following years this competition is sure to intensify. As each seedling grows taller it expands sideways in proportion. After a few years the roots of scores of saplings are interlacing below ground level, and their shoots are mingling in the air above. Because the seedlings in the centre get more light than those on the surrounding rim they grow taller more quickly. The resulting outline of the group has been aptly called an 'inverted pudding-basin'.

Beech can tolerate a great deal of shade but the weaker individuals, which cannot keep any leading shoots up in the sunlit top layer, inevitably perish when they become completely overshaded by their neighbours.

This elimination of the weaker or less favourably placed individuals is a ruthless process. Once an unlucky tree has died its decay begins. Leaves and stems wither, fall and are soon broken down to become part of the forest mould. The roots of the survivors draw on this debris for nutrients and also tap those portions of the soil that the roots of the dead sapling once claimed as their own. Surviving trees can only gain greater living space at the expense of their defeated fellows.

These trends continue as the saplings year by year grow taller. The forester keeping a watchful eye on the progress of his 'natural regeneration group', which is replacing his lost mature beech without expense, refers to the taller survivors as *dominant* trees. Those falling behind in the struggle for existence are aptly called *suppressed*. Long-term observations show that few suppressed specimens ever gain a place in a final crop of timber. Once a tree has fallen behind, it is on its way out.

This fierce mutual competition has interesting effects on the shape of the surviving trees. Only those that grow vigorously upwards can retain a worthwhile place and this favours good straight trees with vigorous trunks of sound timber forms. Those that trend sideways or develop too many side branches soon disappear. The deep shade near ground level kills off the side branches of surviving trees, and these branches soon fall. This 'natural pruning' lessens the size and frequency of knots, which are 'buried branches' in the resulting timber, and so increases its value. Though competition slows down the progress of the tree in its early years, it moulds its form in ways that make it a better timber proposition. The forester may therefore be ready to accept its slow progress in its early years, rather than clear the land and replant with trees at wider spacings.

Assessing the intensity of this competition in numerical terms, the mature beech trees stand at a density of 250 stems per hectare (10,000 square metres). Each therefore needs 40 square metres of growing space. But the seedlings spring up at a density of 100 per square metre. This means that, at the outset, there are 4,000 contestants striving to gain the place once occupied by only one mature tree. All the rest will be eliminated and the great majority will go out in the first few years. Only a few vigorous stems will follow the ultimate victor of the contest up into the main canopy of the beechwood. (Imperial equivalents: 100 stems per acre, 40 square yards per tree, final space; initial density 100 per square yard).

Plantations

Regrowth by natural regeneration is often welcomed in established woods, but when foresters start to establish tree crops for timber production on bare land they aim to avoid the cut-throat competition found in the early years of a natural seedling thicket. Foresters can, it is true, collect seed and scatter it in the same lavish way as a natural 'mast' crop. But this is costly and most of the seed is sure to be taken by birds like finches or by rodents such as wood mice.

To gain the quick unhindered start that is guaranteed by reasonable isolation, foresters normally make plantations by setting out individual trees, raised to the right size in nurseries, at a distance apart found best through long experience. For a typical conifer such as a pine, this is commonly two metres (yards) apart in each direction. This allows each individual tree a growing space at the outset of four square metres (square yards). This area should be compared with a space of 40 square metres (square yards) required by a typical mature pine tree. Plate 48.

At first the young pines appear to be growing in splendid isolation and for a few years each is unaffected by the presence of its fellows. Yet within five years or so their branch tips are meeting above ground and their roots are crossing one another down in the soil below. A few years later the lower branches of the pines start to die, one by one, through overshading. The living green branches above form a continuous, though loosely interwoven, layer of foliage higher up, called the *canopy*. The shade beneath it may be fairly light as with pine or oak, or deep as with spruce, hemlock or beech.

If all the trees remained, none could expand its branches beyond a metre or two on either side without encountering close competition for sunlight from its neighbours. As the trees grew taller, the canopy would rise with them but it would not develop by becoming deeper, and each tree would be restricted to a minimal branch spread. Its roots below ground would encounter similar checks. The outcome, which is sometimes seen in neglected plantations, is a dense crop of tall thin stems of very low value as timber. They lack stability and eventually the overcrowded crop gets blown down.

To prevent this the forester carries out a regular process of *thinning*. Every five years or so after the canopy has formed he marks a proportion of trees, scattered evenly through the crop, for removal. At the first thinning he takes out about 20% of the original number of trees and this, after allowing for around 13% of previous natural casualties, means that only two-thirds of the first stocking remains. Later thinnings, less drastic, remove from 10% to 15% of the survivors each time, until at length only one in ten of the trees originally planted remains. The average growing space has by then increased from four to forty square metres (square yards) per tree. The 'final crop' is usually cut down about ten years after the last thinning, and the land is later replanted. See Figs. 22, p. 226 and 23, p. 227.

Foresters attach great importance to the control of competition among their plantation trees. After measuring and comparing hundreds of *sample plots* over scores of years, they have devised *management tables*, covering all common trees, for different ages of crop and rates of growth. The rate of removal by thinning out is nowadays guided by computer mathematics rather than guesswork. In consequence a great deal is known about the behaviour of trees handled in the various ways that affect interactions between individuals.

The folklore of the woods insists that trees only grow tall if they are 'forced up' by their fellows. But comparisons between hundreds of crops show that those individuals that are given ample space maintain vigour of growth in all dimensions. Their crowns of foliage are taller and *deeper*, from the topmost shoot to the lowest life branch, than those of crowded trees. Their root systems are larger and therefore give firmer root-hold. Most important in economic terms, their timber stems expand more rapidly towards greater ultimate sizes than do those of similar trees that have been given less living space. On many counts, therefore, the forester prefers a wide spacing scheme with frequent *heavy* thinnings because it promises greatest profit.

Inevitably the wider spacing and heavier thinning result in fewer trees to sell. But within known limits the total volume of timber that a crop can produce is not increased by carrying more trees on each hectare. Where the choice lies between the same volume contained in many stems or fewer, the latter course pays better. This is because bigger planks or similar timbers can be sawn from stouter stems with less waste than from smaller ones. Harvesting is cheaper per unit of volume. Therefore a timber merchant will pay a better price for the same total quantity of wood contained in large stems than in smaller ones.

Though the forester cannot greatly increase the rate of total timber production by crowding his trees, he can do so in other ways. He can cultivate the ground by deep ploughing before planting it, to make a greater volume of aerated soil available for the tree roots. If the land is waterlogged he can improve it by deep drainage. If it lacks nutrients he can add them in the form of artificial fertilizers. The biggest changes, however, result from the wise choice of tree to be grown. Given an equal chance, certain trees such as spruce and hemlock consistently grow more timber in the same time than do pine or larch. Among the broadleaved trees, beech, for example, is ranked a heavier yielder than oak.

A common factor that distinguishes the higher yielding trees is usually an ability to tolerate shade. This means in effect that they utilize the energy of sunlight more efficiently than do trees that demand bright light. Those trees that can thrive close together and maintain close association of their individual living branches carry larger volumes of timber in their stems relative to the land area that the whole plantation occupies, than do the kinds that demand greater space for their growth.

Woods of Varied Ages and Species: The Selection Forest

The seedling thickets and the plantations just described are examples of more-or-less even-aged stands of a single species, also called a *pure even-aged forest*. It is more usual particularly in natural, untended woodlands to find the ground occupied by trees of several kinds with a wide range of ages from seedlings to mature giants and declining veterans. In simple terms, this is a *mixed, uneven-aged forest*. Its character is infinitely variable in respect of both mixture of species and mixture of ages and is seldom the same for two years together. Plates 56, 58 and Fig. 16, p. 166.

In one ideal situation, found more often in the textbooks than in the woods, there is a proportional gradation from young small trees, present in large numbers, to old large trees which are fewer and farther between. The forester secures his timber harvest by choosing every few years a quota of mature timber trees for felling, plus a proportion of middle-aged ones that are growing too close together. For this reason, his management is called a *selection system*. Nature obligingly fills in the resultant gaps with seedling thickets wherever mature trees have been removed, or by the vigorous growth of neighbours wherever middle-aged trees have been cut out. The variation in size and character of tree crowns ensures the fullest possible utilization of the available sunlight and hence the maximum timber production from the land concerned.

Selection forests of this kind are found, though only over limited areas, in certain countries that have a long tradition of skilled professional forestry, notably Switzerland and Germany. They have many attractions. The crop is renewed perpetually at no cost. The soil is never exposed to the full force of wind, rain or snow; soil erosion is therefore minimal and a good depth of soft, well-aerated mould, ideal for water retention, builds up and persists for centuries. Natural wild life, both plant and animal, is given continuing though locally varying habitats. Woodland scenery is scarcely disturbed by the occasional felling of selected trees. Light and living space are used at various levels from the ground to the tops of the trees in the most efficient way throughout continuing time without a break. Consequently the rate of total timber production is higher than that of plantations on similar land.

But selection forests also pose many problems. Their satisfactory management demands not merely one skilled forester but a perpetual succession of dedicated silviculturists whose first love is the woods they tend and who come to know every tall tree or clump of smaller ones intimately. Having studied their remarkably complex crop, noting its spacing and the potentiality of each tree or group for development, they must at intervals market both large mature trees and smaller, overcrowded ones. In the past, traditional timber merchants were happy with the resultant mixture of large and small logs of various kinds offered them for purchase because their woodsmen worked slowly with hand tools and horse haulage. Modern concerns are geared to powerful machines handling a large bulk of uniform timber and cannot effectively handle a 'mixed parcel' sale.

In brief, both the timber merchant and the forest owner can make more money by simpler, mass production plantation methods. Hence selection forestry only holds its own where there is some overriding reason – such as the preservation of woodland scenery or the control of avalanches on alpine slopes – that demands perpetual forest cover.

A common fallacy in ecological studies is to regard the selection forest as the normal state of affairs in natural woodlands throughout the world. This concept of *climax forests* in perfect equilibrium with their environment is a Utopian one implying a world without change. If the guiding hand of the forester is removed the composition of the woodland by species, age and size of tree tends to swing towards one extreme or another.

The ideal mixture may change to a pure forest of ageing veterans, all of one kind, with few openings for seedling trees of any species. When these eventually die, decay and disappear, a new kind of tree may invade the territory by natural seeding and produce a new pure forest with only a limited range of ages. This brings us to the principles of ecological succession.

Ecological Changes in Forest Composition

The course of change in the make-up of the tree cover over a given tract of land is best shown by a few examples drawn from classical studies in Europe, North America and tropical Asia. The accepted method of carrying out such studies, within a reasonable span of time, is to compare different stages of the succession on adjacent, comparable areas. This assumes that certain patches of growth are ahead of others through the chances of events.

The Birch–Pine–Spruce Succession

The birch–pine–spruce succession is typical of northern regions such as parts of Canada and Scandinavia. After a felling or a forest fire, the bare land is first colonized by birch, a broadleaved tree of the genus *Betula*, which has remarkable powers of quick invasion. It is regarded as a *pioneer*. Birch seeds are very numerous, small and light, and can be carried by strong winds over great distances. A sprinkling of viable seeds is sure to fall fairly evenly over the bare land surface which is free for the time being from occupation by other surface vegetation such as heather.

Each birch seedling is minute but capable of rapid growth. Within a few years irregular thickets of birch saplings spring up. Like many pioneer trees, birch is a strong light demander and mutual competition between the growing trees soon reduces the number of survivors. The result is an open forest of scattered birch trees with an undergrowth of heather, blue-berries or bilberries that thrive on the well-lit ground beneath. Birch, however, is not a stayer. Its life span seldom exceeds sixty years. If no other trees were present, gaps would eventually appear which would be filled in by fresh birch saplings.

But pines, which are conifers in the genus *Pinus*, are present too. Whilst the birch has been taking the lead as the dominant tree and forming a birch association, or *betuletum*, pine saplings have played a minor part in the plant community. They owe their subordinate position to their slower growth rate in the early seedling stage.

The decline of individual birch trees through deaths due to fungal attack leaves gaps that are soon filled by sapling pines, well placed by accident to exploit an increased supply of sunlight and soil nutrients. If this happens on a general scale as it often does in the northern forests, the character of the whole woodland changes from a birch association to one of pine trees, a *pinetum*. The pines have a longer life span than the birch. They may persist for 150 years. Any gaps they leave are open to invasion by either pine or birch, but as the pine becomes more plentiful it is more likely, short of some major calamity like a massive felling or a forest fire, to maintain the predominantly pine association over a long span of years.

There is, however, a third competitor for this living space. This is a spruce, of the genus *Picea*, which has survived from a previous spruce phase along watercourses on the fringes of the once bare land. Its minute, winged seeds are carried each spring into the pine-birch association. But very few spruces start growth successfully because these tiny seedlings fail to compete with the dense growth of heather and bilberry below the birches and pines. Plate 57.

At a certain stage in the progress of the pinetum, however, the shade on the forest floor may become too dense for heather and its associates and they die out. Spruce seedlings, which have very low light requirements, may then establish themselves in small groups. Gradually despite the competition of the taller pines they will work their way up into the canopy, awaiting their time to become the dominant trees. As each pine matures and falls, or is felled by the timber man, a group of younger spruce replaces it and gradually the forest becomes a spruce association, or *picetum*.

Left to itself this picetum may endure for centuries, as the *climax* phase for the forest. Mature spruce trees bear seed abundantly but cast very deep shade. The first trees to establish themselves in small gaps will always be spruces rather than pines or birches because the latter two need more light. So spruce once established is very difficult to supplant.

Eventually a sudden clearance due to fire or massive felling may expose bare ground over a wide area. This brings us back to our starting point. The threefold succession of birch, pine and spruce will then repeat itself over a time span of perhaps 300 years.

The part played by the ground vegetation is very significant in this progression. Spruce seedlings that sprout on the original bare land get suppressed and killed by the faster growth of heather, grasses and bilberries. But the birch seedlings, and to a lesser degree the slower growing seedlings of pine, hold their own and soon grow safely taller than the ground cover. Spruce, the ultimate climax tree, can only gain a foothold after the heather has been suppressed by the shade of the pines. It is a *successor* tree, never a pioneer.

We can never comprehend the whole story by considering either the individual tree or the trees as a group in isolation. At critical stages in their life histories the chances are their associated soils, climate, plant and animal life may be all-important, at one time or another, for the determination of their success or failure.

Over any given area of the forest the birch–pine–spruce succession is a simple one through the course of time. But over the forest as a whole there will be, at one time, areas at different stages in this succession. The random run of natural events may result in a clump of old birches standing on a hillock, an expanse of middle-aged pines over the adjoining plain and a long tongue-shaped stretch of young spruce running down a nearby valley.

At a first assessment the ecologist, or student of plants in their natural surroundings, may decide that each kind of tree has found its true place, or *niche*, in the scheme of things. In simple terms he may say that the spruce claims the wet ground while the birch tolerates the dry rocky hillock, both in preference to the pine. This may be true, but only for a limited spell of time. A hundred years later the spruce may have claimed all the flat 'pine' land, the pine in turn may have replaced the birch on the hillock, while the birch itself may be found in strength only in the 'spruce' valley which it has colonized following a timber felling.

One is reminded here of a vivid phrase in one of Thomas Hardy's poems:

> *Thus meet we here in this one place*
> *At this point in time, at this point in space*

The character of the association is never the same in two such places, nor for any prolonged spell of time.

The Thorn–Oak–Beech Succession

A common progression of natural forest is found both in Europe and North America where farms are abandoned by their cultivators owing to some change in the economics of local agriculture. For a time the occasional grazing of sheep or cattle may check all young tree growth but once farm livestock are withdrawn from the land trees invade it through natural seeding. They convert farm to forest in a space of thirty years or so.

The typical first arrival is a thorn tree, usually one of the hawthorn genus, *Crataegus*. Its seedlings appear in strength because its seed is specially adapted to transport by birds. Its berry, or haw, has a fleshy pulp that attracts birds in autumn. The hard seed or seeds within have a thick coat that resists digestion. They are either cast aside by the birds or else get swallowed and pass through the birds' digestive tracts, emerging unharmed in their droppings possibly miles from their source. The thorn seedlings that result soon develop spines which deter grazing animals from gobbling them up. Wherever the turf is not too dense, thickets of hawthorns gradually develop, meet and shade the ground. A hawthorn forest, or *crataegetum*, results. It is only about six metres (yards) high but can persist in the absence of taller trees for fifty years or more.

The taller tree most likely to compete with the thorn trees is an oak of one species or another in the genus *Quercus*. The acorn, the nut of the oak, is a large solid seed too heavy for wind transport and having no soft pulp to attract birds. But its very size and substance paradoxically provide the reason for its carriage over long distances. Its main bulk within its hard husk consists of two big fleshy seed-leaves or *cotyledons*. Though unattractive to man by reason of their high tannin content which gives them a bitter taste, acorns are a nourishing food for beasts and birds, including some that travel long distances. This seed dispersal is accidental: the animal intends to destroy the acorn by eating it but sometimes is prevented from doing so by mischance. A typical accident is the death of a wood pigeon which has recently filled its crop with acorns but is later pounced upon by a hawk. The hawk eats the flesh of the pigeon's carcass but rejects the acorns which it finds indigestible. These sprout where the pigeon fell, possibly in a field miles away from the oak forest.

Squirrels hide acorns as a winter food reserve and may either forget where they put them or fail to survive to recover them. Effective agents of acorn dispersal are the jays, birds that deliberately carry acorns in their beaks to open grassland and bury them below the turf, sowing them just as a good forester might do. Their object, apparently, is to recover them next spring when food is scarce for nut-eating birds. The young oak shoots reveal to an observant jay the spot at which the fleshy seed-leaves still lie hidden below the grass. It eats those seedlings that it finds; the rest become oak saplings!

On grassland the young oaks are in immediate peril of being bitten back by grazing livestock. But if they spring up in or beside a hawthorn thicket this danger is less because the spines of the hawthorn deter the cows, sheep, deer or ponies from attacking the seedlings. In effect the thorn trees act as 'nurses' or 'protectors' of the oaks. Some of the oaks, growing steadily taller each year, eventually gain the top of the thorn thickets, usually through some gap, and emerge above it. Oak can grow far larger and taller than hawthorn, often reaching 30 metres (100 feet). The outcome after another fifty years or so is an oakwood, or *quercetum*, with the few surviving thorns reduced to a minor role as bushes, more or less suppressed by the oak trees' shade.

This climax forest of oaks can endure for centuries but in many situations it is liable to be supplanted by beech, *Fagus*. The beech nut like the acorn is a fairly heavy seed, transported in a similar way by jays, squirrels, pigeons and similar creatures. In years of heavy beech seeding, or mast years, some beech nuts are likely to get carried into the oakwood. Those that sprout have little difficulty in starting growth beneath the oaks for beech can tolerate remarkably deep shade.

The scattered beech seedlings grow slowly but steadily taller to become saplings which eventually form an understorey of medium-sized trees below the higher canopy of the oaks. The scene is now set for a 'take-over bid' by the beeches. Whenever an aged oak dies and falls there are sure to be some beeches near at hand which escape damage at the time of the oak's fall. These are ready to fill the space that the fallen oak leaves. Gradually the whole character of the forest changes. The half-grown beeches have a start of many metres in height over any competing young oak trees that might otherwise fill in a clearing. The beeches have already grown taller because they tolerate deeper shade.

Once the beech trees have begun to form their own dense canopy of foliage, no oak seedlings that remain or subsequently arise below it have much hope of survival. In simple terms the beeches 'shade them out'. The end result is a forest of pure beech, or *Fagetum*, the final climax of the thorn-oak-beech succession. Only one other tree may possibly supplant the beech at some far future date. This is yew, *Taxus*, which both casts and tolerates still deeper shade.

Succession in Tropical Forests

Succession follows a similar plan at a faster rate in the forests of tropical regions. Here a common cause of bare land is the practice of 'shifting cultivation' followed by peasant farmers. Within their tribal territory each group selects a patch of tall mature forest, fells the smaller trees and kills any that are too large to cut down by ring-barking them. The farmers burn the debris partly to clear the land and partly to enrich the soil with the nutrients that are held in the timber's wood ash. The destruction of useful timber in this process does not worry them since it has in these remote places few profitable markets, while an abundance of small poles for house building remains available in the jungles around.

After growing a few crops of rice, millet or maize over the next few years, the cultivators find the yield is falling as the fertility due to the wood ash becomes exhausted. Then they move on to fell a fresh patch of tall forest.

The abandoned clearing is quickly invaded by quick-growing trees of relatively small size that play only a minor role in the surrounding high forest. These grow very fast, often two metres (six feet) taller in one year, and within a few years the jungle has reclaimed the cleared ground. Few of these pioneer trees have much potential value as timber, nor do they reach great size or have a long life span. Gradually the real forest giants such as teak, mahogany and iroko infiltrate the so-called 'secondary jungle' that first took over the abandoned clearing.

Typically, the seedlings of these larger or successor trees are able to grow in the light shade of the pioneers, and they appear to benefit from the shelter, humidity and lesser illumination that the first invaders provide. Gradually the saplings of the taller and longer-lived timber trees emerge through the low canopy of the pioneers. Once well-established, they forge ahead, growing far taller and larger than the pioneer stand which they eventually dominate. If this pioneer stand persists at all it is only as a sparse understorey below the main timber crop.

This process is continually going on in different parts of the same forest. The shifting cultivators prefer to make their clearings in the older stands which promise greater soil fertility since they hold more minerals in their wood, and carry fewer stems to kill or cut down on any given area, than do the younger woodlands. The patchwork of old timber, cultivated land and young forest regrowth at various stages is best observed from the air.

Obviously this practice sets big problems for modern scientific forest managers in the tropics. With foresight they can harvest the valuable mature timber stems from each fresh cultivation patch before it is cleared. The ideal solution, seldom practical for political, social and economic reasons, is to ban further shifting cultivation and settle the cultivators in fixed villages elsewhere. Usually this means transferring a fraction of the forest land to the permanent agricultural area of the country concerned.

Shifting cultivation was formerly also practised in European forests before settled communities developed. In North America the system was followed by those Indian tribes that cultivated maize. The successions that took place in these northern continents followed the birch–pine–spruce or thorn–oak–beech patterns discussed above, or some similar progression from light-demanding to shade-bearing trees.

The Individual Tree in the Society

In such considerations of tree communities it is easy to lose sight of the individual trees that build them up. Like separate people in a human society each tree has its own particular life to live as well as its contribution to make to the group. In scientific terms, we must remember its *autecology*, or the environmental complex of the individual, as well as its *synecology*, which implies the environmental pattern of the society of trees, and also their linked plant and animal life, of which this tree forms a part.

Trees demand exacting study in this respect because they grow so large and last so long that they create peculiar environments for their own kind. Typically an individual maple, *Acer*, may progress from a seedling in sheltered shade to a mature, seed-bearing giant in exposed sunlight. During its progress it may spend years in a seedling thicket stage, neighboured by other maples and also by trees of quite different species that restrict its upward and outward expansion. Below ground its roots will live in another changing environment, restricted at various stages by competition with the roots of other trees and plants.

All these factors will be reflected in the growth and form of this tree. For example, its years of overcrowding will be indelibly recorded in a zone of narrow annual rings which will always remain hidden in its inner wood. This zone will hold only short small knots because its side branches were at that period small and short-lived. Subsequent years of free growth will find expression in wider annual rings and larger knots.

71

With smaller, shorter-lived plants it is often possible to link growth with simple factors of the environment. A buttercup on fertile soil grows larger than one on a sterile patch of sand, and one cactus may be stunted by extreme drought while another nearby grows tall because its roots reach some hidden spring of water. But a tree leads a far more complicated life. It is affected by its environment but it also reacts to its surroundings and changes them as it gets bigger. At one stage it may secure ample light, water and nutrients, and at another be deprived of these essentials only to regain them when it outlasts its competitors. A community of trees, with the individuals that compose it interacting with and upon one another as well as with the group as a whole, presents a still more complex structure which exists through fluctuating dimensions of time and space.

Chapter 6

The Soil

THE soil that a tree's roots explore and exploit and in which its trunk gets a secure anchorage is a complex material composed of many elements. It is derived from the basic 'rock' beneath it by a process called weathering, which is intimately affected by surface vegetation. 'Rock' in this context is a geologist's term that embraces softer substances like clay and sand, as well as rock-hard materials. Since trees and forests form major elements in the world's vegetation, it follows that they influence soil formation to an effective degree. Forests not only grow on soil; they help to make it.

Loams

The layman who approaches the study of soils is usually muddled at the outset by that familiar term 'loam' applied, with all sorts of qualifying adjectives like 'sandy', 'clay', or 'peaty' to any soil worth cultivating by a farmer or gardener. On further enquiry he discovers that loams are mixtures of varying proportions of fine or coarse grains of mineral matter, classified as particles of clay, silt, sand and even gravel. They hold varying amounts of 'humus', a handy term covering every kind of organic matter, vegetable or animal, in varying stages of decay. These mineral and organic particles are not packed solid but hold a great deal of pore space. This may be filled with either air or water, and usually both are present.

Soils of this 'loam' type provide the ideal medium for the support of tree life and forest growth. The tree's roots, including their finer elements and the still finer root hairs, can branch out and explore the gaps between the particles of mineral and organic matter. Everywhere they find air which is essential to their life process of breathing. Water is available for intake into the tree's conductive system to support transpiration through the leaves. Because this water has at one stage or another filtered down through the humus-rich surface layers of the soil in which leaf litter and other debris is embodied, it holds nutrients derived from the breakdown of previous plant and animal organisms. Further nutrients in dilute solution arise from the slow disintegration of the mineral soil particles which hold traces of essential elements such as phosphorus.

A fertile loam supporting a forest crop is thus a complex structure in which many factors favour the nutrition of the trees above it. One further essential is the right temperature. If the soil freezes or its temperature falls below 6°C active growth ceases and the roots lie dormant until the earth warms up again.

Brown Forest Soils

It is natural to enquire how such fertile soils arose from the earth's original materials of hard rock, stiff clay or sterile sand. The modern science of *pedogenesis*, literally 'the birth of the soil', explains this and attributes the formation of fertile loams largely to the work of past forests themselves. Under its broad scheme of classification most loams fall into a 'world group' termed *Brown Forest Soils* or *Brown Earths*.

Soil is created by a long chain of physical, chemical and biological processes extending over thousands of years. Exposed bare rock is first weathered by the action of sun, wind, rain and in the colder regions frost, into a softer, broken surface material in which small plants take root. The lowest kinds of plant life, including algae, lichens and mosses are eventually succeeded by grasses and herbs and finally, as the depth of broken-down material builds up, by forest trees. These by reason of their greater size are able to add more substantial amounts of humus each year, largely by leaf and other litter fall. Their roots explore deeper than those of smaller plants and speed up the gradual breakdown of the rocks below. They also transport substantial amounts of organic matter from their crowns down into the soil by the mere process of root growth.

Most of the best farm land in all countries has been won from the virgin forests that created its fertile soil through deliberate clearance by cultivators. In many countries, including the British Isles, little forest remains standing on Brown Forest Soils. Nearly all these soils have become the 'loams' of farmers and gardeners who have forgotten their true origin. Inevitably this Brown Earth group is regarded as an outcome of agriculture rather than what it really is, the bequest of vanished woodlands.

Where a forester is fortunate enough to tend woods which are growing on Brown Forest Soils, there is little he can or need do to increase the health and vigour of his tree crops. They are growing under optimum conditions of nutrition and experience has shown that they cannot be speeded up by either fertilizers or cultivation. The trees themselves restore nutrients by leaf and litter fall and their active roots achieve all the cultivation required.

74

The forester's standpoint here contrasts with that of the farmer. The latter is constantly removing nutrients in the form of crops or animal products such as meat, milk or wool; he must therefore restore nutrients by bringing in manure or artificial fertilizers. The forester leaves most permanent nutrients behind, taking out only trifling amounts of minerals in his timber at much longer intervals of time.

The advance of agriculture, claiming all the better land for food production, obliges foresters in all the more developed countries to deal with trees growing on soils that are much less attractive than Brown Earths. In many countries including Britain and much of North America, it is true to say that land only becomes available for afforestation when its soil or situation is unsuited to sustained farming use. Much of this land in the remote past carried trees of some kind or another. Often it has remained treeless for centuries because of the grazing of farm stock, especially sheep. Foresters have in consequence become experts on the less fertile classes of soil and in methods of improving them at economic costs.

Their methods can be described in three ideas: cultivation, drainage and fertilization. Any two of these or all three may be combined, depending on the nature of the problem. Irrigation, implying addition of water, is rarely applied in forestry. The ultimate goal of forest site improvement is the state of affairs that natural forces have already created elsewhere in the Brown Earth soil group. This is in theory self-sustaining, needing no repeated treatments. Without being sentimental, it is fair to describe those foresters who improve poor soils as 'earth healers'.

Much land lies beyond their effective scope. It may lie too far north, say in Canada or Siberia, or too far up the hills, so that cold climatic conditions rule it out. In the tropics or sub-tropics low rainfall may result in desert conditions that no tree can tolerate. Slopes may be too steep for machinery to operate upon: the basic rock may be too hard and incapable of breaking down to yield soils. Many combinations of these adverse factors naturally exist but elsewhere persistent foresters can achieve miraculous improvements of unpromising land. Trees increase soil organic content in two ways, by the fall of their litter and by the continuous transport of carbon compounds, 'fixed' from the air, down to the roots to ensure their growth.

Blown Sands

Striking successes in land reclamation have been achieved by foresters in many countries who have tamed dunes of loose, blowing sands. Classic examples are found on the Culbin sandhills of northeast Scotland, the

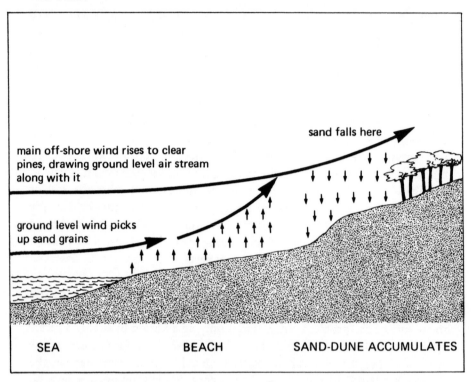

main off-shore wind rises to clear
pines, drawing ground level air stream
along with it

sand falls here

ground level wind picks
up sand grains

SEA   BEACH   SAND-DUNE ACCUMULATES

Figure 10   Sandblow control at Arcachon, south-west France. Offshore winds rise to clear maritime pine trees, *Pinus pinaster*, on right. Suspended sand grains fall and a dune results.

coastal sand dunes that protect the Landes district of southwest France from the stormy Atlantic Ocean, and on the coast of South Australia. These apparently sterile and bone-dry sand grains hold, in the mass, enough nutrients to support plant life and also, except in regions of minimal rainfall, adequate entrapped water. But no normal plants can grow because the constant winds move the free grains of sand both horizontally and uphill, burying small plants. Only a few specially adapted plants such as marram grass, *Ammophila arenaria*, survive by means of a meshwork of underground stems and roots that endure partial burial, then grow up to and through the new soil surface. But such grasses never halt dune movement entirely because the air currents flow between their more or less parallel stalks and blades.

The forester's solution to the dune problem is to thatch the surface of the sand with brushwood, deliberately placed criss-cross-wise. Then, no matter what the wind direction may be, the air currents at ground level no longer move fast enough to stir the sand grains. The surface of the dune becomes static and therefore the movement of the dune as a whole is arrested.

Between the brushwood stems the forester plants small trees, usually pines of a well-proven species such as Corsican pine, *Pinus nigra* variety *maritima*, or the south European maritime pine, *P. pinaster*. He uses small, well-rooted plants, only about 10 centimetres high, and sets them out with their roots deep in the sand during the winter resting season. Surprisingly there is always enough water held by capillary attraction amid the sand grains below the dune's bone-dry surface. The pines take root and grow, slowly at first, then rapidly. Within a few years they form a light but continuous cover over the dune and their foliage reinforces the wind-slowing action of the brushwood thatch. As that rots away, only slowly under the arid conditions of the dune surface, the trees replace it with their own natural debris. Pine needles and eventually dead side branches fall to the plantation floor and create permanent organic cover at ground level. At the same time, the trees are expanding their crowns of foliage above to give lasting shelter while their roots form meshwork in the soil below.

Gradually a true soil is created on the sand dune through the addition of tree debris together with other waste organic matter from the plant and animal life that now appears in the pinewood's shelter. This soil is threaded through by actively growing tree roots which eventually by their own decay carry organic additions down to deep levels. A self-sustaining forest on a self-maintaining soil eventually results. Plate 43.

Clays

The opposite extreme to sands is found in heavy clays which, though composed of small mineral grains that together compose only a soft material, prove a poor substratum for plant growth. Though clays hold water it cannot move freely. Air circulation too is impeded by the close-packed nature of the clay. Deprived of oxygen, roots cannot readily penetrate the material. Clays are usually rich in nutrients but in the absence of active root penetration these cannot be absorbed by the plants or trees.

The farmer's answer to this problem is to cultivate the surface layers yearly, taking advantage of dry spells or periods of frost that make the intractable clay more workable. His cultivations are inevitably superficial, but adequate for shallow-rooted crops.

The forester in contrast must improve rooting conditions to a deeper level. He can only do so by digging a system of open drains, for tree roots would soon clog any pipe or 'tile' drains. He digs ditches, nowadays by machinery though formerly with hand tools, up to depths of $1\frac{1}{2}$ metres. These promote sideways movement of water which is followed or accompanied by air. Tree roots can then penetrate the stiff mass, and once trees become established, they introduce organic matter in root tissue and by leaf- and shoot-fall on the ground surface. The decay of dead roots opens up fresh channels for moisture flow and aerations. Gradually the growing forest changes the inert clay into a 'living' soil in which both plant roots and minute animal life can flourish.

Where the drainage of a clay soil is seriously impeded, the level of the water that saturates it may rise during rainy seasons and fall later. On its upward course it carries with it certain minerals, especially iron compounds, that get deposited in the upper layers giving them a mottled appearance. The resulting soil structure is called a *gley*. Gleys can be improved by drainage where the terrain allows. Otherwise they support only a limited range of trees that are adapted to grow on waterlogged soils.

Gleys and clay soils generally give poor root-hold to forest trees. When they are wet they assume the character of plastic substances rather than true solids. A peculiar danger arises from their ability to shrink in dry weather and to expand again when wetted by heavy rains. The roots of large trees that transpire water rapidly, such as poplars, *Populus* species, promote rapid drying out of soil during hot summers. In consequence the clay shrinks and moves to a degree that can upset the foundations of buildings that stand near such large trees.

Under exceptional conditions of continuous waterlogging, usually associated with clay soils, only specially adapted trees can survive. These include alders, *Alnus* genus; willows, *Salix* genus; the swamp cypress, *Taxodium distichum* of the southeastern USA, and the mangroves such as *Rhizophora* species, in the tropics. Mangroves can even grow when exposed to salt water, which proves fatal to all other kinds of trees.

Peats

A third extreme class of soil consists of peats, which are deep layers of dead plant tissues, with related animal matter, which accumulate where conditions prevent normal decay. This is usually due to the waterlogging of the soil so that there is insufficient air for breakdown of the carbon-rich tissues present. Typically, peats begin to form in hollows with poor natural drainage. The debris of marsh plants fails to break down but it does provide a substratum on which a fresh layer of marsh plants can grow. The flora is limited to specialized plants that tolerate wet, acid soils, including sphagnum mosses, *Sphagnum* species, heather, *Calluna vulgaris*, grasses such as blue moor grass, *Molinia caerulea*, and sedges like the deer's hair sedge, *Trichophorum caespitosum*. These are typical of northern and montane peat beds in Europe, and allied species occur across Asia and North America. Farther south a wider range of marsh-dwelling plants and even trees like alders, *Alnus* species, and willows, *Salix* species, form peats around shallow lakes and slow-moving rivers. These fen peats are, however, less acid and more fertile than the upland peats, and are often reclaimed for agriculture.

Once started the process of peat formation proceeds for hundreds, and even thousands, of years. This can be proved by modern radio carbon methods of dating organic tissues. Peat builds up to depths of two metres or more and covers enormous areas of the northlands. Peat has limited, local uses as fuel for cottage fires, or composts for gardens. Its value for pasturage is very low since it supports no quick-growing, nutritious grasses. Large tracts of peat-covered land are therefore available for afforestation in most northern countries.

Only stunted pines, spruces and birches can grow on undrained peats, which form the *muskeg* typical of the cold zone south of the polar *tundra*. The waterlogging of the peat below the surface layers is the main obstacle to better tree growth. Today this can be overcome by a well-planned system of open drains cut by special ploughs drawn by crawler tractors.

The usual practice is to plough twice. At the first pass a tractor drawing a relatively shallow-digging plough digs drains about half a metre deep at intervals around two metres apart. This throws up long ribbons of peat in which the forest trees are planted, also two metres apart. Then a deeper-going plough, or draining machine, is used to make drains up to two metres deep, at wider espacements. These deep drains cut across the shallow ones and direct the water towards a suitably placed stream. The trees are planted deeply in the overturned slices of turf or preferably set with some roots running right through it to tap the moisture that always collects beneath an upturned sod. As they grow the roots strike deeper into the main mass of underlying peat, now aerated through the outward flow of previously entrapped water.

Peat is rich in nutrients derived from the decay of the plants that formed it. But it is often deficient in the element phosphorus which must then be added artificially at rates of around fifty grams per tree. The stability of the trees, as they grow taller and face the wind, becomes a problem, but luckily the drained peat, with an interlocked system of tree roots, gives better root-hold than the original wet, soft medium.

Chalk and Limestone Soils

A distinct group of shallow soils technically known as *rendzinas* develop over soft chalk and hard limestone rocks in which the main mineral element is calcium, in contrast to the silicon found elsewhere. These rocks and the soils derived from them are strongly alkaline in reaction and very pervious to water. Plate 44.

Bare chalk and limestone, being nearly pure calcium carbonate, $CaCO_3$, supply little nutriment to plants and trees and hold little moisture for their support. Plant life therefore depends for its existence mainly on the thin layer of decaying humus that forms just below the surface turf or forest leaf litter. This never becomes more than a few centimetres thick because the humus breaks down where it meets the unchanged alkaline bedrock. It is usually seen in any cutting through the soil and subsoil as a dark red, brown or black layer. Surprisingly shallow for the plant life it supports, it stands in sharp contrast to the white mineral chalk or limestone rock below.

The plants that thrive on chalk and limestone are specially adapted to grow on alkaline soils subject to severe summer drought. Certain large groups such as the *Rhododendron* genus of the family *Ericaceae* are utterly intolerant of lime and will die wherever alkaline water flows through their rooting soil. In other groups, including grasses and even heaths, occasional lime-tolerant species occur. Forest trees with roots that start shallow and then grow deeper may thrive for several years on lime soils but later fail and die long before reaching timber size. The mechanism of failure is called 'lime-induced chlorosis'. The iron in the normal chlorophyll of the tree's leaves is replaced in part by calcium; the leaf becomes an unhealthy pale green or yellow, and ceases to function normally.

Since the forester cannot change the character of these rocks, he can only raise timber by using trees that are known to tolerate their alkalinity and rapid drainage. These are not always the most profitable nor the most beautiful. Few conifers thrive well on chalk. The few exceptions include: yew, *Taxus* species; western red cedar, *Thuja plicata*; Lawson cypress, *Chamaecyparis lawsoniana*; Austrian pine, *Pinus nigra* variety *nigra*; European silver fir, *Abies alba*; and Atlas cedar, *Cedrus atlantica*. Many others, including most spruces of the genus *Picea*, cannot develop successfully; Scots pine, *Pinus sylvestris*, dies out after about twenty years growth on thin chalk soils.

Broadleaved trees are more tolerant and beech, *Fagus* genus, ash trees of the genus *Fraxinus*, and European sycamore, *Acer pseudoplatanus*, grow readily to full timber size.

Both chalk and limestone provide good root-hold and it is rare for trees to be blown down unless their roots have first decayed and become unsound. In practice foresters can do little to improve lime-rich soils except to maintain continuous forest cover. The leaf litter from tall beechwoods on chalk downs contributes more to their long-term fertility than any process of cultivation or artificial fertilizing.

Podzols

Podzols are a major group of soils associated with forests in temperate lands. Their name is simply the Russian word for 'ash' and is possibly derived from the ash-grey appearance of their leached layers. Plate 9.

Podzols form only on freely draining land by derivation from other forms of soil, mainly Brown Earths. They are easily recognized by their layered structure when a soil profile or cross-section is cut through them. An examination of this explains their origin.

A typical podzol such as is found in a pinewood with a ground flora of heather has on its surface a brownish layer of undecomposed leaves, twigs and other debris that have fallen from the plants and trees above to a depth of one centimetre or so. This merges into a decomposition layer from one to two centimetres thick in which the organic matter is actually breaking down under the action of fungi, bacteria, mites and other forms of minute animal life. This humus layer, which is actively explored by the roots of heather and pine, seeking nutrients, is dark brown to black in colour. It ends abruptly in an ash-grey zone called the *leached layer*. This owes its pale colour to the slow but steady leaching out of minerals by organic acids, derived from the decay of the humus above, as they percolate down through the soil. Its depth ranges around 20 centimetres but is highly variable even on the same site.

The leached layer ends abruptly in a fourth zone, the deposition layer, also called by countrymen the *pan, iron pan* or *hard pan*. In this narrow zone, only around one centimetre thick, certain minerals, notably iron compounds, that have been carried down from the leached layer are deposited to form a hard compacted structure usually coloured rusty red-brown. Though it originates through the percolation of water the hard pan becomes resistant to the passage of water, air and above all tree roots. It forms an effective barrier to drainage, cultivation and the vigorous growth of either farm crops or forest trees. Below it lies the unaltered subsoil of sand, gravel or broken rock from which the whole podzol structure was originally derived.

Farmers avoid podzols because a soil that has become stratified in this way supports neither good grass nor good crops. If its tree cover goes it remains as a waste of heather or heaths, coarse grasses and low shrubby plants like the Scottish blaeberry, *Vaccinium myrtillus*, which tolerate poor acid soils. In extreme cases it carries only mosses and lichens. For this reason extensive tracts of heathy land often become available to foresters at low cost for new afforestation projects.

Cultivation is an obvious method for their improvement. The first ploughs that were tried, drawn by horses, scarcely scratched the surface of both the soil and the problem. Today the ploughs used are exceptionally large with shares that can penetrate, if required, to a depth of one metre. They are drawn by high-powered crawler tractors. The tip of each share ends in a projecting tine of exceptionally hard steel, which cuts through both the tough top soil and the thin though rock-hard pan above the sub-soil. This tip and similar plough parts exposed to hard wear are detachable; the tip has to be renewed at intervals of a week or so.

In practice foresters rarely plough up all the ground in the way that a farmer would do. Instead they are content with a partial ploughing in strips around two metres apart, to match the planting intervals for their trees. Along these strips the huge ploughs rip through the whole layered structure of the podzol, and turn up a high *slice* of disturbed soil. Thus they open continuous gaps through the hard pan which allows penetration of water, air and tree roots to the subsoil below.

The upturned slice of soil, standing about half a metre high parallel to the furrow cut a corresponding half metre deep, provides a good medium for the early growth of young conifers. The former podzol is broken and disturbed to provide a permeable, well-drained medium for tree roots. The competing vegetation of heather and other plants is effectively suppressed for a few years and incidentally the risk of any heath fire spreading is much reduced. The young trees are set about two metres apart in steps cut with a hand tool in the side of the plough slice. Each little tree receives about fifty grams of a phosphatic fertilizer to remedy the soil's deficiency. Then it grows steadily down with its roots striking deep into the disrupted podzol to gain nutrients and a firm anchorage.

Laterites

The tropical equivalent of the podzol is in broad terms a group of soils called *laterites*. In these freely-draining soils the iron salts are carried down to various levels, up to two metres or so, and become spread through soft layers of minerals weathered from the underlying bedrock. When first exposed at a roadside cutting a typical laterite is soft-textured and yellowish brown in colour. After exposure to the air for only a few weeks, the iron components become oxidized, the colour changes to rust-red and the texture changes markedly to a hard gritty gravel. This curious transformation is of great value to engineers who can use weathered laterite to build serviceable roads, able to carry the heaviest lorry traffic, within a few weeks of digging it out.

The growers of farm crops are constantly exposing surface layers of laterite to the air and consequently work with the red, weathered material. This is a good medium for cultivation and yields fair crops when enriched with organic residues or fertilizers. But tree roots strike down into the very different unweathered laterites and on the whole these prove infertile, supporting only moderate tree growth. Laterites are typically associated with savannas of low, stunted trees, though other factors discussed in Chapter 12 are often limiting for growth.

Chapter 7

Climate and Weather

TREES, like all living organisms, can only thrive over a certain climatic range and within this they are subject to the seasonal or exceptional variations of conditions that are generally described as 'weather'. They differ from most animals and plants in their potentially longer life span. Many annual plants such as the common weed groundsel, *Senecio vulgaris*, can flourish indefinitely through one generation after another even though the climate is suitable for their life over only part of each year. By contrast a thousand-year-old tree must have survived all the climatic vagaries of all seasons on its site over a span of years of that length.

This simple fact of climatic tolerance is often overlooked by foresters and even more often by optimistic gardeners who seek to introduce new trees outside their acceptable climatic range. The classic example is the Australian *Eucalyptus* genus, which is constantly being reintroduced to temperate regions such as the British Isles. The well-established pattern is that it survives a series of fairly mild winters, particularly in coastal districts warmed by the Gulf Stream. But in the exceptional severe winter when prolonged frost holds water immobilized in the soil, it dies from drought, rather than from cold. Such winters, while quite unpredictable, occur about every ten years. Since thirty years are needed for a commercial timber crop to mature, it is clearly not worth while to aim for one. A similar pattern of rapid growth until the first killing winter has become evident for *Eucalyptus* even in sunny California.

In general the existence of mature trees gives firm evidence that they can tolerate the climate where they are found. But where trees have been planted by man they may be growing under a climate ill-suited to their flowering and fruiting and they may therefore be unable to complete their full life-cycle unaided. Common examples are the beech trees of the genus *Fagus*, which are often planted for ornament, and even for timber, in regions that are too cold for them to mature their seeds, both in Europe and North America.

Trees unlike smaller plants can adapt themselves to extremes of climate by assuming low bush form or even creeping prostrate over the soil surface to escape the force of the winds. In these stunted forms they can still achieve long life spans and mature their seed. For example in New Hampshire, USA, on the lower slopes of the 2,000-metre Mount Washington the balsam fir, *Abies balsamea*, grows as a tall tree around 30 metres (100 feet) high, regularly harvested for its timber. Nearer the tree-line, or upper limit of tree growth, which here stands at about 1,300 metres (4,300 feet) above sea level, it is reduced by prolonged winter cold and extreme exposure to high winds to a compact bush barely two metres tall. Seedlings that sprout at the extreme, tundra-like limit of the balsam's climatic range grow out sideways into flat woody mats, weighed down through most of the winter by the snowdrifts.

Drought conditions can likewise create miniature, stunted trees, sometimes of exceptional age. Both the long life and the small stature of the bristle-cone pine, *Pinus aristata*, are due to its growth under very dry conditions in the Arizona mountain deserts.

Trees, then, can flourish and reproduce their kind over long spells of time under conditions that effectively prevent their optimum development of size. The extreme conditions found at the limits of their range do, however, over a long series of generations kill out the larger or less tolerant strains. Gradually local varieties emerge, better adapted to cold mountain tops or hot dry deserts than the typical form of the species.

It is not always easy to identify these on their home ground. For example, a dwarf balsam fir found on a mountain top may belong to a montane variety incapable of taller growth no matter how it may be cultivated. Alternatively it may be the offspring of a taller fir in the valley below, from which a seed was wafted by a high wind to a high spot. If this is so, and you collect seeds from its cones and plant the seedlings down in the valley, they will grow to trees of normal size and stature.

Gardeners regularly select and propagate, by seed or by grafting, exceptional strains of common trees to suit their landscape patterns. One common example is the dwarf pyramidal spruce, *Picea albertiana* variety *conica*, which has become adapted on the cold Canadian tundra to growing as a low, round conical bush. It retains this engaging habit when transplanted to a suburban garden with a far kindlier climate. The intense silvery-blue colour of the blue Atlas cedar, *Cedrus atlantica* variety *glauca*, arises from its need to restrict water loss through transpiration on the high sun-drenched mountains of its home in the Atlas Mountains of North Africa; the blue shade is due to wax that both reflects heat rays and slows down the passage of water vapour from the leaf. Happily it is still produced under the cloudier and moister surroundings of urban gardens both in Europe and North America.

Just as gardeners seek races of trees that will grow exceptionally slowly, or with remarkable colours in their foliage, foresters are constantly on the look-out for superior strains of trees that will yield timber at better-than-normal rates. Their task is much harder. It is relatively easy to find a tree that will grow in some odd way that makes no special demands on its environment. It is much harder to find one that exploits its surroundings to the utmost.

But sustained research particularly in Europe has revealed the origins, or *provenances*, of trees that will give the best results in each region. Within the European Economic Community, in fact, it is now illegal for nurserymen to offer trees for timber production unless they can show that they have been raised from seed of the approved origin, or provenance zone, for the region in which the timber crop is to be grown.

As a simple illustration, the experience of the Forestry Commission in Great Britain shows that it can secure vigorous crops of three timber trees, namely the European Scots pine, *Pinus sylvestris*, the western American lodgepole pine, *P. contorta*, and Sitka spruce, *Picea sitchensis* also from western America, by using seed collected in latitudes similar to that of Britain, i.e. 50° north. Seed from the far northlands such as Finland and Alaska yields trees that grow slowly, apparently needing longer summer days. In contrast seed from the far southlands such as Spain or California also yields slow-growing trees, which apparently need warmer summers.

But this simple 'same-latitude' rule is confounded by experience with Norway spruce, *Picea abies*, Corsican pine, *Pinus nigra* variety *maritima*, European larch, *Larix decidua*, and Japanese larch, *L. kaempferi*. Seed of all these is regularly imported from latitudes well to the south of Britain, and produces trees that grow vigorously in their new, more northerly, home. Obviously this is a field in which experience is a better guide than theory.

Many trees have evolved down the ages in frost-free climates and cannot tolerate temperatures below zero Centigrade. The great majority of tropical forest trees fall in this group. In the temperate regions they can only be cultivated in greenhouses and because of their great size they are only seen there, if at all, as young or artificially restrained specimens. Most palms are wholly tropical.

Climate and Micro-climate

In contrast to the main climate of a situation, the *micro-climate* consists of the physical conditions that prevail over the immediate surroundings of a growing plant or similar organism. Micro-climates exist, for example, even among plant communities of low stature such as the grasses of a meadow. But the far greater size of forest trees gives rise to micro-climates that can be very distinct from the main climate around them and present very different circumstances for plant and animal life.

A simple instance is provided by a beechwood, composed of trees of the genus *Fagus*, which cast a heavy shade. If we regard the mature trees as living in the main climate, or *macro-climate*, we will find that they enjoy full exposure to daylight and wind and receive all available rainfall. The humidity of the air varies with that of the surrounding air mass and so do the prevailing temperatures.

A seedling of the same species springing from a nut that has fallen from a mature tree embarks on life in a markedly different micro-climate. The prevailing light intensity is cut down during the summer growing season to about 20% of that found above the canopy of the taller trees and may prove insufficient for the seedling's growth. The amount of rainfall that reaches the forest floor will be reduced through the interception of the leafy canopy above to about 80% of that in the open. Wind speeds will be much reduced, averaging only 50% of the open-country velocities. In the absence of bright sunlight and high winds the humidity of the air will tend to be significantly higher. Air temperatures may be higher *or lower* than those outside the wood. On bright sunny days the shady interior of the wood, as everybody knows, will be cooler than its scorched surroundings. But on cold frosty nights the woodland floor will remain warmer than the open land around it or the tops of the trees above it.

Expressed in the simplest terms the micro-climate of a beechwood floor is darker and calmer than the macro-climate of the beech trees' crowns; though it gets less rain the air is moister and extremes of temperature are modified. It is cooler in hot weather and warmer in cold weather. Altogether not a bad place to live! It is not surprising that primitive men (and modern campers) prefer to pitch their simple dwellings in or beside woods rather than out in open country.

One important point to remember here is that although the mature trees' crowns live in the macro-climate of the region, their roots live within the micro-climate zone of the forest floor. The soil temperatures are those of the shaded forest zone, not those of open country around, and the rainfall received is likewise different. A tree planted in a single climatic habitat gradually develops two such habitats as it grows larger and taller, surrounded by its fellows. It adapts itself to living partially in both.

Under traditional methods of renewing forest crops by natural regeneration, foresters take heed of these changes. For example, by gradually opening up the canopy of a maturing beechwood, felling selected trees here and there, they can allow more light to reach the forest floor, and this will encourage the growth of natural seedling beech. At the same time, they will seek to avoid the creation of a 'frost pocket' in which still air accumulating on a cold night in late spring drops below freezing point and severely injures the young growing shoots of the small trees. They will also aim to avoid too rapid exposure of the forest floor to full sunlight, for that would encourage a too-rapid growth of weeds which would smother their slower-growing young beech.

Under less intensive methods of forest management, the changes of conditions at and near ground level cannot be nicely adjusted in this way. By making larger clearings the forester accepts the fact that he is destroying the remarkable micro-climate found below every tall woodland stand. Having done so he aims to restore forest conditions through the rapid growth by a vigorous tree crop that may benefit from the start from ample light.

The competing vegetation of forest weeds will also benefit even more quickly than the trees. The forester accepts this and makes plans in advance to check their growth by weeding his crop for the first few years after planting it. Experience tells him that if he neglects weeding, most of his trees will be smothered by quicker growing herbs, grasses and ferns such as bracken. But if weeding is done effectively, the trees soon grow safely above all competitors.

Resistance to Extremes of Weather

Even where a tree is growing in a general climate well suited to its needs, it has still to face extremes of weather that can occur unpredictably at any time during its long life span. At this point the student of tree growth finds that one set of data from the meteorologists are of little help to him whereas another may give valuable clues to the real state of affairs.

The unhelpful data are the *average* ones, the various 'means' that meteorologists delight in calculating if only to keep their computers busy! In terms of tree growth, means are meaningless. No tree was ever blown down by an 'average' wind, died of drought during a season of average rainfall or fell a victim to a frosty spell of average intensity and duration.

The valuable information comes from records of extremes. Wind, the most variable factor, can rise to speeds of 150 kilometres per hour in places where the average speed is only 15 k.p.h. Rainfall, though showing a reasonable figure for a whole year, and even for a spell of a few months, may fail completely over a span of several weeks. This can cause thousands of newly-planted young trees or newly-sprouted nursery seedlings to perish from drought. Temperature, though showing levels satisfactory for tree growth over a twenty-four hour spell, can fall to a killing level on a single bitterly cold, frosty night. Less severe frost maintained over a long run of days can have unexpected cumulative effects.

Tree growers, to be successful, must always have these extremes in mind. They must know, too, the stages in a tree's life at which adverse factors can prove critical for its survival.

Light

The intensity and duration of light is one of the most widely fluctuating factors of any tree's environment. Even if there were no clouds in the sky and neither mountains nor taller trees to obstruct the sun's rays, the length of each day and the angle at which the sun's rays strike the point at which a tree is growing are never the same on two successive days of the year. These variations are at their lowest on the equator and at their maximum near the two poles, which are subject to months of perpetual daylight followed by months of perpetual night. Though no trees grow at the world's polar extremes, timber stands of spruces and pines do flourish in Alaska and Norway north of the Arctic Circle at 66° 30′ latitude, and enjoy perpetual sunshine in those 'lands of the midnight sun', though only for a few midsummer weeks.

In certain regions of the world, notably the Pacific coast of North America and the westerly regions of the British Isles, the sun's rays are obstructed for a substantial proportion of the daylight hours by high clouds or low fog. Inland, cloudiness is a feature of most high mountain regions, from the Rockies of North America and the Alps of Europe to the monsoon-swept Himalayas of southern Asia, and at ground level direct sunlight may be obstructed locally by high mountains. These factors are minor elements in the illumination of forests in the tropics where the sun rises swiftly to an overhead position at mid-day, but they can be important in the temperate zones. Fortunately the longest and deepest mountain shadows fall during the winter resting seasons, when the trees are least able to utilize the energy of sunlight.

Overshadowing – an apt term – all these external physical influences is the shade cast by growing trees themselves. Foresters rank trees in two

89

main groups, the *light-demanders* that need full light for vigorous growth but cast little shade themselves, and the *shade-bearers* that both cast and tolerate conditions of minimum illumination. For convenience the degree of shade cast is conventionally expressed by stating the percentage of outside illumination that reaches the forest floor. Below deciduous beech, *Fagus* species, in summer this may be only 20%, and below old yews, *Taxus* species, no more than 10% all the year round. This reduction in light intensity is easily measured by a photometer, or more simply any photographic exposure meter. To take photos within a deep shady wood you need five to ten times the exposure you would require outside.

The implications of this enormous variation in illumination for plant life of all kinds are best expressed by a terse northern English proverb:

> *Under t'beech and t'yow*
> *Nowt'll grow*

Nothing that needs daylight, not even the seedlings of the beeches and yews themselves, can live in their deep shade. Only non-green plants, such as parasitic or saprophytic fungi that exist by the breakdown of woody tissues and need no light, can survive. A curious rarity of European woodlands is the symbiotic bird's nest orchid, *Neottia nidus-avis*, that gives nourishment through its association with beech roots. It lacks chlorophyll, which it could not use in the deep shade, and its leafless stems are white and colourless.

Sensitive, though simple, experiments demonstrate conclusively that the rate of growth of young trees is reduced by reduced illumination. A point is eventually reached, called the *compensation point*, at which the energy received from sunlight and effectively used by the plant is so low that it only balances the energy needed for the life processes of breathing and transpiration. There is no surplus available for growth. Below this point the tree dies. This critical level of illumination is naturally lower for shade-bearing trees than it is for light-demanding ones.

Increased illumination promotes more rapid growth, but not indefinitely. The optimum degree of light for many forest trees is about 80% of the full unobstructed daylight around them. Give them more and they grow slower. This slowing down is probably linked to a temperature effect. The fully-lit leaves exposed to the whole range of the sun's rays become overheated and transpire water too rapidly. When this stage is reached the guard cells on either side of the stomata of the leaf come into action and restrict air flow. Transpiration is slowed down, but so is the free flow of carbon dioxide through the leaf tissues. Growth therefore slows down too, although there is ample energy available from the sun for more carbon fixation.

The deep crown of a large tree such as a beech holds leaves exposed to varying degrees of illumination. Some get full sun, others partial shade, others deep shade. The most efficient are those in the middle. The character of the leaves, on the same tree, is modified to match their degree of illumination and so is their colour. In general sunlit leaves are smaller, harder and paler than shade leaves, which tend to be larger, softer and a darker green. On a copper beech the shaded leaves are not copper but deep green tinged with crimson.

Heat

Heat, another potential source of energy, is essential for tree growth but cannot take the place of light in the all-important process of photosynthesis. You cannot grow green plants in the dark, no matter how you heat their surroundings, but the growth of non-green plants such as the fungi that rot timber is stimulated by high temperatures.

Heat reaches the growing tree in three ways: by direct illumination as heat rays from the sun, by conduction from the air stream that surrounds the trunk, branches and leaves, and through the soil that holds its roots. The three sources naturally interact for heat is highly mobile, always flowing from a higher temperature source to a lower one. Hence, if a sunlit tree trunk becomes warmer than the air around it, it will pass on some of the heat it holds to the air. Conversely, when a warm breeze flows round the same trunk after it has cooled down during a still frosty night the trunk will gain heat from its surrounding air stream.

A tree then can both receive and give out heat. A very significant factor in forest growth is the loss of radiant heat on cloudless nights in cold springs. The foliage and young shoots of a 'frost-tender' tree such as beech may then lose so much heat into outer space that they freeze and die back at the tips. But shoots of the same character below the main leafy canopy remain warmer and survive unharmed.

Fluctuations in heat sources for the living tree may be rapid or slow. The quickest changes occur with radiant heat where the intensity of the sun's rays can be reduced instantly by a passing cloud. There is also a regular cyclic change between night and day. The yearly seasonal change from summer through winter brings changes in day length and also variations in the angle of the sun's rays towards the earth.

Changes due to the surrounding air can also be sudden. Warm southerly winds blowing from the Gulf Stream towards Europe or from the Indian Ocean during the monsoon periods of Asia may suddenly be replaced by icy blasts from the Arctic. Such a change may do little harm if it occurs during a tree's winter resting season. But if it happens at a time of active spring growth, or in a season when fertilized flowers are developing their fruits, as on orchard trees, the effect can be catastrophic.

By contrast the earth around a tree's roots warms up and cools down more slowly. Because of its immobility, weight, water content and sheltered situation it is never subject to rapid change unless it is exposed by some total clearance of all vegetation and litter to direct radiation through its bare surface, either inwards under scorching sun or outwards on cold cloudless nights. Soil temperature is a key factor in the growth of tree roots and also in the establishment of young trees freshly planted in the ground.

During winter frost the roots of frost-hardy trees survive but do not function. Active life is resumed when the soil temperature rises above 6°C. There appears to be no upper limit to activity provided moisture is present in a form available to plant life: hot soils tend to be dry ones but some water is usually present below the surface levels.

Young trees cannot be planted into frozen soils but planting is often done in late autumn or early spring into cold ones. Most fully hardy trees survive an inactive period, but there is a group of sub-tropical trees including the widely planted Californian Monterey pine, *Pinus radiata*, that perish unless the soil is warm enough to allow early root growth.

Temperatures in the above-ground portions of the tree are modified against extremes in various ways. The green leaves, exposed at times to strong radiant heat, are cooled by the process of transpiration of sap; this, like the evaporation of water from the surface of a pond, is a process that absorbs heat energy. The trunk or bole of a tree has a high latent heat content. During life it is saturated with water and has a higher specific gravity, around 1·0, than dry wood substance, which only averages half that weight-for-volume figure. Therefore it needs a long spell of exposure to higher temperatures to warm up and conversely a long spell of lower temperatures to cool down. In summer at least it is usually shaded, by the foliage above it, from extremes of temperature at both ends of the scale, from hot sunshine to sudden frosts. This protection is naturally greater for the evergreen trees that carry foliage all the year round. Finally the twin circulations of sap through the trees' tissues, root sap up through the wood and leaf sap down through the bast, tend to even out inequalities of temperature in different parts of the tree.

All the same, extremes of heat and cold occasionally result in physical injuries. If a shaded tree trunk is suddenly exposed to full sunlight, for example, by felling neighbouring trees that have shielded it, it may suffer *bark scorch* caused by overheating of bark and bast tissues. This causes a serious, though localized, surface wound. Thin-barked trees like beech are most apt to suffer.

Very sudden severe frost can cause *frost crack* due to the exposed outer rings of wood cooling faster than the protected inner rings. A radial crack develops right down the affected stem with a sudden sharp noise like that of a pistol shot.

A far more frequent cause of damage is the killing by sudden local frosts of tender young shoots in *frost hollows*. These are depressions into which cold air sinks, because its density is greater than that of warmer air, on windless nights. If the night is also cloudless, radiation heat loss brings the temperature down below freezing point. Trees growing nearby on high ground escape unharmed, and so do small trees protected from heat loss by an overhead canopy of foliage on taller trees. Frost striking in the vital spring flowering season can prove crippling to the fruit grower as well as to his trees. Wise fruit farmers therefore establish new orchards on sloping land from which cold air can drain away.

Rainfall

The amount of rain that reaches any given site is of critical importance to the life of trees. Throughout the world the total *precipitation*, or combined rain and snowfall, varies from almost *nil* in the extreme deserts to 5,000 millimetres per annum in the monsoon regions of tropical Asia. Variations are remarkably local. Within the small area of the British Isles there are districts on the dry east coasts of Scotland and England that receive only 500 millimetres (20 inches), and others on the wet west coasts of Scotland, northern England and Wales that get 2,500 millimetres (100 inches), or five times as much. Forests thrive in both regions and though the Sitka spruce, *Picea sitchensis*, introduced from America's Pacific rain belt, cannot adapt itself to the drier region, the native Scots pine, *Pinus sylvestris*, thrives in both wet and dry zones.

Thus trees show great adaptability to the amount of rainfall they receive, especially where it is evenly spread around the year. The lower limit for tree growth in arid regions is about 100 millimetres, but this can be tolerated only by trees such as sub-tropical pines and certain species of *Eucalyptus* which are structurally adapted to resist long spells of drought. Most trees have only a limited storage capacity for water within their trunks. A few such as the African baobab, *Adansonia digitata*, and the Australian bottle tree, *Brachychiton rupestre*, develop remarkable swollen trunks that serve as reservoirs during the dry season. On the whole trees rely on the soil to hold the water needed by their roots between one variation and another. Its water-holding capacity is increased by the action of tree roots in increasing pore space since each root leaves an open channel when it dies and decays. It is further augmented by the litter layer that is developed from the tree's annual fall of leaves, twigs and other debris.

Snow provides a valuable source of water for arctic and alpine forests. Though much of its water evaporates, a great deal is released during the spring thaw and percolates into the soil at the season of spring growth when it is most needed. 'Fog-drip' on misty days is locally significant.

The rain that falls on a forest's leafy canopy in summer moves on through several paths. A very little is absorbed by the leaves but much is almost immediately evaporated from them and returns to the atmosphere. This *interception* can account for the whole of a brief shower on a hot day or a small proportion of a long downpour during colder weather. The remaining moisture which is not intercepted by the leaves, or bounces off them, is called the *throughfall* and this accounts for most of the water that actually reaches the ground. During prolonged rainstorms it is augmented by *stemflow*, which is the water that runs down tree trunks after their foliage and branches have been thoroughly wetted by the rain.

At ground level much of the water is absorbed by the litter layer and returned later to the air by evaporation. The remainder which percolates into the soil becomes absorbed into its pore spaces and therefore available for the tree roots. These draw upon the soil-held moisture continually, and the trees' conductive systems carry a steady flow upwards to the foliage of the tree crowns. There it is returned to the atmosphere through the process of *transpiration*.

Depending on the intensity and duration of the rainstorm, there may be *surface run-off*, consisting of water that does not penetrate into the litter or soil, but flows over the surface to the nearest stream. There also may be *percolation*, a much slower and steadier process that carries the water *through* the soil to emerge later in springs that feed the forest streams.

The water relations of a woodland are thus complex. As a broad generalization, forests reduce the amount of water that runs off a given area of land, as compared with alternative ground cover such as grass, because they must transpire more water for their life processes. But they also act as regulators, preventing sudden floods because of their greater capacity for interception by both foliage and litter layers. They are also a most effective shield against soil erosion caused by rapid run-off during sudden heavy storms. This in turn lessens the amount of silt that can be carried downstream to disturb river flow or to fill up reservoirs, possibly to the point where those become useless.

For these reasons forests are accepted everywhere as a desirable form of ground cover for water catchments. It cannot be shown, despite several

94

long-term, large-scale experiments, that forests *increase* rainfall. Indeed, as we shall see in the following chapter, they diminish the usable output of water. But they give long-term protection to land and reservoir at low cost and may bring in revenue through the profitable raising of timber. As side benefits, a tree-lined reservoir has obvious advantages over one surrounded by bare land in terms of landscape and shelter for visitors. In the uplands of Britain nearly all the catchment areas of water supply reservoirs are nowadays afforested, with satisfactory results.

Atmospheric Humidity

Allied to the water that falls to the ground as rain, the water vapour that is held in the air is of immediate significance to plant life. The air is rarely saturated and so it usually absorbs moisture transpired by tree foliage. Hot dry air makes an intensive demand on the living leaf and trees that grow in such surroundings have leaves that are specially modified to resist excessive water loss. Growth is clearly easier in surroundings of humid air and the world's largest trees and densest forests are found in regions of high prevailing atmospheric humidity. These are the rain forests of the tropics, and the rain-drenched Pacific Slope on the west coast of North America. In the British Isles, tree growth is faster along the wet, humid west coast than in drier, sunnier regions farther east.

Wind

Trees by their very nature are organisms that can only flourish in a current of moving air. They grow by abstracting carbon dioxide from it and breathe by taking in its oxygen. The rain that provides their essential water content can only fall when clouds are carried inland by winds blowing off the sea. A tree's leaves are designed to spread their blades in sunlight in a stream of constantly moving air, and its trunk and branches are shaped to resist the forces that the wind brings to bear on this foliage as well as to support it. Tree growers take the wind for granted, knowing that it constantly stirs the tree's crowns without doing any harm, until it approaches gale force.

The highest wind speeds recorded in or near Britain are of the order of 130 kilometres per hour. These were found off the east coast of Scotland at the Bell Rock lightship near Arbroath, in the great gale of 15 January 1968. Curiously this blast blew down few coastal trees thereabouts, though many that stood on exposed bluffs farther inland were laid low. Much higher speeds doubtless occur in the mountains but there are few weather stations to record them. Record gusts up to 350 kilometres per hour have occurred at the observatory on Mount Washington, 2,000 metres above sea level in New Hampshire's White Mountains. This blew down no trees there for the summit carries only low alpine plants and lichens clinging to bare rocks. The tree line lies 700 metres lower down, around the 1,300 metre contour, where balsam firs are shaped into low bushes by the force of the elements. They can only grow to real tree stature below the 1,000 metre level. Plates 45, 46.

Clearly topography has a critical bearing on the wind speeds that trees must withstand. The world's tallest trees, the 100 to 112 metre giant redwoods and Douglas firs of the Pacific slope in British Columbia and the western United States, grow in one of the world's calmer regions, thanks no doubt to the proximity of the mighty Rocky Mountain chain. As one moves into greater exposure trees become more and more stunted. This is true of the high mountain slopes, the cold northern plains, and windswept shorelines in both temperate and tropical zones. On the gale-swept western seaboard of Britain, commercial planting may become impracticable above the 250 metre level. Farther east, under the shelter of higher ground it can safely be taken to twice that altitude. As a guide to the degree of exposure that the trees can accept and still grow at a profitable rate, Forestry Commission researchers set up 'tatter flags' in advance of afforestation. These are simple unhemmed squares of standard white cloth, mounted on pivots. The rate at which they disintegrate provides a fair measure of wind speed and gustiness over a spell of several months.

Trees live in air streams that are capable of enormous fluctuations in velocity. Their branches have amazing natural resilience and absorb the wind's energy like a brake or buffer, by bending before its force, then springing back to their previous position. Only living branches can do this because their wood is saturated with sap and is therefore elastic. Dead timber becomes dry and brittle and though it retains other strength properties it loses this elasticity. The ability of trees to temper or deflect wind forces makes them invaluable as shelter for farm land or urban buildings, as discussed later.

Under the force of a strong wind a tree 'folds up' its branches and foliage rather like the folding of an umbrella. They are pushed upwards towards the main stem to give a more streamlined face to the wind. By lessening the area of leaf-surface exposed to the wind this movement reduces to a marked degree the horizontal force that the tree must bear. Wind tunnel studies by the Forestry Commission have shown that, instead of the wind's thrust upon the tree increasing by the *square* of the wind's velocity, as with other objects, it rises only in *direct* proportion because of the lesser surface on which the air stream is brought to bear. A keen observer can see this happening on any windy day. It is rather like the prudent skipper of a sailing ship taking in sail as a gale approaches.

Windfalls

Most trees unless felled by man are eventually overturned by the wind. Few fall in still air. Surprisingly few get blown down while still in full vigour and health. Windfall, which looks so sudden and dramatic, is usually the last act in a long slow process of decay caused by fungi that has sapped the strength of their trunk or roots, usually both.

There are of course exceptions, and the most frequent arise through poor root-hold on damp ground. This in turn is often the outcome of poor drainage. Roots cannot extend into soil that lacks oxygen, and damp ground, particularly if it is clay or peat, has poor mechanical strength to resist overturning forces. In some situations the forester can improve root-hold by deep drainage. Elsewhere he must accept the fact that once the trees reach a certain critical height the wind force that plays upon them can exceed the resistance offered by the soil.

When root-hold fails, a large slab of earth is torn out from its surroundings and exposed as a big *root-plate*, still firmly attached to the fallen tree trunk. Most fallen trees will be found on examination to have come down in this way. The physical breakage of a healthy stem, known as *windbreak*, is a much rarer event.

Both catastrophes usually occur at a critical point in the swaying of the tree by gusts in turbulent winds. This was once dramatically recorded during a gale that swept a forest in Northern Ireland during the course of a tree-felling competition. When the wind rose so high that it became unsafe for the competition to continue, a cinephotographer trained his camera on the doomed trees. The resulting film showed that they first swayed in a circular fashion until a critical danger point was reached, at which root-hold gave way and then they crashed to the ground.

Most though not all trees fall in the direction of the gale: the air current in that direction imposes the greatest strains. Over a long span of time most trees will fall in the direction of the prevailing wind, which in Britain blows from the southwest. Ecologists, finding that most tree trunks found buried in peat bogs point towards the northeast, have occasionally postulated as the cause a single great southwesterly gale. Just the same result is, of course, achieved by a succession of such gales, which is a much more likely train of events.

Topography influences wind direction, wind force and the incidence of windfalls to a marked degree. At the point where I live on a bluff above a complex of valleys in a range of low hills, the wind is never blowing in a direction constant for my surroundings. A westerly wind, for example, swings to the north and speeds away down a winding dale. Shifts of direction like this, combined with acceleration, can upset otherwise wind-firm trees, even though they endure for only a few minutes. Trees are not 'hit' by wind forces; they are moved *within* air currents.

Current research by the Forestry Commission of Great Britain seeks to establish the critical point at which a tree's root-hold will give way under wind forces. A winch mounted on a tractor is used to exert a sideways pull that can be accurately measured by an electric strain gauge. On 'soft' soils such as peat or clay, root resistance is overcome by a lower force than is needed on 'hard' soils such as sand or gravel. The resistance of the softer soils can often be increased by better drainage to lower their water content.

Another approach to the same problem is to mount an accelerometer on a tree stem, high in the tree's crown. This gives a visual reading of the degree of sway that a tree's crown makes under wind forces on a graph at ground level. It is hoped to establish a relationship between the amount of sway and the tree's stability.

Wind-moulding

One obvious and impressive effect of wind currents on trees that stand in exposed situations is the moulding of their crowns into streamlined shapes aligned to the prevailing, or occasionally to the off-sea, wind direction. This effect is most apparent along coastlines where the physical forces involved are strongly reinforced by the chemical action of wind-borne salt. Small but effective quantities of sodium chloride are deposited as natural aerosols carried inland from wave spray. If rain follows, this salt is quickly washed away and does no harm. But if a dry sunny spell occurs the salt is concentrated on buds and foliage where it can easily be tasted with the tongue. A strong salt concentration scorches the leaves, which turn brown, and cripples the buds. Consequently active growth occurs only on the sheltered, leeward side of the tree, and this results in a one-sided, stream-lined crown. Plates 14, 59.

Trees vary markedly in their resistance or sensitivity to wind-borne salt. Among the broadleaves, elms, *Ulmus* species, and evergreen oaks, *Quercus ilex* etc., are resistant, but beeches, *Fagus* species, and hawthorns, *Crataegus* species, are susceptible. Among conifers, maritime pine, *Pinus pinaster*, and Sitka spruce, *Picea sitchensis*, prove resistant but the similar Scots pine, *Pinus sylvestris*, and Norway spruce, *Picea abies*, prove vulnerable.

Inland, on high mountains or even the ridges of low hills where wind speeds are accelerated by the natural lie of the land, many trees adopt a 'flag-shaped growth' (in German *Fahnenwuchs*) in which the branches on their leeward side grow out sideways far more vigorously than those else-where. This enables the tree to expose a large effective leaf area with less resistance to the prevailing winds than it could do by growing in the normal symmetrical way. The physical forces that cause this directional emphasis on growth are not fully known: probably ice formation on exposed wind-ward buds plays a part in checking new spring growth.

Wind-borne Ice

This brings us to a curious but infrequent form of damage to trees that occurs at near-freezing temperatures when moisture-saturated winds blow through tree crowns. Under certain rare atmospheric conditions this moisture is in effect super-cooled and hence ready to crystallize out on solid objects such as twigs, as hoar frost or rime. The resultant gleaming white twigs and conifer sprays delight the artist and photographer during their brief existence until the next thaw, but the added concentrated weight can have devastating effects on side branches. Normal snowfall, shown in Plate 47, causes no damage, branches bend beneath its weight, then recover.

Chapter 8

Forests and Conservation

FORESTS, despite continued clearances down the ages, still occupy one-third of the world's land surface. They are therefore a major factor in the conservation of the timber, soil and water resources that support mankind. Their distribution is markedly uneven and no longer follows the limits imposed by the natural physical factors of rock, soil, slope, altitude and prevailing climate. Man has everywhere played a part in determining their present extent. It may be a small part as in some tropical rain forests where only two per cent of the natural forest has been cleared for settlement. Or it can be a major part as in the British Isles where the proportion of natural forest *surviving* is only about two per cent of its original extent. Major losses of this kind are often though not always compensated for by planned programmes of afforestation so that man-made forests take the place of natural ones. Alternatively, natural regrowth of forest trees may take over abandoned farm lands.

Why Forests Survive

Within environments where forest growth is possible, forests exist today for one of four reasons:

   a. The land they occupy is not worth clearing for agriculture.

   b. It *is* worth clearing but the local people have not yet developed the resources to do so.

   c. It *was* worth clearing, but fertility could not be maintained, and it was later abandoned to tree growth for technical or economic reasons.

   d. Its value as a resource of timber, soil, water, landscape or recreation, including sport, is held to exceed its worth for other purposes and it is therefore deliberately reserved as forest for all foreseeable future time.

The fourth reason, reservation for intrinsic value, is naturally often applied to certain forests in the other three categories. The politicians who decide these matters find it easy to say at the critical point in time, 'Let us reserve this land as national forest because we cannot possibly use it for anything else', thereby making a virtue of necessity at no cost to anybody. Such courses may be regarded as 'negative conservation'. These forests remain as such because there is *no* acceptable alternative use. It is not surprising, therefore, that in any country with a long history the woodlands are found mainly on the poorest land: in places with steep slopes, poor soils or much bare rock; on ill-drained swampy land or in regions difficult of access – the 'bad lands', in fact.

An elegant example of small scale reservation of land for woodlands is found in southeastern England – in the Weald, meaning 'forest', region of Kent, Surrey and Sussex. Here large-scale maps, on scales of 1:50,000 or over, reveal that the frequent small, unplanted or replanted woods which are fragments of the ancient Saxon Forest of Anderida, or Andredsweald, lie along the steep banks of narrow valleys or dingles. These irregular ribbons of woodland have survived 1,500 years of agricultural encroachment. The Jutish and Saxon settlers who gradually cleared the native oak forests from 400 AD onwards did not find it worthwhile to tackle steep slopes that they could not plough. Modern farmers accept that situation still, happy in the knowledge that the surviving woods make ideal game coverts for pheasants, giving sporting values and often incomes from ground they cannot till.

Sole Use or Multiple Use?

A more constructive approach concentrates on the positive values of conservation. What do forests provide that is unobtainable from any other kind of land use? An immediate question is whether 'land-use' implies *sole-use* for one purpose or *multiple-use* with many benefits obtained simultaneously from the same stretch of ground.

The sole-use protagonists are remarkably numerous and influential, though they are by definition opposed to every sort of multiple-use and also to every other kind of sole-use except the one they favour! But their arguments give us insight into the values attached to forests as a form of land cover. If they are worth defending so stoutly, these values must be high.

It follows that, even if constraints must be applied to certain types of usage, any well-planned system of multiple-use must give a higher overall value to the reservation of land for forestry than any single use can do on its own.

Water catchment is a simple example of a sole-use that has often been allowed to dominate to an absurd degree the whole pattern of benefits that a forest may bring to a community. I know of a beautiful lake embowered in a flourishing forest of oak and chestnut, spruce and larch, within a few miles of Hastings in Sussex, southern England, a seaside resort in a region where such forests and lakescapes are rare. But the lake is a reservoir for domestic water supplies and nobody is allowed near it, even for a distant view, in the interests of keeping the water supply perfectly pure. Here one dominant use makes life easy for the resource managers, but obviously the full value of the forest as a scenic as well as a water conservation asset is not being realized. Why not, with suitable safeguards, make it a tourist attraction, at least for the distant view?

Similar examples could be repeated indefinitely. One amazing instance concerned an old oak and hornbeam coppice called Ham Street Wood, some 100 hectares (250 acres) in extent, close to the south coast of Kent in southeastern England. A rare insect hitherto recorded only on the Continent had been collected there, having no doubt been blown across the English Channel by some strong gale. A dedicated entomologist then campaigned for the whole wood to be declared a National Nature Reserve, as the only British station for one rare insect!

If such a claim were pressed for every rarity, no forest could ever be used for any purpose save as an insect preserve. In the event these woods did become a Nature Conservancy reserve but with far wider objectives than the provision of a home for one rare invertebrate.

Wilderness Conservation

Advocates of what is broadly called 'wilderness' present a powerful political influence in many countries, particularly the United States of America. The concept has deep emotional appeal. What a splendid thing to set aside, in our overcrowded modern society, torn by every sort of stress and strain, some vast expanse of virgin forests with lakes and mountains never trodden nor explored by man! Let there be no roads, trails or footpaths, and if possible no aeroplanes overhead!

Here we will preserve wild nature as a heritage for the future. Nobody, no, *nobody* will be allowed in, *ever*, except for some obscure long-haired or densely-bearded *researcher*. Even he will have to get a permit from the Department of Conservation or whatever, specifying exactly what he may research. In the nature of life such high-powered, permit-worthy researchers usually win speedy promotion to a professorial chair in some distant, busy university where they never find time to return to the wilderness.

So much for the favoured few. What of the value of the wilderness to the rest of mankind? Frankly it is hard to see much gain on the credit side. Without access there can be no appreciation of beauty. The secluded wilderness is like a national picture gallery with all its doors permanently barred. Equally there can be no harvest of timber for every fallen tree must be left to rot and nourish native fungi and invertebrates. Wild life cannot be controlled either. For better or worse it must find its own balance, or imbalance, within the reserved wilderness.

Inevitably the neighbours of the wilderness lay blame on it for every excursion of hungry birds or beasts. The reserve, they assert, breeds 'vermin', a handy term for every unwelcome creature. Every effective reserve must by definition form a reservoir for rare animals, and these are sure to trespass beyond its boundaries unless checked by some artificial barrier such as an elephant-proof fence. Deer will certainly wander far from the cover of their sanctuary to feed on farm crops. Predators from foxes and lions to egg-stealing carrion crows will venture far from their safe wilderness lairs or nests to raid hen-runs, sheep flocks or pheasant preserves several kilometres away.

Human life may be at risk also. A rubber estate where I once worked in Malaya lay close to a vast state forest in which tigers were strictly preserved. Only one Indian lad was lost in the four years that I was there, but other estates were from time to time less fortunate. A wild life reserve may also form a reservoir for pests or diseases that attack people or their livestock. A well-known example is the tse-tse fly of tropical Africa which multiplies as a disease-carrying pest of antelopes in game reserves, then emerges to attack domestic cattle.

There is the constant risk of the reverse movement of people from out-side the reserve into the wilderness. Poachers neither need nor heed permits. The temptation to take something of value from the reserves is always present and often irresistible. Furs have a ready sale and flesh a delicious flavour. From the days of William the Conqueror, who enacted harsh game laws to protect the deer of England's New Forest soon after 1066 AD, the preservers of wilderness wild life have had a difficult task. Modern transport and modern weapons have made it no easier. A poacher with a rifle slung out of sight beneath his workaday car is a different proposition from a horseman bearing only a bow-and-arrow, and may prove far more elusive.

Intensive Research Woodlands

A variant of the wilderness reserve, which may be created within it or else as a quite separate entity, is the intensive research woodland. An excellent example is Monks Wood, owned by the Nature Conservancy Council close to the town of Huntingdon in the lowlands of eastern England. It covers 160 hectares (400 acres) on a gentle slope of clay soil running down towards the flat fenlands. Monks Wood was once the timber and firewood reserve for the medieval abbey of Sawtry nearby. There is a remarkable representation of broadleaved trees native to the eastern English lowlands including scarce species like wild service tree, *Sorbus torminalis*, aspen, *Populus tremula*, and dogwood, *Cornus sanguinea*. The main components are hazel, *Corylus avellana*, which has been harvested for centuries by the coppice method (see Chapter 9), and taller oaks, *Quercus robur*, grown as timber trees. All the flora is native and unplanted and has survived from prehistoric times.

A modern laboratory block with administrative offices has been built beside the wood, which has in effect become an open-air laboratory itself. The tests, trials and enquiries started within the buildings extend there into the natural environment that the Conservancy was established to study. Conversely, lines of research prompted by observations in the wood may be pursued indoors.

While the situation described may seem obvious, anyone who has encountered the cloistered isolation of many academic biologists will realize at once how valuable this immediate contact with real life can be. I once studied zoology under a famous but fossilized professor who would not let house martins nest on the outside of his brand-new million-pound university building, though he encouraged his students to dissect their dead bodies inside!

Where woodlands are concerned it is particularly important to have a living forest at hand because woodlands are the most complex and changeable of all possible environments. It is fatally easy for an enquirer in his concentrated study of a particular plant or animal to divorce himself entirely from the surroundings in which it lives out its natural life. Leaves never fall in a well-tended laboratory nor do flowers burst forth in spring. The isolation essential to fruitful academic studies often leads research men to ignore simple factors such as the weather or the complex interactions of other plants and animals on their chosen subject of study.

It is obvious, then, that a major forest resource is the continuance of reserves in which forest life itself may be studied. It is a major, primal type of environment for myriad forms of life on earth, and man cannot gain a true understanding of himself without first discovering what happens in the forest which was, after all, his ancient home.

Understandably, intensive studies of this kind cannot be effectively pursued without some restriction of public access. At Monks Wood a permit system is used. If the land is legally free for all to come and go, appeals may be made for co-operation. On Mont Ventoux in the south of France I came across a series of elaborate experiments on the control of a processionary moth attacking pine trees, which involved the caging of insects close to ground level. Notices had been set up asking parents to restrain their children from meddling with these cages. Fortunately French children usually seem to behave responsibly!

A perennial problem in all such intensively-researched areas is that the enquirers create for themselves a false environment. As an example, a generous benefactor gave Oxford University a fine broadleaved forest called Wytham Wood within a few miles of the city of Oxford. The University decided to turn it into an open-air ecological laboratory for its biological scientists and as a result much valuable research has been accomplished there. But the intensity of study is such that critics complain that it has become impossible to walk through the wood without stumbling over some automatic recording device or even a somnolent researcher! A point is reached when the monitoring of what goes on becomes itself a factor of the environment. There is always a risk that over-intensive research may defeat its own ends. Even the setting up of nest-boxes as an aid to the study of bird life alters the natural pattern, as extra birds immigrate to use the boxes.

Soil Conservation and Erosion Control

Forests do not simply conserve soil, they create it. In Chapter 6 we discussed how soils are formed through the interaction of organic matter, brought into being by tree growth on the bedrock of the land. This invaluable resource on which all terrestrial life depends can be quickly dissipated by erosion, which implies the wearing away of its surface layers by water, frost or wind.

Examples of soil erosion occur all too often wherever the land is stripped bare of its protective cover of vegetation. It occurs most rapidly in tropical countries with seasonal heavy rains, or occasional heavy thunderstorms and is naturally most serious on sloping ground. Rain, falling faster than the soil can absorb it, runs downhill with ever-increasing speed and its ability to carry soil grains in suspension increases rapidly with its velocity. The theoretical mathematical increase of water's ability to move obstacles is that of the sixth power of this velocity. This means that a mere trickle will carry grains of clay or silt, a steady flow will move sand or fine gravel, but a torrent can transport boulders.

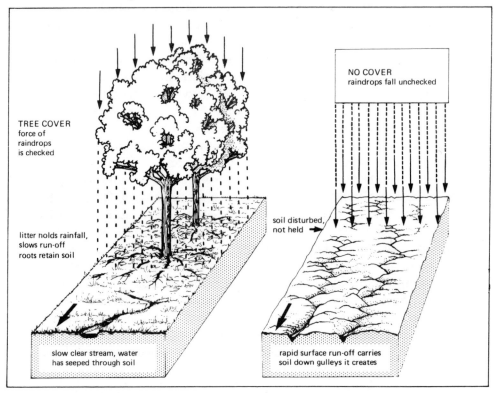

TREE COVER
force of
raindrops
is checked

NO COVER
raindrops fall unchecked

litter holds rainfall,
slows run-off
roots retain soil

soil disturbed,
not held →

slow clear stream, water
has seeped through soil

rapid surface run-off carries
soil down gulleys it creates

Figure 11   How tree cover checks soil erosion. Leaves check force of raindrops. Litter holds rainfall and slows surface-water run-off. Roots retain soil.

Gully erosion occurs wherever the downward flow of water is channelled into hollows. Its concentrated volume enables it to cut into the surface of soft earth and once it starts to move hard stones these act like digging tools cutting into the soil below. Where soil depth allows, fantastic steep-sided gullies, often two to three metres deep, may be excavated in one rainy season by a succession of storms. The process is only stopped when the sub-soil is cut through right down to hard rock where such material exists. Where several gullies meet and the terrain allows, wide ravines many metres deep may be cut out.

Sheet erosion, still more serious, arises where the whole surface of the soil is carried away, grain by grain, by the downhill movement of storm water.

It usually follows naturally on gully erosion, with the soil particles being washed into the ever-deepening channels. Sheet erosion removes the whole basis of land fertility for both forestry and agriculture. It may end with the total exposure of worthless bare rock.

Eroded soil is carried downstream and eventually deposited wherever the speed of the water current slackens. The main burden is dropped only a few kilometres from its place of origin, close to the point where the rivers or short-lived seasonal torrents leave the hills for the plains. Here it may spread out over valuable pastures or arable land carrying crops and ruin them. Alternatively it may build up in mudbanks, sandbanks or shingle beds in the courses of large rivers, and cause disastrous floods. If it is carried as far as a reservoir it will collect behind the impounding dam and eventually make the whole reservoir useless for water storage. Ultimately the finer elements get carried out to the sea where they build up in deltas or else become permanently lost to the land. Eroded soil becomes a major liability to the whole river valley system in which it occurs, causing serious economic loss and often creating flood dangers for the inhabitants.

Forest is the ideal anti-erosion cover for mountainous land. The leafy canopy of the trees, and even their branches during seasons when certain trees stand leafless, breaks the first force of a rapid downpour of rain or hail and lessens its capacity to cut into bare soil. Even more valuable is the layer of leaf litter that forms wherever trees stand and shed spent foliage, whether they be deciduous or evergreen. This mulch of slowly decomposing, fibrous organic matter makes an ideal check to rapid movement of water, even downhill. It can absorb the first downpour and then, when saturated, oblige the surplus water to trickle gradually, drop by drop, from one leaf element to another, never gathering critical speed. In the event most water is directed downwards into the soil to emerge as springs later. Only a small proportion even in the heaviest storms trickles away over the surface. This valuable litter layer renews itself at no cost. As its lower elements decay to form soil humus, fresh leaves fall annually to replace them on the surface.

Farther down within the soil the meshwork of large and small tree roots forms an excellent barrier to soil movement even under the influence of flowing water. This organic barrier is self-renewing also. As one group of roots ages, dies and decays, a fresh group develops to exploit renewed leaf litter. The channels left by dead roots of all sizes enable rainwater to percolate deep into the soil structure and so help to reduce the volume of the surface run-off. Man himself could not devise a better medium for checking soil erosion at sub-surface level and any materials that he might set in place would prove perishable in the long run. The forest root network is perpetual, and will be renewed indefinitely so long as tall green trees flourish overhead.

Downstream, riverside trees play a very important part in checking soil erosion along streams and river banks. Certain trees are by nature adapted to grow best beside running water. Willows of the genus *Salix*, poplars of the *Populus* genus and alders of the genus *Alnus* are typical examples in temperate zones. In the tropics many palms such as those of the *Nipa* genus have a riverain distribution, while others like the coconut palm, *Cocos nucifera*, are at home along estuaries. Such trees root in wet soil provided that the moisture is moving sufficiently freely to bring them oxygen, and they benefit from the nutrients that the currents transport. Willows even develop peculiar pink roots that gain water and dissolved mineral salts directly from a pond or slow-flowing river.

The network of roots that such trees develop along the banks of swiftly falling streams having steep gradients is of prime importance in checking the erosion of those streamsides. In effect, the stream-bed is 'anchored' at a certain level in the bottom of its sloping valley. The stream cannot cut freely into soil or rock and must swerve from side to side to find a free channel around tough roots. This deviation slows down its current and drastically reduces its erosive power. In hilly country streamside trees should never be removed without regard to the likely consequences of exposing streambeds to unleashed erosive forces. Alas! many drainage engineers and farm efficiency experts fail to grasp this point. They strip off the efficient tree cover and then instal costly concrete barriers to repair the damage that results to both watercourses and the land itself.

Farther downstream where broader rivers flow through wider courses, streamside trees stabilize sandbanks and help to hold the wandering river in an established course. Their removal in the interests of faster discharge may be followed by serious erosion, the formation of fresh unstabilized sandbanks in inconvenient places and resultant flooding of broad stretches of farmland after the uncontrolled river has burst its banks. In general riverside woodland should be conserved and respected as an essential factor of stream-bank control.

If the course of a stream is dammed at any point to provide a reservoir as a source of irrigation water, hydro-electric power or water for general domestic and industrial use, the silt derived from eroded soil must inevitably build up behind the dam. This will inevitably, in turn, reduce the water-holding capacity of the reservoir and eventually shorten its service life.

Silting up may be long delayed, for example in situations where feeder streams flow over hard rocks that they cannot readily erode. Alternatively where feeder streams are cutting into easily eroded soils it can be rapid: some otherwise excellent river dams in the western mountains of North America have been rendered useless through silting within twenty years of their construction. Forest cover, as we have seen earlier, is the ideal protection against soil erosion. Wherever dams are constructed the river authority should always consider how far the forests upstream can be conserved as such, and preferably in perpetuity.

An exceptionally rapid form of soil erosion occurs in high mountain regions subject to regular snow fall and ice action. Examples are the American Rocky Mountains, the European Alps and similar ranges, and the Asiatic Himalayas. The daily alternation of frost and thaw which occurs in the warmer months, between the upper limit of the forest and the level of perpetual ice and snow, is constantly dislodging rocks from crag faces. Winter snowfields create *avalanche* conditions when they start to melt in spring. Rapid thaws and even thunderstorms give rise to torrents that course down the steep slopes. Plate 49.

Forests can do nothing to halt such erosive forces above the tree line, but on the lower slopes they prove an invaluable protection against loss of soil. The snow that falls on them is trapped between their stems, and when spring approaches it melts slowly because it is always shaded from direct sunlight. Most of the resulting water trickles slowly down into the soil, to emerge harmlessly from springs lower down the valley. The mobile mass of loose snow that constitutes an avalanche can rarely gain momentum within the forest itself, though it may shoot rapidly downhill through any gap in the woods. For these reasons forests in the Swiss Alps and similar territories are carefully conserved as *protection forests*. No clear felling is permitted and management is aimed at the constant regeneration of the woods by seedlings arising amid established trees.

Water Resources

There is a widespread but poorly-based belief that 'forests increase rainfall', but, as we have noted in the last chapter, this cannot be substantiated on any major scale. Locally they do so, but usually in circumstances that make little difference to the total environment. In dry tropical climates moisture-laden clouds may fail to drop rain even where they rise to cross mountain ranges, becoming cooler as they go, because of the heat reflected from bare sun-baked rocks. Where forests grow less heat is radiated because more is absorbed by the darker and 'deeper' surfaces. This may make a difference to the critical degree of humidity that causes the clouds to form raindrops.

Rain then falls over the forest, but not elsewhere. The deserts around get little benefit.

A very different circumstance arises in continuously moist regions such as the Pacific seaboard of northwestern North America, which receives a high rainfall, around 2,500 millimetres (100 inches) per annum. Here constant transpiration from the forests helps to maintain air humidities, but the tallest forests are only 100 metres (330 feet) high and the heavy rainfall results from the ascent of moisture-laden clouds, from the Pacific Ocean, over the Rocky Mountain chain, which averages 2,000 metres (6,600 feet). The giant trees are still insignificant in their physical and meteorological context. It is hard to see how they can affect the main course of events even though they do promote mists and local showers.

Large-scale experiments have been carried out over long spells of time at carefully selected sites in North America and South Africa to compare the rainfall and stream-flow regimes of 'parallel' water catchments. The idea, simple in conception but difficult in practice, is to take two similar river basins both carrying forests, remove the forests from one and see what happens. It has proved hard to find pairs of river basins that do, in fact, receive the same year-round rainfalls even *before* any forest cover is removed, and this factor confounds whatever change in rainfall may result from removing forest cover. No statistically sound changes of rainfall have been ascertained so far.

But differences in stream-flow patterns are clear and consistent. *Where forests have been removed* and the land is left under some alternative vegetation such as grass, every rainstorm is followed by rapid run-off from the land, and the stream that drains the basin reaches a peak of discharge within a matter of hours after the storm concerned. This peak is followed by a quick fall to a low level.

Where forest cover has been retained most of the storm-water is held by foliage, litter and soil, and it can only percolate slowly to the springs that feed the stream. In consequence days may elapse before the down-stream discharge rises slowly to a low peak followed by an equally slow decline.

In other words, the forest slows down and regulates the discharge of rainwater from the land surface that receives it. This has important consequences for the whole river system downstream. Floods are less frequent and therefore stream bank erosion is less. There is a more regular supply of purer water than can be obtained from bare catchment areas. All forms of river use, including fishing, navigation, hydro-electric power and the abstraction of supplies for farm irrigation or domestic use, benefit.

Water supply managers, however, are also concerned with the *total yield* of water from any given area of land. Here it must be conceded that the output from a forested catchment is commonly lower than that from a catchment under grass. In simple terms the trees use more water: they return it by evaporation and transpiration from their foliage to the atmosphere.

On the immediate credit side forests check the silting up of reservoirs, and a water engineer may be content to accept a lower-than-maximum water yield in return for the longer service-life of a costly dam. He may also regard the forest as an effective reservoir in itself. By retaining or establishing forest cover he may get by with a smaller reservoir and a cheaper dam because there will be no sudden peaks of stream-flow that must be captured behind it.

Overall, the advantages of maintaining forest cover over water catchments, in terms of storm-water control, prevention of erosion, timber output and the provision of scenery and recreation are so great that they are almost universally accepted world-wide. Even in the hotter and drier countries such as Australia and South Africa where water yields can be a critical factor, forests are held to be the best possible form of land use for water gathering grounds. In Britain nearly every suitable major upland water catchment, whether it be for domestic supplies or hydro-electric power, has been systematically afforested with conifers since the dams and reservoirs were constructed during the past hundred years.

The Recreation Resource

Mankind in this modern world of stresses and strains, unpleasant working conditions and crowded living places, feels a constant need for rest and recreation. Forests are uniquely well fitted to meet this. They are beautiful, airy and silent, meeting at once our needs for refreshing sights, ample fresh air and quiet. Many forests are so vast that they challenge man's physical capacity to explore them. A multitude of people may be absorbed in a large woodland without disturbing one another. Each group is hidden from the next by green screens of leafy trees. Plate 63.

Many kinds of recreation in the forests call for little organization or equipment. The first basic need is a right of access which may be free or subject to various degrees of control. This is often a crucial point in the conflict between sole-use and multiple-use management. No advocate of the sole-use of a forest for any other purpose, whether it be water supply, game preservation, timber production or some cherished nature reserve really welcomes any recreational use except of course by himself! If challenged he will claim to support recreation, implying thereby the healthy amusement of a scientist, a sportsman or a water engineer, but the sole-use approach remains, by definition, a selfish one.

The legal right to access, or to debar access to others, varies markedly between different countries. In North America, Scandinavia and much of Europe there is a long-standing tradition of free access to all forests except where specific exclusions apply. In Britain, by contrast, woodlands are generally assumed to be reserved to owners and occupiers unless specifically declared open to others, though traditional rights continue over common lands, some of which are well-wooded.

After the *right* of access, the next essential is a *means* of access, which in terms of modern transport usually means a car park. Enquiries reveal that relatively few people visit forests by other means, such as by train, bus, cycle, horse, or even on foot. A major reason for favouring the car is the ease with which it transports, in one package, the less mobile members of each group, whether they be infants or grandparents. It also carries the refreshments, which leads us to the third main need when the forest is reached, a place to picnic. At all well-frequented forests two further amenities become essential, namely, litter baskets and toilets. Any forest manager who encourages public access is required, sooner or later, to provide these three first essentials, which all cost money. Not surprisingly the provision of access points to forests is mainly the concern of public authorities. Few private landowners are ready to incur the necessary trouble and expense. In practice it is rarely practicable to make any charges and the very existence of access tends to lower the capital value of the woodland concerned as well as to complicate its management.

Woodland access poses real problems in modern, highly mobile societies. Given cars, people flock like birds to the choicest viewpoints and it is very difficult to resist public demands on national or communally-owned forests. Severe recreation pressures build up in Britain at well known centres such as the New Forest in Hampshire and the Forest of Dean in Gloucestershire, both of which have been made accessible from London and other large cities by motorways. In California the limit is reached in the groves of tall redwoods and giant sequoias, where visitors have to be restricted to paved walks in order to safeguard the soil on which the perpetual life of the forest depends.

Relatively few visitors set out on long walks through forests but thousands love to follow a short, signposted trail. The Nature Trail movement has enabled a multitude of people of all ages to appreciate the wealth of interest that the woods hold. Since human guides are few and hard to organize, visitors are encouraged to buy simple pamphlets telling them where to go and what to see. At a few selected forests, especially in America, displays illustrating wild life are mounted in small museums which are manned at busy times by knowledgeable wardens.

Active sports that can be followed in woodland surroundings include horse-riding, cross-country walking and running. Orienteering, an exciting cross-country racing contest in which competitors must find their way round a rugged course by using map and compass to plan their routes to hidden markers, is particularly well-suited to wooded country. Water sports including bathing, swimming, dinghy sailing, fishing and water skiing gain interest and appeal from forest surroundings, and so do snow sports such as tobaganning and skiing. Plate 16 shows orienteering.

The pursuit of game is the leading traditional recreation in all wooded country, but it is a pleasure that relatively few people can enjoy. Quite simply in these times of easy transport there are not enough beasts and birds to go round. Rationing is accomplished by various methods in different countries. These include very short 'open' seasons for particular creatures, as in many States of the USA, and the need for special permits. Such measures are essential where the quarry is found in publicly-owned forests, especially where these are open to all comers. An alternative followed in certain countries, and particularly in Britain, is to restrict the right to hunt or shoot to the landowner or others authorized by him. This results in strictly controlled and closed-off pheasant preserves in which game birds are artificially raised to provide a few days of exciting shooting each year for a small group of sportsmen. The resulting sporting values, which find expression in money rents, are so high that it pays landowners to maintain suitable woodlands mainly as cover, or *covert*, for the pheasants. Broadleaved trees are preferred, especially species like oak and beech which provide nourishing acorns and nuts. Substantial wages are paid to skilled resident gamekeepers.

The study of the trees and the wild life amid them is itself a fascinating form of recreation. It can be greatly assisted by photography both to record whatever is observed and as an appreciative skill that provides endless challenge and enjoyment. Artists find exquisitely beautiful scenes to draw or paint in woodland surroundings and achieve the ultimate means of expressing the emotional appeal that forests present to man. Poetry can rival pictures, but woodland poets are rare and need a sympathetic human speaker, or singer, to give true expression to their sentiments. The appeal of the coloured painting is, by contrast, immediate.

People like to *live* in forests as well as simply visit them or look at them. Woods make ideal camp sites, particularly when they are situated beside lakes or mountains. Sympathetic planning can enable a large number of campers to enjoy such rewarding environments without intruding upon each other's immediate surroundings. Camping is one of the few forms of forest recreation that can be planned to pay its way, for people with cars, tents or caravans expect to pay for their placement overnight in return for simple amenities. Further developments are the provision of log-cabin type residences as summer holiday homes and forest motels. This kind of accommodation provision leads naturally on to simple shops and restaurants. The latter can profit exceedingly from their forest surroundings, though the best meal in the woods is the one you cook yourself over a log fire.

Timber Production and Combined Resources

Timber production need be discussed only briefly here since it is considered fully in a later chapter. The efficient growing and harvesting of wood is the most economically profitable use for most forests. Whatever other resources are exploited, timber production should be retained wherever possible in the interests of meeting commercial demands and worldwide shortages – or to put it more simply – human needs. This can mean sole-use for timber raising, a dual purpose such as timber combined with game preservation, or ideally a multiple-use regime in which recreation and water conservation unite with the enhancement of scenic values to make an ideal forest, meeting many human demands. This should be the goal of every true forester but circumstances will severely tax his skill and patience as he seeks to achieve it.

Part 3

The World's Forests

Chapter 9

Broadleaved Forests of the Temperate Zones

TALL deciduous broadleaved trees form the leading element in the forest cover over most of lowland Europe and North America, besides those Asiatic lands such as China that lie within the temperate climatic zone. South of the equator they are only major constituents of smaller forests, notably in southern Chile, Argentina and New Zealand. The word 'temperate', implying little change, is misleading, for the yearly march of the sun from south to north, then southwards again, ensures that trees live through cool springs, hot summers, mild autumns and cold winters.

Their main adaptation to this annual climatic rhythm is the development of a deciduous leaf which functions for one summer only and is then discarded. This leaf has no particular protection against water loss, nor is any needed, because rainfall is adequate throughout its life spell and water can readily be obtained by roots active in warm soil. This kind of foliage is called *mesophyllous* in contrast to the *sclerophyllous* or leathery foliage borne by evergreen broadleaved trees.

Each autumn the leaves fall and the trees stand with bare branches all through winter. At that time of year the soil water supply is even more adequate but trees cannot draw upon it when it is frozen in the form of ice in the soil nor indeed at any time when soil temperatures lie below 6°C. All reserves needed for next spring's growth must be stored in the woody tissues of trunk, branches and major roots.

Economic Value of Broadleaves

The annual fall of the leaves may be regarded as a source of loss to the forest, making deciduous trees less efficient as producers of timber than their evergreen counterparts. This loss is however offset by the regular return of mineral nutrients to the soil. One must remember also that evergreens show a like pattern of leaf fall, the only real difference being that evergreen leaves remain alive and functional for several years instead of for merely one season. The evergreens can, however, make use of occasional warm spells when photosynthesis is impossible for the leafless deciduous kinds. It remains broadly true that deciduous broadleaved trees cannot match evergreens on similar sites for rate of timber production. Under commercial forests their volume yield is rarely more than half that of conifers. Height growth may be similar but the increase in thickness of the stems, which contributes more to the volume, is nearly always significantly slower. Only poplars rival the conifers in this respect.

In order, then, to get logs of equivalent size to those of coniferous or softwood trees, the forester must keep most broadleaved trees growing for a longer spell of years. He may look for their maturity as prime timber at an age around 100 or 120 years, instead of sixty or seventy years for the conifers. The financial return on his investment is thus delayed and as soon as he takes compound interest into account his calculations will show that broadleaved forests 'can never pay', whatever likely price he may eventually secure for their timber. This economic argument is somewhat academic because the life of a broadleaved tree crop in the temperate zone is, so far as its owners are concerned, a two-generation affair. The man who plants it passes it on to his heirs. The man who fells it obtains it as an inheritance rather than an investment. Changes in money values and socio-economic conditions over any given century have usually resulted in broadleaved forests proving highly satisfactory investments, or inheritances!

The broadleaved trees of the temperate zone produce highly variable timbers which contrast with the more uniform woods of the conifers. Until the development of metal, concrete and plastic technology during the present century, they played essential parts in industry and transport for which no acceptable substitutes could be found. This gave these timbers a high scarcity value. Today the demands for specialized hardwoods are less, but some still continue and help to maintain high timber prices. Examples are ash and hickory for tool handles, oak for wheel spokes, ladder rungs and the staves of sherry casks, and walnut for gun stocks. Because of their intrinsic beauty and scarcity, many choice hardwoods have also gained a luxury value. They may be used in the solid form to construct sound sturdy furniture of, say, maple, elm, ash or birch, or be applied as veneers that may include highly figured 'flamy' birch or rich brown cherrywood, tinged with green and gold.

Coppices and Pollard Trees

A remarkable character of most temperate-zone broadleaved trees, which is found in very few conifers, is their ability to sprout, or *coppice*, from their stumps after their main trunk has been cut down. They send out shoots from dormant buds around the face of the cut so that a single large stem is replaced by a group of smaller ones, each competing with one another for space, light and nutrients. If these in turn are cut back, a few months later a second cluster of coppice stems springs up. This process can be repeated indefinitely for a span of time measured in centuries. Repeated cutting-back appears to rejuvenate the coppice stump or stool, giving its active outer zones of sapwood and bast a virtually unlimited span of life, while below ground the lesser roots are renewed like the shoots above. Plate 31.

The ability to 'coppice' gave broadleaved trees particularly oak, sweet chestnut, hazel and willow, an important economic value to early communities. Provided they did not need large logs people could harvest the timber and firewood they needed by the planned, repeated coppicing of reserved woods. The word 'coppice' came into the English language from the Norman French verb *couper*, 'to cut', which gives a clue to the date, probably within a century or so after 1066, when the practice entered into estate policies. In modern French, however, the same method is called *taillir*, also meaning 'to cut', and the noun for French coppices or copses is *taillis*.

The output of coppices consists of small poles suitable for fencing and for minor building framework, as in cowsheds or peasant cottages, and a variety of lesser rods or wands that can be applied to interwoven hurdles or baskets of many kinds. Hurdles were widely used, in all wooded regions and from early prehistoric times, for portable fences or as wattles in wattle-and-daub buildings. When daubed with clay and set in a timber frame they made sound, durable, fire-proof wall panels. Cleft rods also served as laths and spars for tiled or thatched roofs and 'brooches' for thatching hay-ricks and corn-ricks.

Besides constructional material coppices yielded a steady, dependable supply of firewood, essential before the end of the last century when the earth's reserves of coal and oil remained virtually unexplored. They provided warmth for winter and year-round fuel for cooking and industry. Charcoal obtained from wood (see Chapter 20) was an essential raw material for all medieval economies. It provided the fuel for metal working, baking, pottery, glass-making and cooking food. It served also as a chemical agent for 'reducing' all metals from their ores, including the iron on which all Iron Age civilization depended. Besides enabling man to make plough-shares, charcoal made possible the forging of swords and the casting of cannon. It was also an essential ingredient of gunpowder and hence a munition of war.

A further invaluable industrial chemical, that could be obtained more dependably from regular coppicing than from felling full-grown trees, was tanbark. The barks of oaks, *Quercus* species, and sweet chestnuts, *Castanea* species, are particularly rich in tannins which are essential for the tanning of hides to make leather. This was needed for harness as well as for footwear and clothes.

Pure woodlands of coppiced trees, also called 'simple coppice', could not supply the large timbers needed for house-building or ship-building. The practice therefore developed of leaving selected tall trees, usually oak or ash, to grow on to maturity amid the coppiced stems. These trees were known as 'standards' and the system that employed them was called 'coppice-with-standards'. An ideal oak coppice, cut over for poles, firewood and tan-bark every fifteen years, could carry a regular sprinkling of standard trees, of all ages up to ninety years, reserved at each cutting-over of their neighbouring stumps.

After every cutting of the coppice, cattle, sheep, and other livestock had to be kept out of the woods for several years so that they could not bite back the young sprouts or 'spring' from the stumps. This was done either by fencing or herding. Where this was not practicable, as for instance on common lands open to the grazing of cattle having many owners, an alternative system called 'pollarding' was followed. Pollarding, from Norman French *poil*, meaning 'head', implies the 'beheading' of a tree at a height of about two metres above ground level. Most broadleaved trees, unless too old, respond by sending out a cluster of vigorous shoots from dormant buds just below the cut. These shoots grow into a mop-head of small branches, all safely above the reach of browsing cattle or deer. In effect you get a coppice crop raised two metres above the ground.

The hornbeams, *Carpinus betulus*, of Epping Forest, northeast of London which were lopped for centuries to yield firewood, are a classic example of pollarding. Over much of England and northern Europe isolated pollards or small groups are frequent around farmsteads. They served as a handy, perpetually renewable, low-cost source of wood for cottage fires, which was cut in summer and stacked to season for the following winter.

A remarkable feature of pollarding is that it rejuvenates the tree concerned, just as coppicing gives fresh life to a stump. The stoutest and probably the oldest oaks in Britain are all pollard trees. The current record of 13 metres in girth is held by a farmstead tree at Pontfadog near Chirk in North Wales. As coal and other fuels became available, countrymen ceased to lop such trees and their last sprouts developed into enormous limbs. The resulting picturesque oaks and beeches attract artists who mistakenly believe ·they show the tree's natural form, not something moulded by man.

A variant of pollarding sometimes practised even today in Europe and

Asia is called 'shrouding'. It involves the cutting back of side branches rather than the top ones. This encourages the tree to put out a fresh crop of young side shoots each spring. Elms, *Ulmus* species, are the trees most often shrouded, and the usual object is to provide foliage and soft green shoots as fodder for goats.

With such varied uses for the shoots and stems grown so regularly and in such profusion by coppicing and allied methods, it is not surprising that large areas of broadleaved forest were converted to them. In Britain in 1914 no less than 40%, or 500,000 acres out of 1,250,000 acres of *broadleaved* forest, were classed as coppice or 'scrub', which usually meant neglected coppice. In France in 1823 the corresponding proportion was no less than 80%, or 400,000 hectares (one million acres) out of 500,000 (1,250,000). By 1900 the French area included a considerable extent of *robinie* coppice, formed by the deliberate planting of a fast-growing introduced American tree, the black locust, *Robinia pseudoacacia*, as a source of rural firewood.

One of the merits of coppice where it is wanted, but a great drawback when it ceases to be harvested, is its extreme persistence. Cut it back as often as you like and it will sprout once more. The physical removal of its large, deeply-rooted and tenacious stumps is a formidable and costly task even with modern equipment such as bulldozers. The most effective modern method is to poison the stumps with a chemical brush-killer such as 2,4-D. This is expensive to purchase and apply but cheaper than hard hand labour. More gradual methods include grazing by livestock and the singling out the shoots so that one from each stump eventually becomes a single tall timber tree.

The general decline in demand for coppice products as modern technology finds alternative materials has resulted in widespread surpluses of broadleaved coppice throughout western Europe. Most of this is neglected or used only for the sport of pheasant shooting. Its conversion to un-coppiced woodland, technically called 'high forest', proceeds slowly and patchily. Left alone most coppice would eventually 'graduate' into high forest, but oak, for example, would require about 200 years! One effective method of changing this forest liability into an economic asset, now widely practised in France, is called *enresinement*, meaning increasing the share of conifers, known to French foresters as *essences resineuses*. It involves partial clearance followed by the introduction of shade-bearing conifers such as Douglas fir, *Pseudotsuga menziesii*, from the western USA. This quick-growing conifer casts a deep shade and can suppress the coppice once it has overtopped it.

A fundamental reason for the vigorous growth of coppice and lopped trees is their retention of living and active root systems. If a wood is clear-felled and the land replanted with small trees, there is a period of low production of timber during which the trees build up their root systems. This does not happen if the crop is coppiced, for the 'working capital' of fully developed roots is retained intact and unharmed.

European Broadleaved Forests

The temperate broadleaved forests of Europe form a wide though irregular band stretching from west to east from the Atlantic coast of France to the steppes of eastern Russia. The British Isles except for the Scottish Highlands are included in this band and so is Denmark, south Sweden and even the southern tip of Norway. The northern fringe of the broadleaved zone where it gives way to coniferous forest trends southwards, as one moves east, into an increasingly continental climate with harder and longer winters. From 60° latitude in Norway it falls to 50° in central Russia. Along high mountain ranges it has definite altitudinal limits, but these vary with latitude and local topography. In the Alps, for example, broadleaves may thrive up to 2,000 metres above sea level on the southern slopes of sheltered valleys, but fail to reach 1,500 metres on the exposed, cold northern flank of the same range. At its upper limits, the pure broadleaved forest merges into a mixed woodland of broadleaves and conifers and eventually gives way to pure coniferous stands. In broad terms only the Pyrenees, the Alps and the Caucasus mountains have their upper levels wholly outside the broadleaved forest zone.

The northern and upper altitudinal limits are set by cold, or more probably by the shorter growing seasons that are forced on these deciduous broadleaved trees by low temperatures. The critical point is the number of days over which prevailing temperatures normally rise, not above freezing point, but above the level of 6°C at which active metabolism begins. Where this active period becomes short, the evergreen conifers, having the advantage of perpetually-ready leaves, gain a competitive advantage.

The southern limits of temperate broadleaved forests in Europe and western Asia are set by summer rainfall. As one moves south towards the Mediterranean, this becomes insufficient for transpiration to be sustained through the growing season, and ordinary broadleaved trees, lacking modifications to resist this stress, die of drought. The broad geographical southern limits of continuous temperate broadleaved forests are the Pyrenees, the Alps, and a line running eastwards from Venice towards the northern shores of the Black Sea. But there are many major exceptions to this rule. Where mountains rise high enough to give cooler summers and to induce more ample summer rainfall, broadleaved forests can again flourish. There are, for example, thriving beechwoods on the flanks of the Pyrenees and the Alps, the Italian Apennines, the Balkan mountains and the Caucasus.

In some regions, therefore, the broadleaved forest fails to go far up the mountains because they are *too cold*; in others, by contrast, it runs high up them because they are *cooler* and moister than the plains below.

Deciduous oaks are of two main species, namely pedunculate oak, *Quercus robur*, with stalked acorns and sessile oak, *Q. petraea*, which has stalkless ones; these are usually considered the typical trees of European temperate broadleaved forest. They and their allies occupy the central zone of this woodland and usually gain dominance over the better sites and soils.

Beeches of the genus *Fagus* and ash trees in the *Fraxinus* genus show more tolerance of lower temperatures and calcareous soils. They become locally dominant over chalk and limestone rocks and flourish higher up the mountains, also farther north. But the main broadleaved trees near the northern and high mountain limits of this forest are birches in the genus *Betula*. Plates 11 and 15 show beech forest. Plate 62 shows birches.

Sweet chestnut, *Castanea sativa*, though not native north of the Alps, was carried beyond them 2,000 years ago by Roman legionaries who used its nuts as a staple ration; it has since become extensively naturalized.

Associated with these five leading groups of broadleaves are many others that occupy smaller, more irregular areas, often on specially suitable ground. In marshes or near running water grow: alders, *Alnus*; willows, *Salix*; and poplars, *Populus*. On higher, better drained land one may find maples, *Acer*, including the European sycamore *A. pseudoplatanus*, now widely naturalized in the British Isles. Elms, *Ulmus*, appear in more fertile situations. Planes, *Platanus*, native to the Balkans, have been artificially established in many northern countries. Plate 30.

Everywhere the European broadleaved forest has been disrupted by clearance and settlement. It builds up by leaf fall and root action the very desirable Brown Forest Soils or Brown Earths described in Chapter 6, the 'loams' that arable cultivators seek. Wherever men farm, they can do so most profitably and with the highest reward for their labours by clearing broadleaved forest to win land. The better the forest, the more fertile the resulting soil. Given three thousand years of agricultural development, it is unlikely that much natural broadleaved forest could have survived unless it were given deliberate long-term management and protection.

This protection has taken three forms: ownership by the state, ownership by local communities and ownership by individual private landlords. The relative importance of each depends on the political structure and history of the country concerned. It may vary from about 98% *private* ownership, as in Britain as recently as 1920, to 100% *state* ownership, as in Soviet Russia today. In the United States of America both the federal government and individual states can and do own forests.

Ownership by the national or state authority, or by far-sighted private individuals, may have long-term objectives that match the hundred-year life-spans of broadleaved trees. But rural communities seldom look so far ahead. Their main needs have always been for the small poles and firewood yielded by coppice trees. This helps to explain the large areas of coppiced woodland found across Europe.

Communal ownership has another advantage for the preservation of forests against incursions by graziers and cultivators. Woodland in which all the farming members of a commune have a share cannot be destroyed by any single individual. Any man who steps out of line and seeks to enclose forest for farming is promptly restrained by his neighbours, rightly jealous of their own rights. Preservation of communally owned woodland demands eternal vigilance of the sort which is rarely lacking in any peasant community!

It was the social and economic structures of rural communities that preserved broadleaved woods as local sources of timber supply right through the Middle Ages. In more recent times all concerned have realized the need for long-term plans to ensure the survival and welfare of such woodlands.

Broadleaved Forests in Asia

The varied topographical and climatic make-up of the great Asiatic continent gives scope for temperate broadleaved forests to flourish in curious places. In Asia Minor and the Caucasus these forests grow in the cooler, higher rainfall regions of the mountain ranges and this pattern continues across northern Persia. The mighty 3,000-kilometre-long Himalayan chain running across the north of India carries an almost continuous strip of temperate-zone broadleaves on its foothills, sandwiched between the cold coniferous forests higher up and the tropical broadleaved jungles lower down. These forests, though broken by the rugged mountainous topography, continue eastwards through southern China. Over most of China, however, whatever broadleaved forests grew originally have been swept away by thousands of years of close settlement and intensive cultivation. In Japan, similar close utilization of the more fertile lower ground has long confined broadleaved forests to the lower slopes of the mountains, but there are extensive forests of Japanese oak nowadays exploited commercially as a furniture and joinery timber that has been exported on a large scale to Europe and America.

Asia's broadleaved trees are with few exceptions members of the same genera that are found in Europe. This applies all the way from the Mediterranean zone in the west to the Pacific seaboard on the east. The species show minor differences from each other which are due to their development from common ancestral stocks in regions that later became isolated from one another by world-wide climatic changes.

North American Broadleaved Forests

On the North American continent the main temperate broadleaved forest forms a huge oval zone reaching inland from the east coast. Its northern limits are the coniferous forests north of the St Lawrence river in Quebec, extending west into Ontario. On the west it is bounded by the prairies beyond the Mississippi. To the south it merges into the region of pines and evergreen oaks of Florida and neighbouring southeastern states. It is a rich and varied forest resource, holding all the Eurasian genera of broadleaved trees with a wider range of species, and in addition several important genera never found in northern Europe or Asia.

This American forest is remarkably rich in oaks of varied characters and properties, each adapted to a particular region. The red oaks like *Quercus rubra* are remarkable for the brilliant colouring of their autumn foliage; their timber is not remarkably strong or durable and serves mainly for cheap furniture or flooring. By contrast the white oaks like *Q. alba* have exceptionally strong, durable and workable timbers, and are used for exacting constructional work, lasting fencing, high-grade furniture and staves for whisky casks. Maples, of the genus *Acer*, flourish in remarkable variety and rival the red oaks in the brilliance of their leaf colour every fall. They yield sound, hard timbers. The sugar maple, *A. saccharum*, is the source of maple syrup and sugar obtained by tapping trunks in spring. Birches grow on the upper hill slopes, alders flourish by watersides, and beeches, ash trees and elms form shady groves in sheltered valleys. Plate 19 shows maples.

Broadleaved trees peculiar to North America include the beautiful tulip tree or yellow poplar, *Liriodendron tulipifera*, which bears saddle-shaped leaves and greenish-yellow goblet-shaped flowers resembling tulips. The robinia or false acacia tree, *Robinia pseudoacacia*, also known as black locust, bears masses of showy white blossoms shaped like sweet peas in June, and yields a tough, golden-brown timber. Hickories, of the genus *Carya*, have compound leaves like those of walnut and yield an even tougher timber, better than all others for its resistance to impact when used for the handles of hammers, axes, or picks. Incidentally it is always preferred for making lacrosse sticks, as this is a game invented by American Indians needing a very shockproof implement for carrying and launching the ball.

The British and French settlers who established the first colonies on North America's eastern coasts encountered many trees that had been familiar to them, though as somewhat different species, in their European woodlands. They quickly adapted their well-known crafts to the new materials and added new ones learnt from the Indians around them.

As soon as they landed the settlers set to work felling and clearing oaks for building houses, fences and protective stockades. The adaptability of the native American timbers to familiar uses proved a valued asset to the newcomers who had the tremendous advantage over the Indian of iron tools and the skills to apply them. Oak was cleft for clapboard to make house walls, roofing shingles, ladder rungs and wheel spokes, and was soon being given its traditional place in shipbuilding. Birch yielded abundant slow-burning, long-lasting winter fuel and also tough waterproof bark that could be used, as they learned from the Indians, to construct remarkably strong yet light canoes. Native ash and hickory provided tough tool handles. Tan-bark needed for turning hides to leather was easily obtained by stripping from the stems of indigenous oaks. Wood ash from the brushwood fires proved a valuable fertilizer, rich in potash and phosphorus, and some was even exported to Europe in return for necessities such as tools and guns.

The slow but steady clearance of the eastern North American broadleaved forest provided all these requirements for the developing settlements. It also gave the colonists exceptionally rich soils, deep Brown Earths which held the accumulated nutrients of thousands of years under forest cover. Aided by this rich bounty, farming flourished as the clearings were extended and has been maintained successfully in many regions for over 350 years.

During the present century there has been some recession, particularly in the New England states, because agriculture has become less profitable there than in regions of better climate farther west or south. As a result, centuries-old farms have been abandoned, and the broadleaved forest has come back. The first invaders are usually alders, which colonize marshy patches of pastures. Then come birches on the drier soils, maples everywhere, several kinds of oaks, and finally beech, ash and hickory. This 'secondary forest' shows promise of restoring the splendid primeval native stands, though much of it is in practice felled far short of maturity for profitable use as pulpwood for paper-making.

Two other kinds of North American temperate broadleaved forests merit brief mention. One is the sprinkling of alders, willows, poplars (or cotton-woods) and maples that grow in the valleys of the Rocky Mountains where conifers play the leading part. The other is the broad belt of hardy birches and aspen poplars that runs across the continent south of the cold tundra intermixed with hardy evergreen spruces and low junipers. Plate 62.

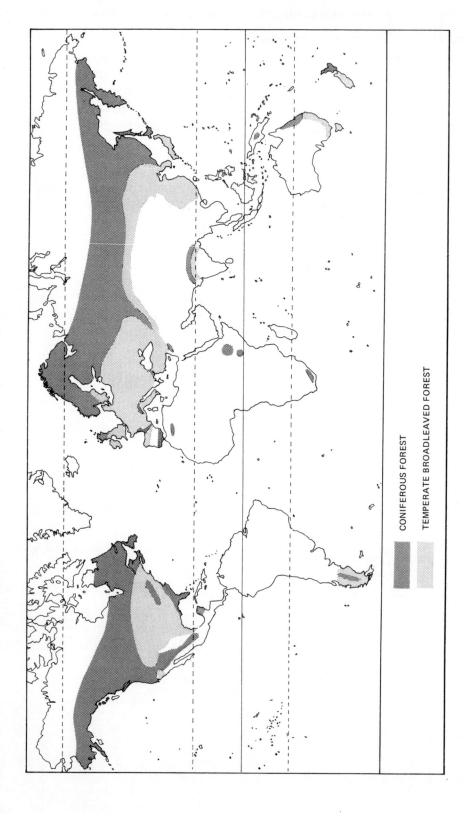

CONIFEROUS FOREST

TEMPERATE BROADLEAVED FOREST

Figure 12 World distribution of coniferous forest (dark shading) and
temperate broadleaved forest (light shading). Where the two meet, they merge.

Chapter 10

Coniferous Forests

FORESTS of cone-bearing, needle-leaved trees, also known as softwoods or gymnosperms, cover enormous areas of the world's cooler regions. Most are evergreen. The deciduous habit is only found in a few specialized genera such as larches, *Larix*, which grow in places like the high Alps where they cannot gain or hold moisture during the winter.

Northern Coniferous Forest

The largest expanse of northern coniferous forest, sometimes called the *taiga*, reaches right across northern Europe, Asia and America. It extends from the Scottish Highlands and the coast of Norway to the east of Siberia and the northern islands of Japan, a total distance of some 7,000 kilometres (4,350 miles). Farther east beyond the Bering Straits it continues through Alaska and right across Canada and northern New England to Newfoundland, a further 7,000 kilometres (4,350 miles). Its width from north to south varies from 200 kilometres (130 miles) at its oceanic fringes to over 1,000 kilometres (650 miles) within Asia and 1,500 kilometres (950 miles) in western North America.

Towards the north this taiga is bounded by the colder, more arctic *tundra*, which is frozen for most of the year. This is a region of stunted vegetation, dwarf birch and juniper, with many heaths, mosses, lichens and bog plants. On the south it merges gradually into the temperate broadleaved forests or else in regions of lower rainfall gives way to prairie or steppe.

The northern limits of this huge coniferous forest are fairly constant for there are few mountain ranges in the sub-arctic. Close to the Atlantic and Pacific Oceans it goes well beyond the Arctic Circle, and up to latitude 68°. Within the Eurasian and American continents, where there are no great water masses to moderate winter cold, the dividing line between taiga and tundra comes as far south as 65° latitude in central Siberia, and 60° around Hudson Bay in central Canada.

On the south, however, the fringes of the northern conifer forests are far less well defined. Along mountain chains such as the Urals on the frontier of Europe and Asia, the Rocky Mountains of western North America and the Appalachians farther east, it extends southwards, below the tree-line, to latitudes around 40°. Detached ranges of high mountains where the altitude creates cold local climates, also carry extensive conifer forests as islands within a broadleaved sea. European examples are the Pyrenees, the Auvergne massif of central France, the Alps, the Italian Apennines, the Carpathians, certain Balkan ranges and the Caucasus. Asia holds huge conifer forests along the mighty Himalayan chain, and also in Turkey, Iran, Mongolia and on the mountains of Japan. In America they are found in similar isolation along the Allegheny Mountains of the middle-Atlantic states. Plates 2, 13, 15.

Four genera of conifers play a leading part throughout all these regions, namely: *Picea*, the spruces; *Abies*, the silver firs; *Pinus*, the true pines; and *Larix*, the larches. Lesser groups with a more localized distribution are: *Pseudotsuga*, the Douglas firs; *Tsuga*, the hemlocks; *Thuja*, red and northern white cedars, Plate 56 and the true cypresses which comprise two genera, *Cupressus* and *Chamaecyparis*, certain cypresses and Atlantic white cedars, Plate 63.

The large spruce genus *Picea* is remarkable for its homogeneity. Though diligent botanists have split it into some thirty species, most are little more than regional forms adapted to local climates. All bear solitary needles on little woody pegs that give their twigs a rough 'feel' after they have fallen away. Spruces bear cylindrical cones that droop downwards. Their trunks hold pale, rather soft timber that is, however, strong enough for many types of building, joinery and box-making work. Spruce wood, also known in the trade as 'whitewood', is an ideal raw material for making paper, cardboard, chipboard, wood-based textiles such as rayon, and wood-based film like cellophane. The vast spruce forests of Scandinavia, northern Russia and North America are therefore of great commercial value to the countries concerned. The typical European species is the Norway spruce, *Picea abies*; white spruce, *P. glauca*, is a leading kind in eastern North America while Sitka spruce, *P. sitchensis*, forms valuable forests of giant trees in the Pacific seaboard from Alaska south to California. Plates 36, 57.

The silver firs such as *Abies alba* in Europe, *A. balsamea* in eastern North America and *A. grandis* in the west of that continent resemble spruces but bear their needles directly on their twigs without pegs. Their large cones stand upright but are rarely seen since they break up after ripening in autumn. Silver fir wood is like that of spruce and has similar uses. Plate 58.

Pines in the large *Pinus* genus bear their needles in groups of two, three, or five, according to the species. Their youngest first-year seedlings, however, carry solitary needles. Pine cones taper to a point, many being in fact almost truly 'conical' in shape. Pine timber being basically stronger than that of spruce is preferred for heavier construction, fencing, transmission poles and railroad sleepers or ties. It has a resinous heartwood which is darker in colour than the sapwood around it. The heartwood has only moderate durability but the wood as a whole is easily treated with preservatives that ensure a long service life out-of-doors. Pine can also yield paper and rayon and overall its commercial value is high. The typical European species is Scots pine, *Pinus sylvestris*, a two-needled species. The eastern North American white pine, *P. strobus*, a five-needled species, is the best-known American kind in the northern zone. Plate 59.

Larches, represented by European larch, *Larix decidua*, and the American larch or tamarack, *L. laricina*, both differ from other common conifers in being deciduous, shedding their needles each autumn. These needles, being short-lived and having little need to check water loss during their summer activity, are soft in texture. Most are borne in pretty clusters or rosettes, though those near the shoot tips and also those on seedlings are solitary. Larch cones are barrel-shaped. Larch timber, which has a naturally durable, dark heartwood, is tougher than most other conifers and can serve exacting uses. It is chosen for example for the planking of wooden fishing craft, still built even today on both sides of the Atlantic. The American name for larch, 'tamarack', comes from the American Indian word for the tree; so does the American name for the tree's timber: 'hackmatack'.

Sub-tropical and Southern Hemisphere Coniferous Forests

The conifers' evergreen habit and ability to restrict water loss within their tough leathery needles enable them to grow south as well as north of the main temperate, broadleaved forest zone. Certain species have become adapted to the Mediterranean climate described in a later chapter, while others flourish in the sub-tropics. The cedar forests, *Cedrus* species, of Mount Lebanon (*C. libani*), the Atlas mountains of North Africa (*C. atlantica*), the Troodos mountains of Cyprus (*C. brevifolia*) and the Indian Himalayas (*C. deodara*) belong to this sub-tropical group, though they can be grown successfully in temperate climate gardens. Each has evolved on its own 'island' of mountains, with cold snowy winters but intensely hot sunny summers, from some ancient common ancestral stock.

America holds a group of 'southern pines' such as the Florida long-leaf pine, *Pinus palustris*, which form extensive open woods on poor sandy soils where they can tolerate severe droughts, though they are not frost-hardy.

Other species are found in Mexico. Their old-world counterparts are the maritime pine, *P. pinaster*, the stone pine, *P. pinea*, the Aleppo pine, *P. halepensis*, and the Bosnian pine, *P. leucodermis*, all natives of the Mediterranean shores. The southern ranges of the great Rocky Mountain chain in California, Utah, Colorado, Nevada and New Mexico hold a fascinating group of sub-tropical conifers including the Colorado blue spruce, *Picea pungens*, the lovely fir, *Abies amabilis*, and the long-lived bristlecone pine, *Pinus aristata*. Plate 18 shows maritime pine forest.

In Asia the sub-tropical conifer woods are less well-marked due to the monsoons that promote wetter climates. The Japanese cedar, or sugi, *Cryptomeria japonica*, is however an outstanding example of a sub-tropical conifer that forms valuable timber-yielding forests.

Within the warmer tropical zones, sub-tropical conifer forest is isolated on islands at high elevations where the climate is too cold for tropical rain forests to grow. The podocarps, a handy term for members of the genus *Podocarpus*, which have yew-like foliage and fruit like plums and are unknown in the colder north, form considerable evergreen forests on the mountains of Ethiopia, east and central Africa, Chile and also in Malaysia, the Phillipines, New Guinea, northern Australia and New Zealand. In South Africa they come down to sea level, being represented by the yellow-wood, *P. falcatus*, at the Cape of Good Hope.

This brings us to the conifer forests of the southern hemisphere which grow mainly under sub-tropical conditions. They are of much lesser extent than their northern counterparts owing to the smaller land masses. New Zealand has on its North Island valuable stands of kauri pine, *Agathis australis*, which belongs to a genus unknown in the northern hemisphere. The large genus *Araucaria*, likewise confined to the southern half of the globe, has an important species, *A. bidwillii*, on the mountains of Queensland. It is best known by its aboriginal name of *bunya-bunya*. The sub-tropical pampas of Brazil and the neighbouring South American states are the home of Parana pine, *A. brasiliana*, a valued softwood timber that is exported on a large scale.

The most familiar member of this remarkable *Araucaria* genus is the monkey-puzzle tree or Chile pine, *A. araucana*, which forms considerable forests on the southern Andes range in both Chile and Argentina. Its odd name was bequeathed by an English wit who saw a specimen being planted in Victorian days as an ornament to a country house lawn and remarked, 'It would puzzle a monkey to climb that tree!' It originates in a cold, snowy region (where there are no monkeys) and the bizarre branches extend indefinitely, branching at intervals in a geometric fashion. The large, triangular scale-like leaves have a long life span, even for evergreens, and may persist for over ten years. Eventually the monkey puzzle bears separate male and female flowers, usually on separate trees. The female flowers ripen slowly to huge cones, large as pineapples, which hold big edible seeds, long a staple food for the Araucanian Indians who give the group its name.

Life in the Northern Conifer Woodlands

Few people apart from the foresters who work in their midst understand the rhythm of life in the conifer woods. Being evergreen they appear to change little with the seasons and to bear no obvious flowers, while their younger seedlings are hardly ever observed, even by knowledgeable naturalists. In fact the conifer forest is a place of constant growth and change, more rapid in some respects than the broadleaved woodland.

The warmth of spring prompts each conifer shoot to burst the winter resting bud at its tip and for a few weeks the bright green of the soft, newly expanded needles stands out against the darker green of older foliage. After this sudden outburst of growth, which may extend the length of a branch and the height of a tree by anything up to one metre, further extension ceases. By mid-summer the shoot has laid down a cluster of resting buds at its tip in preparation for a similar rapid spurt of growth in the following spring. During the summer the nourishment needed for the rapid growth of next year's buds into shoots is accumulated and stored within the tissues of twig, branch and trunk.

The markedly seasonal shoot extension that is typical of all coniferous trees results in a geometrical pattern of branching in which each year's growth is seen as a branchless length between the nodes from which whorls of side-branches originate. Hence it is usually easy to tell at a glance how fast most conifers are growing, for they mark the passage of the years on their shoots as well as by the hidden rings of their timber. This is clearest in youth, becoming less obvious amid the branches of an old, slow-growing individual.

The natural processes of regeneration among the conifers are adequate for the perpetual renewal of the forest unless it is faced with some exceptional calamity such as a fire or a deliberate widespread clearance by man. Male flowers are borne abundantly by sizeable trees each spring and scatter abundant pollen on the winds. Female flowers, usually borne on the same tree though on separate leafy shoots, regularly ripen ample fertile seed. In general both the small scales at the tip of each cone and the similar small scales at its base prove infertile, but each of the larger scales part-way along the cone's mid-rib matures sound seeds. With most species the seeds are two in number and winged. Enough are carried by the wind to all chance gaps or small clearings in the woods to restore the full stocking of trees.

The ease with which coniferous forests replace their losses is hard to appreciate in Britain where natural regrowth is unusual and local. The best examples are found in the pinewoods of the Scottish Highlands. One reason for the frequent failure of conifer seedlings in the British Isles is the mild winter which enables competing weeds to outgrow the little trees and smother them. Other causes are the presence of rabbits, deer, sheep, and even the black grouse and capercaillie, large game birds that readily eat both conifer seed and seedlings. Beasts and birds by their grazing or browsing take a heavy toll of the potential tree crop and often eliminate all potential recruits to the timber stand.

But these British conditions are exceptional. Elsewhere in its enormous range the conifer forest replaces itself readily through the reliable growth of its abundant seedlings. Any clearing in an Alpine, Scandinavian or Canadian forest is quickly re-populated by saplings. These spring from seedlings that are not checked by faster growing grasses or herbs nor even smothered by ferns such as bracken. Minute first-year seedlings are immune to winter cold and frozen soil and persist unharmed under a deep blanket of white snow. Competing plants, browsing animals or greedy insects may kill them but they appear immune to harm by the elements.

The northern conifer forest as a whole is in fact able to withstand severe winters better than any other kind of woodland. Though its foliage, with the sole exception of the larches, is evergreen, it is able to hibernate. Each tree is in effect refrigerated or cold stored from November until April. Little harm is done by the most severe and prolonged frosts known, even in regions such as central Siberia and Canada where winter temperatures fall to $-50°C$. Not only is life held in suspense but sap is immobilized. Tree roots cannot gain water from frozen soil, but equally the foliage does not lose water to the cold atmosphere.

Evergreen leaves and branches support a heavy weight of snow which does no damage unless it builds up to a burden that fractures stems or trunks, which rarely happens. The snow is probably protective: it lessens transpiration from leaf surfaces, for that cannot occur to any significant degree until the snow itself has evaporated – a very slow process at low temperatures. The snow may also insulate the leaf tissues against the worst extremes of low temperatures since it is a poor conductor of heat.

Little research has been done on the hibernation of evergreen conifers. Not surprisingly, physiologists prefer to investigate the life of trees during more active seasons when there is 'something going on' and they do not have to wear thick fur coats to brave the icy weather.

Experts in seed storage have, however, discovered that conifer seeds can – as one would expect from simple forest observations – withstand long spells of freezing cold. Seed of most species is stored commercially in refrigerated chambers, kept at temperatures only a few degrees above freezing point. Seedling trees and young transplants can also be cold-stored without loss of life. This has become a standard commercial practice in countries like Canada and Scandinavia where the practical planting season was formerly very short. By holding back planting stock in a cold store the planting season may be extended beyond the normal March and April period, just after the spring thaw, right into May and June. Both seed and plant storage systems employ polythene containers to retain moisture in the plant tissues. Plants, however, must never be exposed to the sun while enclosed in polythene bags as they then heat up rapidly and are killed outright in a few hours.

Exploiting Coniferous Forests

Historically, the world's conifer forests represent a frontier to man's advancing civilization. He did not develop his agriculture and crafts within them but moved into them from regions of better soil and kinder climate. This usually implied a migration towards the north or higher up the mountains. A feeling of awe still persists when fir forests are mentioned. In the imagination they are limitless, trackless and snowbound, the haunt of wild deer, wolves and outlaws. This attitude continues into the present day even after they have all been surveyed and photographed from the air, mapped and assessed as sources of commercial timber.

Settlers in northern or alpine regions have always preferred to clear broadleaved woodlands such as birch forests for cultivation because these provide richer soils than the conifers can do. This is due in part to the broadleaves' situation on gentler slopes with a greater depth of soil than the conifers, and in part to the rich Brown Earths that evolve beneath broadleaved cover. By contrast the conifers commonly promote the formation of podzols, layered soils with a succession of infertile strata (see Chapter 6). Villages and homesteads were therefore built on better soils though often on the fringes of the conifer forests. These remained and to a large degree still remain intact, with few clearings for cultivation.

Until trade developed during the later Middle Ages coniferous forests were regarded as low-value assets to those countries that owned them. They provided what were then regarded as limitless supplies of logs for fencing or the building of houses or ships, though birch was better for firewood. In many regions their softwood timber might be had for the taking for there was more than enough for all local needs. Trappers seeking furs, sportsmen shooting grouse, and berry-pickers roved through these forests, but even in winter the ring of the logger's axe was rarely heard.

The first demands for softwood on a scale that led to exploitation of coniferous forests came from the growing towns and seaports of the more prosperous agricultural lands of Europe, Asia and North Africa. Wood was needed for building houses and warehouses and for the planking, masts and spars of trading ships or warships. These needs often arose at a distance from the forests and water transport became a key factor in meeting them. Timber is well suited to movement down rivers since logs float, or across seas as it is readily stowed on ships. Historically the trade began in the days of the great Babylonian and Egyptian river basin empires, along the Rivers Euphrates, Tigris and Nile. There is a famous biblical example in the contract made by Solomon, king of Israel, with Hiram, king of Tyre, for the supply of cedar timber from Mount Lebanon for the building of the temple at Jerusalem. This provided for the regular floating of the material coastwise down the Mediterranean sea. The classical civilizations of Greece and Rome likewise made massive demands on the forests within trading distance of their cities.

In the Middle Ages the towns and seaports of the fertile European plains drew heavily on the northern coniferous forests of Scandinavia and the Baltic and also on mountainous woodlands like the Black Forest of southern Germany that could supply their needs by transport down great rivers like the Rhine.

With the discovery of the New World the need for timber in Europe soon found expression in the felling of coastal forests in eastern Canada and the United States. Eventually, after the opening of the Panama Canal, it became profitable to ship lumber from the western seaboard of North America both to Europe and also to the eastern United States, and this trade continues. The building of railroads during the nineteenth century opened up great areas of inland forests, both in America and eastern Europe, and even in Asiatic regions such as the Himalayan foothills of India. Finally, during the present century road vehicles were developed to the point at which relatively few conifer forests remained 'inaccessible' in the commercial sense.

As soon as coniferous forests became valuable they were claimed by owners of various degrees. Unexplored and unoccupied land is generally held in political theory to belong to the state in which it lies. This position is still maintained in Soviet Russia and Siberia, the Canadian northlands, and to a lesser degree in the national parks, the national forests and the state forests of the United States. Many European and Asiatic countries also retain large areas of national forests. Devolution to other ownerships has been a long and varied process down the ages. In Europe many forests are *communally owned*, which means that a local community replaces the state as a joint owner. In North America and Scandinavia large tracts of productive forest have been made over, often in perpetuity, to commercial timber companies who have proved ready to exploit them in return for a royalty on timber, often described as 'stumpage'. The feudal system of land ownership whereby noblemen held land, originally in return for military service to the king as head of state, led to great expanses of European forests becoming in effect the personal property of rich and powerful individual landowners. This process was carried to the extreme in Scotland where at the start of the twentieth century *all* forests were privately owned.

The character of the forests' ownerships has proved significant to their present condition and future prospects. A forest can be destroyed by unplanned and unregulated felling in a few years but takes a century to recover, if it ever does. In the Old World many private landowners and communities conserved their spruce, pine and fir forests with commendable care. A common tradition was that each farmer could cut only enough timber for immediate use on his property, for example in house building or fencing, or as fuel. Exports to other districts required the consent of either the communal council of a communally-owned forest, or the landlord of a privately-owned one. Owners of both these types had a *conservative* approach to timber felling in the widest sense of the word. The men who mattered under communal control were the elders of each group, who were concerned with continuing supplies of wood for their sons and grandsons rather than with prompt profits. Therefore they did not favour major clearance or overcutting of any kind. Landowners in an age of inherited wealth and privilege likewise sought to provide for future revenues for their heirs, though there were noteworthy exceptions who devastated their forests to get cash to aid political ambitions, wage wars or live extravagantly beyond their real means.

The general outcome was the establishment of the principle of *sustained yield* whereby the forest was only cut at a rate that could be sustained, in perpetuity, by its fresh growth. First the leading landowners and later the communities engaged skilled professional foresters who could calculate the *allowable cut*, regulate the fellings and encourage regrowth to ensure maximum production for the foreseeable future. This practice saved and safeguarded coniferous forests over most of Europe.

This sustained yield principle was naturally adopted by state forest authorities. They first applied it to the management of their own properties and later enforced it on all the privately owned woodlands in their jurisdiction. In Britain for example it is illegal to cut down any substantial area of woodland without a licence from the Forestry Commission. Before such a licence is issued, the owner must either present a management plan for his wooded estate as a whole or else agree to accept replanting conditions (where appropriate) that ensure the restocking of the cleared land with a fresh timber crop.

In North America things have not gone so well. The first reaction to the discovery of vast and apparently limitless conifer woods was that they provided an inexhaustible asset. They had cost nothing in human effort to create. They could and should be cut for the highest profit and then left for nature to replenish the bounty. At first the settlers made only reasonable clearings but as the power of the timber cutters increased through better organization, techniques and transport, this wasteful approach gained momentum. Labour, capital and equipment became highly mobile. The slogans of the commercial companies were brief and to the point:

Cut out!

Get out!

Inspired by quick profits, and showing no responsibility for the maintenance of forests for future generations, the lumber concerns first devastated the larger pine and fir forests of the northeastern United States and eastern Canada. Leaving a legacy of scarred timberless land they moved on to the mid-west and the southeast, then to the eastern slopes of the Rocky Mountains. As these reserves neared exhaustion they extended their operations along the Pacific seaboard from California north through Oregon, Washington and British Columbia to Alaska, making inroads into the finest evergreen forests the world has ever known.

This horrifying and utterly wasteful attack on a fundamental resource is only just now coming to an end. Concessions are still being worked out on old leases that make no provision for the restoration of the timber stands concerned. Although the alert was sounded in the opening years of the present century it has taken a generation – a whole seventy years – for the message to sink in and become effective in forest management practice. A tradition of wanton exploitation cannot be reversed in a day.

In the United States the leading figure in the fight for the conservation of forests was Gifford Pinchot, who was appointed the first Chief of the United States Forest Service in 1905. Gaining the sympathy and support of President Theodore Roosevelt, he put in train a long succession of moves given effect through new federal and state laws that eventually safeguarded the surviving forests from unplanned and irresponsible onslaught.

In broad terms, lumber may no longer be cut without provision for replacement. The heavy task of replenishing the forests lost during generations of wanton cutting remains but is being tackled on an impressive scale.

America and Canada still hold considerable areas of what are called *first-growth forests*, implying virgin forests in which no commercial fellings have ever been carried out. The term *second-growth forest* implies stands of timber that have sprung up following a first clearance. There are often surprising differences between the two types. First-growth conifer forest can hold enormous Douglas firs, *Pseudotsuga menziesii*, or Sitka spruce, *Picea sitchensis*, up to 300 years old and 250 feet high. Conifers in second-growth forest rarely approach half that age or size. Certain tracts of the first-growth, primeval forest have wisely been reserved in national parks as a heritage for the future, since they cannot again be created for another 300 years or more. Future timber-growing will inevitably become concentrated in the second-growth forest, with management and machinery geared to trees of lesser sizes than occur in the virgin stands.

In some regions, notably the Pacific seaboard slopes of the Rocky Mountains, second-growth stands arise regularly and reliably through natural seeding and regeneration of cut-over land provided the clearings are not too large. Elsewhere it can only be secured by artificial restocking.

The Fire Peril

Fire plays a significant part in the life of most conifer woods. The resinous character of their foliage makes coniferous trees inflammable whenever the humidity of the surrounding air falls to a low level. This happens relatively infrequently in regions of high rainfall and constant mist or cloud, such as the western slopes of the Rocky Mountains in North America, the Alps and similar high mountain ranges of Europe. Western Scotland, Wales and Ireland are likewise regions of high humidity and low fire risk. The opposite state of affairs arises over inland plains in both the North American and Eurasian land masses, in the hot southlands of the Mediterranean zone and California, and seasonally in eastern Canada and the United States, also in the eastern regions of Britain and the lowlands of Europe and northern Asia.

The fuel that sustains a forest fire consists of living leaves, the dry debris of faded leaves and small dead twigs, and even peat in the soil, rather than the timber itself. The blaze can only be sustained by the movement of wind through the stand of trees. If it does not spread it dies out, through lack of fuel. Dangerous conditions arise when a hot dry wind blows through the woods bringing in fresh oxygen to feed the conflagration and carrying away the resulting carbon dioxide gas. As each flame, itself a mass of burning gases, approaches fresh dry fuel, this fuel is heated to the point at which its volatile components are transformed to gases, which at once ignite and are swept forward by the wind. An essential requirement for a really dangerous fire is dry air. If the air has a high humidity much of the total heat is used up in warming the water vapour that it contains.

Disastrous fires, some caused by natural factors such as lightning strikes but most by human carelessness, have devastated many large tracts of coniferous forests particularly in the inland regions of North America. Moving at a pace of four or five miles an hour, they may involve hundreds of square miles of land within the space of a few days. In the early days of pioneer logging they often raged unchecked until they met some natural barrier like a broad river, a mountain range, or a prairie that held no more fuel. Today they are fought by every means at man's disposal – including water tanks, aircraft and bulldozers. The main tactic continues to be the arrest of the fire at some man-made or natural barrier. The clear felling of a swathe of trees across the path of an advancing fire, followed by the bulldozing of a strip of inflammable litter right down to the mineral soil that cannot burn, is a well-tried method of limiting a fire's advance – provided enough men and machines can reach the critical places in time.

Though wildfires have made terrific inroads into reserves of conifer timber in many regions, the overall situation is not unduly alarming. Despite all precautions and constant vigilance by fire watchers standing on high fire towers, or circulating as they do in Canada in fire-spotter aircraft, thousands of square kilometres are destroyed each year. But this loss amounts to less than one per cent of the world's reserves and the fire loss is in fact exceeded by that due to insect attacks and fungal diseases.

This low rate of fire loss is only achieved by the constant vigilance of the forest authorities. Fire enters into all their thinking and every scheme for a new planting or management plan for existing conifer forests includes provision for keeping fire risk as low as possible. Every plan includes a system of fire breaks at which a blaze can be halted, access routes for men and machines and provision for constant vigilance and reporting through all the dry seasons of the year.

Chapter 11

Mediterranean Zone Forests

THE countries that border the Mediterranean Sea in southern Europe, northern Africa and western Asia have a characteristic climate regime and their region has provided the name for similar climatic zones elsewhere. Briefly, the 'Mediterranean climate' involves very hot, dry, cloudless sunny summers and warm, humid, rainy winters. Frost and snow occur only on the mountains, the lower ground around sea level being normally frost-free.

Mediterranean-type climates occur elsewhere at roughly the same distance north or south of the equator on four other continents. In South Africa they are found across the southern portion of the Cape province forming a region that has proved particularly well suited to European settlement. In Australasia they occur in the south of the states of West Australia, South Australia, Victoria, Tasmania and the south of New South Wales, all again well-settled regions. North America has a large region of Mediterranean climate in California and its neighbouring states, and South America a smaller zone in southern Chile.

The Mediterranean Sea is often aptly regarded as 'the cradle of civilization' for it was here that people of varied origins were able during a spell of around one thousand years preceding the birth of Christ to develop the technical skills that led to marked political, artistic and religious advancement. Its climate enabled men to grow corn, vines and olives and to raise flocks and herds of sheep, goats and cattle in quantities that left a surplus of food, wine and leisure for enjoyment and the evolution of culture. This progress was only achieved at the expense of the natural forests, which were gradually devastated down the centuries until only scattered fragments remain.

The principal agent in this widespread destruction was the domestic goat, traditional source of milk, cheese, flesh and hides for shoe-leather or water bottles. Goats, originally creatures of sub-tropic mountain grasslands, kill trees by biting back all young sprouts within their reach or by ring-barking any individuals that bear soft bark – which means most young trees of any species. When kept in sufficient numbers they prove the ideal means for transforming forests into grassy steppes. Once this grassland becomes overstocked it is damaged in turn by too-rapid grazing breaking through the turf, aided by the goats' sharp hooves. Erosion of the exposed soil then follows its disastrous course. There are, of course, other destructive forces at work on the forest, including clearances for arable culture, vineyards and orchards, timber harvesting and – most rapid and disastrous – fire. But the goat remains as the major cause of forest decrease and change for he is always present under the protection of his peasant herdsman.

All round the Mediterranean we are dealing with forests affected by human interference, by man himself or his animal agents, which include not only goats but also cattle, horses, donkeys and even camels. In many regions all the original tree cover has gone and its character can only be judged from remnant trees elsewhere.

Tree Modifications under Mediterranean Climates

A tree that flourishes under the peculiar Mediterranean climatic regime must have exceptional physical characters. It must be evergreen in order to utilize both winter rainfall and summer sunshine. It must also be drought-resistant for otherwise it will perish in the long, hot, dry summer. These factors affect both broadleaved trees and conifers. The typical modification for broadleaved trees, as compared with their fellows in the main broadleaved zones of cooler or moister regions, is a thick, leathery and waxy leaf. A typical example is the evergreen oak, *Quercus ilex*, in contrast to its northern counterpart, the pedunculate oak, *Q. robur*. The evergreen oak restricts water loss by developing a waxy coating over its leaves. These are dark green above with paler undersides, clad in hairs that slow down air. The stomata through which it breathes are situated on the shaded lower surface and their apertures can be readily reduced to lessen the escape of moisture whenever the air gets very dry.

An inevitable consequence of the development of waxy leaves is that the foliage as a whole becomes highly inflammable. The leaves of the pedunculate oak will never burn until they have fallen from the tree and faded: during their active life their water content relative to their dry matter is too high to permit combustion. But the reverse is true of the foliages of evergreen oaks, trees of the *Eucalyptus* genus and most other evergreens of Mediterranean-type forests. All these hold so much fuel that they burn fiercely whilst still green and attached to their tree. I have seen holly trees, *Ilex aquifolium*, flare like torches when swept by fire in the New Forest of Hampshire, in southern England. Certain ingredients of the waxes are readily volatilized by rising temperatures, and advancing flames ignite a combustible mixture of air and gas. This explains the appalling ferocity of bush fires in, for example, Australia or California. All these evergreens are continually menaced by forest fires, and the risk increases with greater human activity.

Another regular character of Mediterranean climate broadleaved trees is a remarkably hard, dense wood, having close but indistinct annual rings. This appears to be a consequence of year-round growth. All these timbers make excellent firewoods. Holly, for example, will burn readily when freshly cut, and does not need to be seasoned to have its moisture content reduced first. As constructional woods the Mediterranean hardwoods make sound, solid furniture and hard-wearing floors, but are considered too heavy for general use, say, in box-making. Their rate of growth is naturally slow and the annual yield from any forest area is low in proportion.

The bark of broadleaved trees in this warm zone is exceptionally thick and waterproof. The best developed example is that of cork oak, *Quercus suber*, which is harvested commercially for making into bottle stoppers. See Plate 37.

Coniferous trees adapted to the Mediterranean region show parallel modifications of form and growth. A revealing contrast is that between the Nootka or Alaska cypress, *Chamaecyparis nootkatensis*, also called 'yellow cedar' and 'stinking cedar', which originates under the cold moist climate of Alaska, and its relative the Monterey cypress, *Cupressus macrocarpa*, native to sunny California. Though both have scale-shaped leaves those of the northern Alaskan cypress build up into flat, fern-like, loose and open fronds exposing a large surface to the atmosphere, while Monterey cypress has leaves that clasp the stem all round, creating a narrow cylinder of foliage that presents a minimal area to the air.

Pines in the genus *Pinus* show a different kind of leaf modification directed to the same end. Taking the Scots pine, *P. sylvestris*, as representative of the cooler and moister conditions of northern Europe, one notes it has numerous short, flat needles that allow fairly free transpiration of water. By contrast the maritime pine, *P. pinaster*, of the Mediterranean zone has fewer, longer needles that readily become in-rolled lengthwise. This device restricts water loss from those stomata that lie on the needle's upper surface and the overall exposure to drying air currents is less. The maritime pine has thicker bark than the Scots pine, a further device to check water loss. The timber of the maritime pine is more resinous than that of the Scots pine and it has more strongly marked zones of dense summerwood in its annual rings. These features too appear to be a consequence of the climate in which it grows for it yields more resin, commercially, in the hotter part of its climatic range. Its thick bark helps to protect its trunk against sun-scorch and minor fires.

Shrubs are prominent in the Mediterranean zone forests and all show adaptations to its climate. Many members of the large genus *Rhododendron* have thick, leathery evergreen leaves and develop very hard, dense timber in their tortuous stems. Others, like the Spanish broom, *Spartium junceum*, have rush-like foliage in which all leaves are suppressed; their thin green stems achieve photosynthesis with minimum water loss. The gorse or furze bushes in the *Ulex* genus have green leafless shoots modified into sharp spines to deter browsing beasts, and waxy surfaces that check water loss, though they make the whole gorse bush highly inflammable. Bushy species of *Erica* like the tree heath, *Erica arborea*, bear short in-rolled leaves; the woody roots of this shrub, known in French as *bruyère*, yield the 'briar' for smokers' briar pipes. Tamarisks of the genus *Tamaris* have similar scaly foliage, evergreen in some species but not others. Their name is derived from a Hebrew word meaning 'sweeping broom'. All such trees with rod-like stems and few leaves are sometimes referred to as 'switch plants'. The common yellow-flowered brooms of the genus *Sarothamnus* are further examples though they occasionally bear trifoliate leaves on their rod-shaped stems.

Mediterranean Trees in Horticulture

Trees and shrubs that originate in various countries with Mediterranean-type climates have become prominent in the horticulture of temperate lands because of their evergreen habit. Many can be grown artificially much farther north than their homelands. The British Isles are particularly favoured here, for the Gulf Stream ensures relatively mild winters. They already possess a sprinkling of Mediterranean trees including holly, box, *Buxus sempervirens*, and strawberry tree, *Arbutus unedo*, besides two ever-green shrubs, gorse and broom. These have been reinforced by the addi-tion of evergreen oak, many species of *Rhododendron*, and two evergreen shrubs in the rose family or *Rosaceae*, namely the cherry laurel, *Prunus laurocerasus*, and the Portugal laurel, *P. lusitanica*. All these become natural-ized and spread freely through the woods; in fact the common rhododen-dron, *R. ponticum*, becomes a serious weed where it monopolizes good timber-growing land. Pines from the warm south flourish too, and Corsican pine, *Pinus nigra* variety *maritima*, has become a source of commercial timber. Cypresses are represented by the Californian Monterey cypress, *Cupressus macrocarpa* and its hardier hybrid the Leyland cypress, *Cupresso-cyparis leylandii*, derived from a cross with Nootka cypress.

1 This tall ash, *Fraxinus excelsior*, has outgrown neighbouring oaks and beeches to expand its crown, to flower, and to bear seeds. Cherkley Woods on the North Downs of Surrey, England.

2 These weatherbeaten Scots pines, *Pinus sylvestris*, near the timberline at 2,500 metres (7,500 feet) elevation in the Pyrenees National Park, reveal long struggles with poor soil and harsh environment. Pont d'Espagne, southern France.

3 *Above left* Tree trunks hold leafy crowns aloft in forest canopies. Californian ponderosa pine, *Pinus ponderosa*.

4 *Above right* Woody stems are eventually decayed by fungi. Fallen beech, *Fagus sylvatica*, on Box Hill, Surrey, with ash seedlings invading the clearing.

5 *Below left* Roots of yew, *Taxus baccata*, anchoring a tree to Wealden sandstone. Wakehurst Place, Sussex, south-east England.

6 *Below right* Vegetative shoot (above) and fertile fruit-bearing shoot (below) of apple, *Malus* genus.

7 *Above left* Seeds of ash, *Fraxinus excelsior*.

8 *Above right* Root initials appearing on a cutting of a *Cotoneaster*.

9 *Below left* Leaf litter, dark humus layer, pale leached layer, and darker bedrock of a podzol soil on a Greensand formation, near Abinger, Surrey.

10 *Below right* Flowers of crab apple, *Malus pumila*, showing petals, stamens and ovaries.

11 Succession in broadleaved forest. Following the felling of a mature ash (above) and beech (below) this clearing will be invaded by saplings of both species, also by yew. Box Hill, Surrey, springtime.

12 Young Scots pines springing up from seed shed by taller parent trees. Wotton Common on the Greensand Ridge of Surrey.

13 Mountain conifer forest in southern
Europe. Silver fir, *Abies alba*, near
Cauterets in the Pyrenees National Park,
southern France.

14 Wind moulding of tree form. A
hawthorn, *Crataegus oxyacantha*, bent
sideways by salt-laden winds off the Irish
Sea. Galloway, south-west Scotland.

15 Mountain forests of beech and silver fir, interspersed with hill pastures below rocky summits, provide ideal territory for summer recreation. Le Lac d'Estaing, Pyrenees National Park, southern France.

16 The start of an orienteering contest, strenuous cross-country running guided by map and compass, through sprucewoods in the Queen Elizabeth Forest Park, Aberfoyle, central Scotland.

17 Temperate broadleaved forest. Woods of oak, *Quercus robur*, seen across a replanted clearing in the Forest of Gresigne, Dordogne, central France.

18 Southern conifer forest. Maritime pines, *Pinus pinaster*, established on the sand dunes of the Landes, near Soustons in Aquitaine, south-west France.

19 *Opposite* Temperate broad-leaved forest. Woods of maples, *Acer* species, around Wyman Lake in northern Maine, USA. The log raft consists of spruce, floated downstream from conifer forests, higher in the hills.

20 *Right* Sydney blue gum, *Eucalyptus saligna*, a rapidly-growing broadleaved evergreen tree adapted to the Mediterranean-type climate of Australia.

21 *Below* Holm Oak, *Quercus ilex*, native to the shores of the Mediterranean, bears dark evergreen, leathery leaves that resist summer drought.

22 *Above left* Feathery-foliaged Canary Island date palm, *Phoenix canariensis*, cultivated for garden ornament throughout the tropics.

25 *Below* Savanna grassland in Rhodesia. Short-boled *Acacias* resist fires and browsing beasts.

23 *Opposite above* Fiercely-armed Karoo thorn, *Acacia karroo*, under desert conditions in South Africa, beside a dark green naboom or candelabra tree, *Euphorbia ingens*.

24 *Opposite below* Palm-like cycads, *Encephalartos* species, form typical undergrowth in tropical forests.

26 *Right* Hybrid black poplar, *Populus* 'Robusta', grown on well-watered farmland for shade and timber.

27 *Below* Pulpwood removed from a profitable thinning of a farm woodlot in Quebec Province, Canada. Mainly red pine, *Pinus resinosa*.

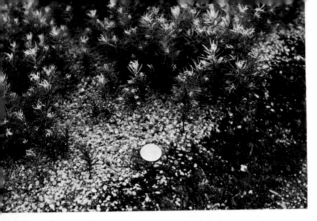

28 One-year-old seedlings of Douglas fir, *Pseudotsuga menziesii*.

29 Watering young oaks, *Quercus robur*, grown in containers for planting on difficult sites.

30 Transplanting conifer seedlings by machine in a forest nursery, Aberdeen, Scotland.

31 Regrowth of coppice shoots six months after cutting the fence stakes seen stacked beyond. Sweet chestnut, *Castanea sativa*. Stanstead Park, Hampshire, southern England.

32 Peaches, *Prunus persica*, in flower in an orchard at Fransch Hoek, Cape Province, South Africa.

33 Orange trees, *Citrus auriantica*, ripening fruit in an irrigated orchard at Mazoe, Rhodesia.

34 *Left* Blue Atlas cedar, *Cedrus atlantica glauca*, grown as an ornamental specimen in the grounds of the Royal Horticultural Society, Wisley, Surrey.

36 *Opposite* Felling a fifty-year-old Sitka spruce, *Picea sitchensis*, introduced from Alaska, in Dartmoor Forest, Devon, south-west England.

35 Planting Lawson cypresses, *Chamaecyparis lawsoniana*, from California, to re-stock a clearing in Alice Holt Forest, Hampshire.

37 *Above left* Cork oak, *Quercus suber*, stripped of its valuable bark. Soustons, south-west France.

38 *Above right* Tapping a maritime pine for resin in the Landes Forest, south-west France.

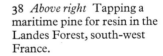

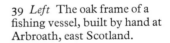

39 *Left* The oak frame of a fishing vessel, built by hand at Arbroath, east Scotland.

40 *Below left* Cross-cutting oak logs in a sawmill yard at Stafford, north-west England; note grapple crane.

41 A mature oak, 150 years old, in Alice Holt Forest, Hampshire. Planted on the advice of Admiral Nelson, circa 1800, to provide timbers for wooden warships. Now 28 metres (78 feet) high, it has a clear bole 18 metres (55 feet) long, due to overshading and suppression of the lower side branches by its neighbours. Its crown of branches and foliage is 10 metres (33 feet) wide, and equally deep.

42 This new-felled Scots pine (*Pinus sylvestris*) log shows the annual rings of 80 years' growth on its butt. The pale band of each ring is *springwood*, the dark band is *summerwood*; the darker central zone is *heartwood*, transformed from paler *sapwood*; annual rings run through both.

43 Corsican pines, *Pinus nigra* variety *maritima*, planted on pure sand blown in from the sea at Dunragit, Galloway, Scotland. They gain moisture through long roots in damp sand below the arid surface, and will eventually stabilize the shifting dune.

44 Downy-leaved oak, *Quercus pubescens* (left), growing on Carboniferous Limestone in the *garrigue* woodland of the Dordogne, central France. Despite the rock's open character, the tree roots exploit only the shallow dark surface zone of the *rendzina*.

45 *Top* Stunted growth of balsam fir, *Abies balsamea,* normally a tall forest tree, at 1,300 metres (4,000 feet) elevation on Mount Washington, New Hampshire, USA.

46 *Centre* The ultimate timberline. At 1,600 metres (5,000 feet) on Mount Washington, balsam fir is reduced to a prostrate form by wind, snow and ice.

47 *Bottom* Northern and mountain evergreen trees are adapted to carry substantial weights of clinging snow. The branches of this North African Atlas cedar, *Cedrus atlantica,* normally ascending, flex downwards but recover later. Coulsdon, Surrey.

48 Plantation of North American Douglas fir, *Pseudotsuga menziesii*, in Alice Holt Forest, Hampshire. Foresters space trees regularly! Mature oaks beyond.

49 Avalanche tracks at the timberline near Arosa, Switzerland. Wherever spruce trees, *Picea abies*, gain a foothold on screes of loose rock, snow melts slowly in their shade and avalanche risk is reduced. Litter and roots check downhill movement of snow and stones.

50 Testing pine seed for germinative capacity at a research station.

51 Detail of a test batch of 100 seeds, now sprouting.

52 Strange tree forms adapted to the dry climates of South African deserts and savannas. Left, a tree aloe, *Aloe bainesii*; right, a baobab, *Adansonia digitata*.

53 Stool beds for regular production of cuttings of desirable kinds of trees. One year's growth of young shoots is cut off at the base annually, then cut into short lengths. Left, poplars, *Populus*; right, willows, *Salix*.

54 Exceptional growth forms of common trees, usually propagated by grafting. Below, weeping birch, *Betula pendula* variety *pendula*. Right, upright or Dawyck beech, *Fagus sylvatica* variety *fastigiata*, at Box Hill, Surrey.

55 Artificial aspects of arboriculture. Top, planes, *Platanus × hispanica*, pleached to make an overhead sunshade for the market-place of Soustons, south-west France. Centre, limes, *Tilia × europaea*, severely pruned to make an arbor at Reigate Priory, Surrey. Bottom, yews, *Taxus baccata*, pruned to represent peacocks, also at Reigate.

56 *Above* Two northern white cedar, *Thuja occidentalis*, seedlings springing from naturally sown seed at the base of a birch. Mont Orford, Quebec.

57 *Right* A sapling of the black spruce, *Picea mariana*, springs up where its predecessor fell and decayed. The dark 'v' shows where fungi rotted two branching limbs. Flying Moose Mountain, near Orland, Maine.

58 *Left* A ten-year-old balsam fir, *Abies balsamea*, struggles up through a thicket of northern red oak, *Quercus rubra*; once free, its later growth will be vigorous. Ellsworth, Maine.

59 *Below* A group of white pines, *Pinus strobus*, withstanding severe exposure to Atlantic gales 150 metres (450 feet) up on Flying Moose Mountain, Maine. Note wind-moulding of branches to the right.

60 *Bottom* A thicket of white poplar, *Populus alba*, a European species, widely naturalized in North America, beside a salt marsh near Chatham, Massachusetts. Many stems spring from a common root system.

61 *Above left* Native Honey locust, *Gleditsia triacanthos*, framed by the foliage of Tree of Heaven, *Ailanthus altissima*, a naturalized species introduced from China. Brewster, Massachusetts.
62 *Above right* American elm, *Ulmus americana*, planted to shelter a homestead.
63 *Below* Natural stand of paper birch, *Betula papyrifera*, in the Mastigouche Park, Quebec.

64 *Above* Cyclists take their noonday meal in the shade of Atlantic white cedars, *Chamaecyparis thyoides*, beside Scargo Lake on Cape Cod, Massachusetts.

65 *Below* Logpiles at the paper mill, Groveton, New Hampshire.

66 *Bottom* Traditional use of wood in a New England homestead. Brier Farm, at Brewster, Massachusetts, dates back to the seventeenth century.

In America it is realized that the southland trees from sunny California can only be taken north through a limited range of *hardiness zones*. These run farther north near both east and west coasts than they do in the heart of the continent, owing to the effect of the oceans which modify the extremes of climate.

A constant feature of Mediterranean zone trees is that though they will often survive short, severe frosts they cannot endure prolonged ones. This is apparently a drought effect rather than a cold one. They cannot replace from a frozen soil the minimal quantity of water needed to maintain life even under their low transpiration regime. During the exceptionally prolonged six-week spell of frost that struck Britain in February and March 1962, Monterey cypresses in the colder districts withstood low temperatures but were killed later on by cold drying winds.

The Australian genus *Eucalyptus* has proved for this reason very disappointing when transplanted outside its native continent. In Britain even the hardiest species are only dependable close to the southern or western coasts that are warmed all the year round by the Gulf Stream. In America well-established eucalyptus groves have occasionally been wiped out by prolonged frosts, even in California. On the continent of Europe the genus is not reliably hardy anywhere north of the Alps.

All trees and shrubs of the Mediterranean zone are considered 'difficult' to transplant by foresters and gardeners who work in regions colder than their homelands. For this reason they are usually raised as seedlings in pots so that a ball of soil accompanies them and they are rarely planted 'barerooted'. Cultivators in the warmer countries where they are native seldom encounter this difficulty and regularly transplant bare-rooted stocks. Apparently these trees cannot readily take up moisture from *cold* soil but have no problems in getting it from *warm* soil even though the latter may look very dry.

Maquis, Garigue, Oakwoods and Pines
Round the Mediterranean Sea

The greater part of the forests that once surrounded the Mediterranean Sea have been reduced through intensive exploitation by timber harvesters, cultivators and pastoralists, aided by uncontrolled fires, to two types of relict – or derelict – forest known in France as *maquis* and *garigue*. Maquis occurs largely on limestone rock and has a dominant plant element of scattered knee-high shrubs, interspersed with evergreen trees of low stature. Typical species are myrtle, *Myrtus communis*; box, *Buxus sempervirens*; wild olive, *Olea europaea*; evergreen oak, *Quercus ilex*; strawberry

Figure 13 Detail from a classical Greek vase of the pre-Christian era, showing the harvesting of olives, *Olea europaea*, by beating branches. This method is still practised today.

tree, *Arbutus unedo*; oleander, *Nerium oleander*; and laurel, *Prunus lauro-cerasus*. Undershrubs are remarkable for their aromatic scents for they hold essential oils that help to check water loss. It is a refreshing experience to walk through their midst trampling their foliage underfoot and releasing clouds of strong, fresh perfume. They include fragrant rock roses such as *Cistus ladaniferus*; wild thyme, *Thymus vulgaris*; wild lavender, *Lavandula spica*; rosemary, *Rosmarinus officinalis*; and wood sage, *Teucrium scorodonia*. Many of these have cultivated counterparts that are used as herbs in cookery. Conifers are represented by shrubby junipers like *Juniperus communis* which also bears fragrant foliage. The tough foliage that this vegetation discards rots down rapidly on all calcareous soils and no substantial layer of humus develops.

Garigue is regarded as degraded maquis, the outcome of long sustained grazing by goats and sheep, and repeated fires. It has been described as 'forest without trees', bearing only woody shrubs and herbs adapted to live through blazing hot summers, unaided by overhead shade. The vegetation includes scrubby heaths of the *Erica* genus, including *E. arborea* and *E. multiflora*; a quaint juniper, *Juniperus phoenicea*, which has scale-leaves clasping its stem and red-brown berries; the pistachio-nut tree, *Lentiscus terebinthus*; and the winter-flowering dark-green laurustinus, *Viburnum tinus*.

Wherever grazing pressure slackens and fires do not rage too often the garigue is colonized by evergreen species of oaks. The most widespread and persistent but useless kind is the chermes oak, *Quercus coccifera*, which forms a low spread of shrubby branches carrying leaves with spiny edges: it spreads by underground roots that send up suckers. Rather taller is the pubescent oak, *Q. pubescens*, while the evergreen oak, *Q. ilex*, ranks as a timber tree. Cork oak, *Q. suber*, the valuable source of commercial cork, grows wild locally. Plates 21, 37.

Three pines also invade the garique. First to arrive on acres swept by fire or abandoned by cultivators is the scrubby Aleppo pine, *Pinus halepensis*, which ripens very numerous wind-borne winged seeds. It has no timber value but does serve as a pioneer aiding the advance of the main forest. Maritime pine, *P. pinaster*, which has much larger needles, cones and seeds and yields a useful resinous timber, also comes in as a wind-borne invader. More valuable still is the stone pine, *P. pinea*, which has large globular cones and big edible seeds that bear only a rudimentary wing: they are gathered, sold and eaten as pine nuts, pine kernels, *pignons*, or *pinocchi*. It is also called the 'umbrella pine' or *pin parasol* because of the shape of its spreading crown. Italian cypress, *Cupressus sempervirens*, a species with dark scale-like leaves clasping its stem, is found in several forms. Those with spreading crowns yield sound timber while those with an upright slender habit like Lombardy poplars contribute a characteristic note to the Mediterranean scene.

A feature of most ground floras under these forest types is their open character. The cover of trees and shrubs, tall or dwarf, is rarely continuous and gaps between them often support short-lived annual flowering plants, tufts of low grasses or bulbous plants like cyclamens, with pretty spring or autumn blossoms.

Madrone Scrub and Conifers in California

The Pacific madrone tree, *Arbutus menziesii*, gives its Spanish name to a type of vegetation, the madrone scrub, found amid the Mediterranean climate zone along the Californian coast. It is a tall evergreen that resembles

147

the European strawberry tree, *A. unedo*, and belongs to the same family, the heaths or Ericaceae. Madrone has a thin, flaking rusty-red-brown bark, dark oval evergreen leaves and white flowers like those of lily-of-the-valley, carried in dainty bunches. These are followed by clusters of round red fruits resembling strawberries. It forms dense scrub on dry sun-drenched hillsides, occasionally growing on the best sites to 30 metres tall and over one metre thick. Though forming picturesque scenery it has little economic use save as firewood or as a protector of the soil against storm erosion. The growing tree itself is highly inflammable and the madrone bushlands, also known as *chapparal*, are apt to be swept by fierce blazes.

Evergreens associated with madrone include the California live-oak, *Quercus agrifolia*, and several related oak species. Common shrubs are California-laurel, *Umbellularia californica*; Christmas berry, *Photinia arbutifolia*; and beautiful blue-blossoms or California lilacs, *Ceanothus spinosus* and its allies.

Evergreen conifers include several pines adapted to this hot summer climate, notably Monterey pine, *Pinus radiata*, and bishop pine, *P. muricata*, both of which bear large persistent cones that may not open fully for several years after ripening. Ponderosa pine, *P. ponderosa*, is a major timber resource. The quaint single-leaf pinyon, *P. monophylla*, which has the two needles of each pair fused into one, yields edible seeds, long appreciated by the local Indians. Typical cypresses are the rugged Monterey cypress, *Cupressus macrocarpa*, and the Gowen cypress, *C. goveniana*. The incense cedar, *Calocedrus decurrens*, which as its name suggests bears fragrant foliage, forms magnificent columns of deep green, fern-like leaf-fronds. The mighty giant sequoia, *Sequoiadendron giganteum*, and its even taller relative the Californian redwood, *Sequoia sempervirens*, are also adapted to the prevailing Mediterranean climatic regime. Both bear very thick bark as a protection against sun-scorch and forest fires.

Evergreen Forests of the Cape Province, South Africa

The southern portion of the Cape Province from Cape Town east towards Knysna enjoys a Mediterranean-type climate with enough rain to support evergreen forests. Because they are isolated these consist of trees, shrubs and flowering plants unique to the region. Near the Cape the woodlands have been much diminished by fellings for timber following extending settlement over the past 300 years, and the survivors hold on mainly in deep, inaccessible gorges called *kloofs*. Around Knysna, however, valuable native forests have been preserved, both as a source of timber and a tourist attraction.

Figure 14   *Left*, giant sequoia, *Sequoiadendron giganteum*, from inland
California, can grow stouter than any other tree. *Right*, Coast redwood,
Sequoia sempervirens, can become even taller (details page 31). Specimen trees
at Alice Holt Forest, Hampshire, planted around 1875, with cones and foliage *below*.

149

The characteristic woody plants of the region are the proteas, members of the family Proteaceae which is unique to the southern hemisphere. They are mostly shrubs but a few, notably *Protea arborea* or *waboom*, reach tree size and yielded timber for the early colonists. The proteas have hard, leathery, drought-resistant leaves and showy round flower-beads which vary in colour with the species and are often gathered for decoration. The silver leaf tree, *Leucadendron argenteum*, owes its lovely colour to a coating of fine hairs that serves as a protection against drought. Other broadleaved evergreens are the red-berried Cape holly, *Ilex mitis*, and the beautiful lilac-flowered Cape chestnut, *Calodendrum capense*. The stinkwood tree, *Ocotea bullata*, an evergreen member of the laurel family or Lauraceae, yields a beautiful timber that draws its name from its powerful smell when freshly cut; it varies in colour from gold to brown and black and has always been highly prized for furniture making. Two evergreen conifers native to the Cape yield good constructional timbers: the Clanwilliam cedar, *Widdringtonia cedarbergensis*, which resembles a cypress and bears hard, round, woody cones; and the yellowwood, *Podocarpus falcatus*, which has yew-like foliage and fleshy fruits.

Eucalyptus Trees and Evergreen Shrubs in Australia

The huge genus *Eucalyptus*, unique to Australia, is well adapted to Mediterranean-type climates which occur both in southwest and southeast Australia. It consists of evergreen broadleaved trees and shrubs with a thick leathery texture and a bluish-green waxy surface. These leaves hold fragrant eucalyptus oil; these and waxes in the leaf help the leaves to hold water during long, hot, dry summers. But they also render the foliage highly inflammable since the heat of advancing fires releases the volatile, highly combustible gases that make Australian bush fires so devastating.

A peculiar feature of *Eucalyptus* foliage which we noted in an earlier chapter is that the leaves hang downwards allowing the sun's rays to pass between them. This lessens the temperature of the leaf surfaces and so reduces transpiration, but in consequence the trees shed little shade to relieve the scorched traveller. The giants of the group are the karri gum trees, *Eucalyptus diversicolor*, which reach heights of 80 metres and girths of 10 metres in west Australian timber lands. Plate 20.

Associated with these 'eucalypts' or gum trees there is a varied array of other leathery-leaved evergreen shrubs and small trees, many having brilliantly coloured flowers. The banksias or tree-honeysuckles of the genus *Banksia* grow as creeping woody plants, shrubs or tall trees, all bearing tough evergreen leaves. In spring and summer they open conspicuous upright flower spikes ranging in colour from yellow, through brown, to orange and crimson. They are named in honour of Sir Joseph Banks, the botanist who accompanied Captain Cook on his voyage of exploration in 1770 and found his first specimens, amidst a wealth of other unfamiliar flowers and trees, at an anchorage that was aptly christened 'Botany Bay'.

The aboriginal Australian name of *waratah*, meaning 'seen from afar', has been preserved for a beautiful evergreen bush known to science as *Telopea speciossima*, which also aptly means 'striking tree seen from afar'! It bears stiff dark green leaves on upright stalks topped by the glowing crimson globes that are its flower heads. The Australian golden wattle bush, *Acacia pycnantha*, bears round 'powder-puff' clusters of gay yellow flowers and grey-green, drought-resistant foliage consisting of flattened blades or phyllodes, that transpires less moisture than conventional acacia foliage.

Improving the Timber Output from Mediterranean-type Forests

Overall the forests of these dry-summer, moist-winter countries as we know them today are a poor resource for the timber grower. Over vast areas the vegetation consists of scrub or bush, often over-grazed or swept by fires, and interspersed with stretches of low heaths, aromatic herbs or bare rock. There is little litter and no real depth of developed, humus-rich soil. So long as grazing and burning proceed unchecked very large areas of land yield little or nothing of value to mankind.

By planned protective measures, coupled with the choice of the right trees from among the many that thrive in various Mediterranean climate countries, modern foresters can transform the whole scene. Their main plantation trees are pines of the genus *Pinus*, cypresses of the *Cupressus* group and *Eucalyptus* species. The Monterey pine, *P. radiata*, which as a wild tree is restricted to a small coastal zone of southern California, has been planted on a vast scale in Spain, Italy and in fact most countries bordering the Mediterranean sea. In the southern hemisphere it has been widely employed in Chile, Argentina, South Africa, southern Australia and New Zealand. It is distinguished by its emerald green foliage with needles grouped in threes and large persistent woody cones. It often achieves three metres of height growth in a single season with no side shoots between successive annual branch whorls. The timber it yields, though coarse and open-grained, has proved adaptable for many varied commercial uses as building timber and wood for packing cases and paper pulp.

From the same small coastal area comes the dark green Monterey cypress, *Cupressus macrocarpa*, which has proved a worthwhile timber producer both in southern Europe and south and east Africa. In America it is scarcely planted except for ornament or as a sturdy screen, while in Britain it is barely hardy.

The *Eucalyptus* species that has been planted most widely in southern Europe, Africa, India and South America is the blue gum, *E. globulus*. It quickly becomes a tall timber tree, and it can also be coppiced to yield, repeatedly, heavy crops of poles, firewood and pulpwood.

Trees native to the Mediterranean region have proved successful timber producers even when transplanted outside their original climate, particularly on the savanna lands of sub-tropical regions. Under sound management wherever they are grown they quickly create a deep layer of leaf litter and a true forest soil, while their forest cover helps to maintain moister conditions even through the drier months of the year.

Savannas, Thorn Forests and Desert Trees

ON either side of the equator there are large climatic zones that receive only seasonal rainfall: these are called *Savanna Climates*. They stand between the constantly moist tropical rain forests and the arid deserts like the Sahara that support scarcely any vegetation at all. Their seasonal rainfall is linked to the apparent movement of the sun from north to south and vice versa. When the midday sun is actually overhead, or nearly so, its intense heat causes warm, light air to ascend from the land and cooler air to draw in from the oceans, bringing rain clouds. But when the sun has swung north or south again there is little wind, few clouds and no rain. There is thus an alternation of hot rainy weather with warm dry seasons.

Between 5° and 15° north latitude in the northern hemisphere two dry seasons occur. There is a short one when the sun has moved north to the Tropic of Cancer, which it reaches late in June, and a long one when it has gone south to the Tropic of Capricorn, late in December. The converse situation is found in the southern hemisphere, with a short dry season in December and a long one around June. To the north and south of the 15° parallel of latitude, a single long dry season occurring in the 'winter' months, which are still very hot, is the rule.

Under these climatic conditions we find existing at the present day a peculiar type of open woodland with scattered trees growing amid grasses or low scrub, known as a *savanna*. This word is of Caribbean Indian origin and was first applied to wooded grasslands in Central America and the West Indies. It is now used to cover enormous areas of similar open woodland in other continents too. South America has two well marked savanna zones, one around Venezuela to the north of the Amazon rain forests, the other on the southern side of these rain forests, occupying most of central and southern Brazil. In Africa the savannas form a great arc on the north, east and south of the tropical rain forests that border the west coast. The southern half of India is largely savanna country and so are the interior zones of Burma, Thailand and Vietnam. There is also a narrow fringe of savannas along the northern coast of Australia.

Trees that grow under these conditions must be able to survive either two short droughts every year or one long one, in hot climates under cloudless skies. They fall into two distinct foliage types: some are deciduous and shed their foliage as the dry season approaches so that they do not transpire water when the soil is dry, while others are evergreen but have hard *sclerophyllous* leaves adapted to resist water loss. The soft-leaved evergreens of the rain forest cannot exist on the drier savannas, where they would die of drought. The hard leaves of evergreen savanna trees are often edged with prickles that make them unpalatable to browsing animals. Thornbearing trees are also common and characteristic of the savanna zone.

Theories of Savanna Origins

The open character of savanna forest was often attributed to the tree's difficulty in gaining enough water for survival during the dry season. If trees stand far apart, the argument went, each will tap a large area of ground with its extensive root system. Taking the year as a whole there is enough moisture for *scattered* trees but not for any close stand. This theory is nowadays neatly exploded by professional foresters who grow close crops of timber trees in savanna country with no apparent difficulty. Their plantations are of two kinds, the sub-tropical pines such as *Pinus canariensis* from the Canary Islands and *Eucalyptus* species from Australia. Both are adapted to resist seasonal drought, the pines by their narrow needles and the eucalypts by their hard, waxy blue-green foliage. But the common indigenous savanna trees are equally drought-resistant and should, in theory, stand equally close.

The forester achieves success with his close-ranked timber trees simply because he gives them protection against fire and browsing animals. It must therefore be factors such as these, and not the seasonal droughts, that give to the savannas their park-like character. In fact the fires and the browsing are inter-dependent. Most savannas are regularly burnt with one of three objects in view: their inhabitants seek to clear their tall growth as an aid to hunting game, to improve grass and browse for their livestock or to cultivate the land with arable crops.

The savanna forest, therefore, is not a natural climax but the outcome of hundreds or even thousands of years of human interference. Botanists can only guess what the original plant cover looked like. In the dry season this vegetation, unlike the constantly moist rain forest, burns easily. When flying over the savannas of Angola in West Africa by night during the dry winter season, I was amazed by the extent and size of the bush fires. Whole tracts of country were aflame. In consequence, the trees one finds surviving are those that miraculously resist fire. Isolated trees can do so because only low grass around them burns, but those in groups prove mutually destructive. Their combined open lattice-work of combustible twigs and foliage is an ideal structure for the build-up of high temperatures, as I have found when fighting actual forest fires elsewhere.

The inhabitants of savanna country and their remoter ancestors have been working out how to utilise bush fires for a surprisingly long time – probably since man first learnt how to make fire himself. Recent discoveries of early man made by palaeontologists in East and South Africa have proved the savanna zones to be one of the major cradles of mankind. Here he could pursue game, gather seasonal fruits and gradually develop the skills that led to a less precarious life as a herdsman and cultivator. Today there are still the Bushmen who have scarcely progressed beyond this primitive stage. They were originally savanna hunters and food gatherers but have been driven into desert regions like the Kalahari by stronger, more advanced tribes that pasture cattle and grow grain.

Amid the drier savannas continuous tree cover is found only along watercourses where it makes up the so-called 'galleried forest'. This is often held to prove that moisture is insufficient for tree growth elsewhere. In fact the terrain along streamsides is often marshy and unsuited to the spread of fire while the trees may be of different, less flammable species than those growing on drier soil. Away from the riverside trees must be able to survive seasonal droughts, which means that their foliage must be protected by waxes or resins and hence it is highly flammable.

Savanna trees develop characteristic forms that have survival value in their perilous habitat. The deciduous *Acacias* often grow in shapes resembling an open parasol. They have a squat trunk from which a dense head of branches radiate in all directions. The gap between the foliage and the ground keeps the leaves safe from all browsing beasts except giraffes. It also makes fire injury less likely for only the trunk is vulnerable at ground level and this forms thick, light, corky bark that acts as a fire shield. Plate 25.

The African baobab, *Adansonia digitata*, develops a huge swollen trunk in which it stores moisture, drawn in by its roots during the rains, through the dry season. Its foliage looks very sparse for its size and its thin branches taper to narrow extremities resembling roots – a pattern that led someone to describe it as 'a tree planted upside down'. Primitive hunting tribesmen sometimes tap the trunk to gain water during droughts; they also gather the baobab's fleshy fruits as a staple article of food. Plate 51.

African doum palms such as *Hyphaene theobaica* branch repeatedly – an unusual growth habit for palms. Each arm ends in a tuft of leaves that looks very small for the length of woody trunk that supports it, but this miniature foliage lessens water loss in the dry season. The South American carnauba palm, *Copernicia cerifera*, has broad fan-shaped leaves which are clad in a coating of wax that checks water loss. This is so plentiful that it is gathered commercially for use in shoe polish – for a purpose where man wishes to keep water *out* just as the palm wants to keep it *in*.

Dracaenas or dragon trees, which are monocotyledons related to the lilies, are able to flourish through the dry seasons because of their palm-like habit of growth. They bear close tufts of sword-shaped leaves which have a tough skin and a leathery texture adapted both to store water through spells of drought and resist its loss to a dry atmosphere. The New Zealand cabbage palm, *Cordyline australis*, is a well known member of this group.

Because of the wide espacement of their trees and bushes and their low stature, savannas have an orchard-like character. The lower vegetation of grasses and herbs flourishes in the gaps between the trees and supports in many countries a dense stocking of wild animals. The savannas are the homes of the African antelopes and giraffes, which are preyed upon by lions and hyaenas. In Australia they form kangaroo country. The growth of grasses is seasonal but the low trees help the beast to survive periods of food shortage by providing browse.

Regeneration of savanna trees from seed is difficult because the saplings must grow up through a vulnerable stage when they are liable to be bitten back by grazing animals. In practice the less well-armed species survive by growing up through thickets of spiny kinds. When, as usually happens sooner or later, the protective thicket is destroyed by a bush fire, the taller and thicker-barked trees survive, usually isolated from their fellows. The composition of this open woodland is constantly changing from point to point as new groups of tree and thorn-bush gain height, growing rapidly during rainy seasons. But the incidence of fire and grazing changes the character of each group. It may survive only as a single isolated timber tree, or vanish entirely, being replaced by grass.

The character and botanical composition of savanna woodland varies markedly with changes of soil and seasonal rainfall. In the direction of increasing rainfall it merges into rain forest or monsoon forest, though the dividing line may be remarkably sharp. In the direction of decreasing rainfall it changes gradually to wooded grassland, 'bush' or thorn forest. There is a bewildering range of character over the several continents in which Savannas occur, and a variety of names for local variants. In Brazil the savannas are called *campos*, in Venezuela *llanos* and in Burma *than-dahat* or *indaing*.

None of these local variations is exactly comparable with any other, nor is their floristic composition ever identical. Each represents an 'in-between, stage in the transition from high rainfall regions, with humid atmospheres' to dry deserts. In Burma, for example, savannas lie in regions with annual rainfalls *below* 2,000 millimetres, where they replace monsoon forests, but *above* 800 millimetres, where they have to give way to thorn scrub or grassland.

One widely accepted theory of savanna formation is that it is caused by deterioration of dry tropical forests under constant clearing and burning by man. Only the tougher trees have survived but the grassland resource that results has proved invaluable as a source of game, fodder and arable land. The primitive cultivators and herdsmen who have made their homes in the savannas for thousands of years are unable to maintain soil fertility for more than a few years at a stretch. They are essentially shifting cultivators or nomad graziers and they move on from time to time allowing the land to revert to bush or scrub. The trees play an essential role in restoring fertility. They are also the source of the timber needed for simple buildings and tools and of the firewood needed for cooking meals.

Under modern advanced husbandry all this can quickly be changed. Good farm management maintains soil fertility by such means as deeper cultivation, rotation of crops, planned stocking and the application of artificial fertilizers chosen after scientific analysis of the soil. Where the land is devoted to timber raising the foresters stop the perpetual succession of fires and establish continuing crops of high-yielding trees, typically pines or *Eucalyptus* species. The combined output from farm and forest far exceeds that from inefficient shifting cultivation and enables the peoples concerned to advance from subsistence economies to the more secure enjoyment of regular crops providing regular surpluses of food or wood for trade. The savannas, though they still cover enormous areas in most tropical and sub-tropical lands, are in retreat before scientific agriculture and forestry. Eventually they may survive only as game reserves.

Thorn Forest

Close to the arid deserts of the world with virtually no rainfall there are regions where between 100 and 800 millimetres of rain are received each year, often in the form of sudden and infrequent showers. The few stunted trees that survive under such conditions are all modified in their growth habit to resist both drought and attacks by browsing and grazing animals, hence the name 'thorn forest'. Plate 23.

Where there is no continuous plant covering over the soil and it is more or less completely exposed to the elements, it may consist of nothing more than loose grains of sand. These can be freely transported by the winds, forming moving sand dunes. Under the intense illumination of the ground by a burning sun in a cloudless sky, most plant litter breaks down before it can become incorporated as humus into the soil. Constant evaporation of what little water is received and the lack of steady percolation through the soil often result in the surface layers becoming saline. They hold such a high concentration of sodium chloride and other mineral salts that only specialized plants, known as 'halophytes,' can survive.

Where plant growth exists in these semi-desert regions it consists mainly of grasses and low spiny herbs such as cactuses, that are specially adapted to long dry spells and peculiar soil conditions. But in some regions trees do exist, if in remarkably modified forms. Even in the cool northern temperate zones of Europe, Asia and North America there are thickets of the sea buckthorn, *Hippophaë rhamnoides*, which shows all the characteristics of a semi-desert thorn forest tree. Low in stature, it bears grey-green scaly foliage that resists water loss through transpiration. Every twig is armed with vicious spines that defeat browsing beasts. The extensive root system ramifies through loose sand and helps to fix it in place. In the cool north, sea buckthorn grows typically on seaside sand dunes, which explains its name, and there it shows tolerance of wind-borne salt both on its leaves and in the soil. In the sub-tropics it is found in dry sandy regions, often also with saline soils. Each tree is either male or female and the latter sex bears juicy yellow berries that attract wandering birds and ensure the buckthorn's spread.

The large genus *Acacia*, of the Mimoseae sub-family of the family Leguminosae, is a major element of thorn forests in many hot dry lands. Its characters include 'powder puff' flower clusters, usually bright yellow, which are often used for decoration as 'mimosa blossom'; each puff is a group of small flowers with minute petals which owe their attraction to dense tufts of golden stamens. Most acacias have finely-divided doubly-compound leaves, but in certain Australian species this foliage pattern changes abruptly as each individual tree gets older. The adult foliage then consists of *phyllodes*, which are technically leaf-like leaf-stalks. These present a lesser surface to the air and help reduce water loss by transpiration. Many acacias develop vicious thorns up to five centimetres long from stipules at the leaf base. In some South African species such as the karoo thorn, *Acacia karroo*, these present a really vicious armament allowing no openings for the soft lips of browsing antelopes. One species, *A. sphaero-cephala*, develops huge thorns with hollow bases which serve as a home for

158

ants. The ants in return protect their host plants from attacks by other leaf-cutting ant species: biologists call this a *symbiotic* relationship, meaning 'living together'.

In Australia, several species of *Acacia* form *mulga* scrub which becomes virtually impenetrable where the shrubby trees grow closely together, and is naturally resistant to kangaroo attack. *Brigalow* scrub consists mainly of one species, *A. harpophylla*. Northeast Africa along with Arabia and parts of northwest India is the home of the gum arabic tree, *A. senegal*, which is tapped commercially for the pale yellow gum that oozes out of incisions made in its bark. This odd substance, the tree's natural defence against wounding, is a pale yellow, glass-like material which is tasteless, odourless and slightly soluble in water. It is harvested by nomad tribes, who claim sole rights to their territorial groves, and it is used as an adhesive, as an ingredient of inks, medicines, polishes and size, and as a glaze in confectionery.

Though the timbers of acacias and other small, rugged thorn forest trees have few applications in modern commerce, they are invaluable to the few primitive people who inhabit the dry country where they grow. They provide the substance of tools and weapons, building materials and firewood. From the supple stems or leaves of certain species craftsmen make baskets for storage and traps for game or fish. Selected woods are used for carving ornaments or to construct musical instruments. Certain trees yield edible fruits. Others provide drugs or the poisons that are sometimes used for tipping arrows by the hunters of game. Local peoples have scores of uses for the sparse produce of their forbidding thorn forests.

Specialized Trees of Semi-Deserts

Regions that are too dry for even thorn forest to survive still hold a scattered stocking of woody plants. One characteristic group are the aloes of southern Africa, stately plants belonging to the lily family, or Liliaceae, in the class of Monocotyledons. Some species, such as *Aloe castanea*, have a single, undivided stem; others, such as *A. ramosissima*, are bush-like because of repeated branching; a third pattern is found in the kokerboom, or quiver tree, *A. dichotoma*, which has a central upright trunk topped by a broad head of branches. In all three types the stems end in tufts of stiff grey-green sword-shaped leaves, thick and succulent. Faded leaves bend down against the stems and persist for many years, acting as a shield against intense heat. Above the leaf-tufts stand the flower-spikes, frequently branched like candelabras and each bearing scores of bright orange flowers. These yield abundant nectar which is sought by long-beaked birds, especially the brilliantly coloured hovering sunbirds, as well as by bees and similar insects. Plate 52.

The genus *Cotyledon* in the family Crassulaceae provides quaint succulent trees such as the *butterboom* or butter tree, *C. paniculata*, of the Cape. This grows up to three metres tall with an odd, squat trunk up to half a metre in diameter. The branches, which are short and stubby, bear very stout oval leaves that hold much sap in their soft tissues. Butter trees eventually open panicles of pretty tube-shaped red and yellow flowers. Smaller *Crassula* bushes are often grown as greenhouse plants by gardeners in temperate lands.

The large family Euphorbiaiceae includes many cactus-like spiny plants mainly in its large genus *Euphorbia*, and some of these are large enough to rank as trees. A typical species, *E. ingens*, native to southern Africa, develops a short woody stem and then branches repeatedly into a candelabra of leafless upright branches, each angular and ribbed with hard spiny edges. If any animal is bold enough to bite into this tough tissue it encounters a blistering, toxic sap.

The most fantastic of South African desert trees is one that actually buries its woody stem deep in the sand. This is the miracle plant, *Welwitschia mirabilis* of southwest Africa, a primitive tree related to the conifers. It grows under extremely dry conditions and all that appears above the surface is the top of its trunk, which may be one metre wide. This bears only two huge leaves, broad green ribbons that extend continuously, never falling; they may become four metres (12 feet) long and at their tips they gradually get worn and ragged, being torn by the winds and eventually fading. Male and female flowers, resembling those of conifers, appear on separate plants. Male flowers are pink and female ones green, and the latter ripen into cones holding winged seeds. This bizarre, stump-shaped tree can attain great age: carbon dating has proved relatively small specimens to be 700 years old and larger ones have ages estimated at 3,000 years!

In the American tropics and sub-tropics the place of the aloes is taken by yucca trees, which also belong to the Liliaceae in the Monocotyledon group. Some, like the aloe yucca, *Yucca aloifolia*, of Florida, have single woody stems up to eight metres tall topped by a tuft of tough leaves and a tall spike bearing white flowers. Others develop much-divided trunks. The most picturesque of these is the Joshua-tree, *Y. brevifolia*, found in the Mojave Desert of Arizona, which bears quaint mop-heads of short, stiff leaves, spiky enough to deter grazing beasts, and waxy white flowers followed by large brown seed pods.

The American counterparts of the African *Euphorbias* are the tree cacti, queer leafless plants bearing vicious spikes in clusters all along the ridges of their angular stems. These stems are green since in the absence of leaves they carry out the vital process of photosynthesis. The saguaro, *Cereus giganteus*, of New Mexico, USA, and northern Mexico, forms a huge single trunk up to one metre (one yard) thick and may attain a height of 16 metres (50 feet). Towards its summit this trunk sometimes divides into several upward soaring branches. The leafless stems bear at their tips short-stemmed white flowers followed by red, fleshy, edible berries. Other tall cacti have clusters of erect spiky stems and the genus *Senita* has been aptly christened the 'organ-pipe cactus'.

Australia is the home of a remarkable group of desert trees known as grass-trees, members of the genera *Kingia* and *Xanthorrhaea* in the family Liliaceae. Each tree consists of a slender stem up to six metres tall topped by a large mop of grass-like leaves which droop downwards when they fade and eventually hide the tree trunk. This foliage is often scorched by bush fires and its charred appearance has earned these trees their nickname of 'blackboys'. One or more flower stalks grow up from the grass-tree's foliage tuft, and expand large round knob-shaped flower clusters at their tips. Grass-trees grow extremely slowly and counts of the leaf-scars on their trunks, when compared with the current rate of leaf production, show that they can attain enormous ages; one estimate suggests 4,000 years, which puts them in the same record-breaking class as the giant sequoias and bristlecone pines of America.

Longevity appears a common feature of semi-desert trees. They have become well adapted to their harsh environment and can stay alive for centuries. But the minimal water supply inevitably restricts their rate of growth: they can add only a few centimetres to their height and a few millimetres to their diameter during each annual growing season. It is indeed marvellous to find trees existing at all in terrain that can only support highly specialized smaller plants.

Chapter 13

Tropical Rain and Monsoon Forests

TRUE tropical rain forests are confined to regions near the equator that enjoy both high temperatures and abundant rainfall the whole year round. The monsoon forests occur in regions of southern Asia and eastern Africa that receive the more seasonal rains brought by monsoon winds. The stronger southwest monsoon blows across the Indian Ocean towards the Himalayas from June to October and is the source of exceptionally heavy rains in the hills from northern India east to southern China. The less powerful northeast monsoon blowing from October to March carries rain clouds in the reverse direction towards the East African mountains.

Climatic Features

Regions of constant year-round rainfall occupy relatively small proportions of the four tropical continents. They are found in Central America and the Amazon basin of South America, along the western side of central Africa, throughout Malaysia and Indonesia and at the northeast corner of Australia. Adjacent areas with short dry seasons also support rain forests but those with long dry seasons carry only savannas, discussed in the last chapter. The ideal rain forest receives 2,500 millimetres (100 inches) of rain annually, spread evenly around the year.

Temperatures in the typical rain forest are remarkably constant, both round the clock and round the year. In West Malaysia, for example, just north of the equator, the lowest temperature each night averages 20°C and the highest temperature by day 32°C. This fluctuation is repeated daily the whole year round with neither cold nor hot seasons nor markedly wet and dry ones. Cloud cover helps to regulate extremes of temperature, but sunshine generally prevails, broken by heavy showers during short, violent thunderstorms.

Day-length, though nowhere constant anywhere on the globe, is remarkably even all the year round. Even at the equator the sun is directly

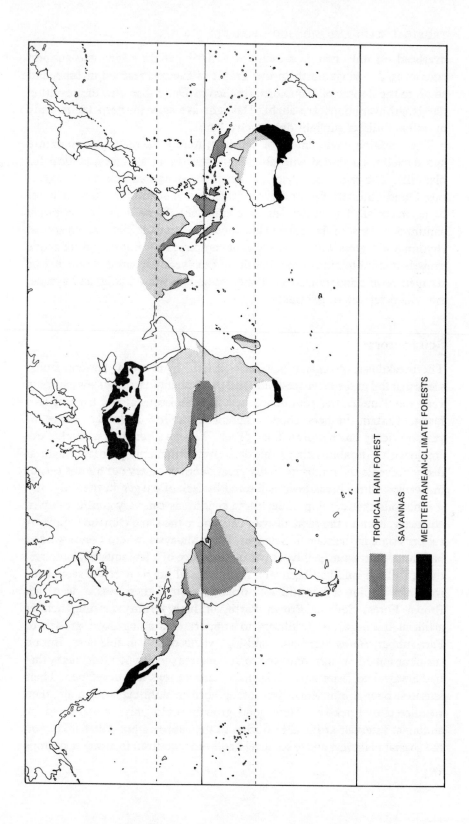

TROPICAL RAIN FOREST

SAVANNAS

MEDITERRANEAN-CLIMATE FORESTS

Figure 15 World distribution of tropical rain forests, *medium shading*, savannas, *pale shading*, and Mediterranean-climate forests, *black.*

overhead on only two days each year; that is, at the spring and autumn equinoxes. It swings north to the Tropic of Cancer, reached in June, and south to the Tropic of Capricorn, reached in December. But the resulting day-length variations are slight. Daylight averages fourteen hours daily overall and direct sunlight only twelve hours.

The resulting environment of constant, mildly fluctuating temperature and daylight, combined with abundant moisture at all times, is ideal for plant life. The rain forest that develops is the richest expression of vegetation found on earth, both in terms of variety of species and total mass of living material. The growth of its component plants, however, is rarely continuous. Most of them show, like those of temperate climates, an annual rhythm of progress with short spells of complete rest. But periods of active growth amount to nine or ten months of each year in contrast to the five or six months of temperate zones. Plates 22 and 24 show a palm and cycads, two characteristic tropic trees.

Soil Factors

The breakdown of organic material – leaves, spent twigs, flowers, fruits, seeds that fail to sprout successfully and the timber of large logs – is naturally very rapid under the continuous heat and moisture of the tropical rain forest. Certain timbers show inherent durability and take scores of years to decay on the forest floor. Teak, *Tectona grandis*, is a notable example with a durability that rivals oak. Overall the rapid process of natural decay prevents the build-up of any great depth or reserve of humus except in swamps where breakdown is limited by lack of oxygen in the soil.

The soils that develop under these conditions can vary considerably in character, even in the same district and under the same climatic regime. A rubber estate in the state of Selangor, West Malaysia, where I once worked had three contrasting soil types within the space of a few square kilometres, though all the land had been won from tropical jungle over the same bed-rock. On the lower but still well-drained ground there was a deep rich Brown Forest Soil, or Brown Earth, of high fertility needing neither artificial drainage nor fertilizers to support continuing good growth of Para rubber, *Hevea brasiliensis*, and high yields of its valuable latex. But on the occasional low hills, only 100 to 200 metres (300 to 600 feet) high, that had always had faster natural drainage, laterite soils had developed. Their laterites, poor in nutrients, were orange-brown until exposed to air, then weathered to brick-red. Here good growth could only be sustained by adding at intervals artificial fertilizers to the rubber crop. The flat land on the coastal plain just above sea level had been won from freshwater swamps and had an apparently inexhaustible store of nutrients derived from the decay of jungle vegetation. Deep drains were needed to enable the rubber tree roots to exploit its fertile, dark grey, humus-rich soil, but no artificial nutrition was ever required.

Such variations in the soils that support and are themselves created by the tropical rain forest are commonly obscured by its vigorous and apparently homogeneous growth. The forest forms an active complex for the exchange of nutrients which can persist indefinitely in vigorous action unless disturbed. Tribes who practise shifting cultivation, clearing patches for the growth of food crops over a space of a few years, can draw on these nutrient reserves indefinitely, provided they constantly move to fresh land. The forest restores available nutrients by regrowth after the cultivators move on. But permanent clearance of the rain forest does not invariably provide land fertile enough for sustained agriculture. Many tropical countries show devastated areas where permanent settlements could not be maintained. On many lateritic areas, for example, rapid erosion of the soil under high rainfall, falling as violent showers, can rapidly dissipate the valuable fertility reserve. On the estate just mentioned, contour trenches had been dug at great expense to check erosion and conserve humus on all the lateritic hills.

The Structure of Rain Forest

Flourishing tropical rain forest is remarkable for its layered structure with different kinds of plants forming communities at different heights. As a rule the main *canopy*, that is, the continuous cover of tree foliage that prevents the sunshine reaching the forest floor, is not made up of the tallest trees. This contrasts with the canopy structure of forests in the temperate zone. In the tropics the main, least-broken cover is found mid-way between the ground and the summits of the true forest giants, at a height averaging thirty metres. It is rarely a level formation: usually the trees that compose it vary in size and height. Their essential feature is that their crowns touch those of neighbouring trees at either the top or base of their extent so that no large gaps occur.

Trees that compose the main canopy are of two kinds. Some are trees of species that hold the second rank in stature, which have attained their maximum development. Others are trees of species that can attain a much greater size in the same situation but have not yet done so. These are still on their way up.

Above the main canopy the *emergent trees*, those that have grown through the canopy and reached their full potential height of 50 to 60 metres (165 to

200 feet), stand in all their splendour. They are commonly isolated from their neighbours and are free to expand their enormous crowns of foliage. Being free of competition at their summits they grow rapidly to immense size though none attains the dimensions found in the giant sequoias and coast redwoods (*Sequoiadendron* and *Sequoia*) of the Californian temperate forests. The maximum diameter of any rain forest tree is probably 5 metres (16 feet) against 7·6 metres (25 feet) for a giant sequoia. The

Figure 16   Conventional transect drawing of a tropical forest in Guatemala, Central America. Giant emergent mahogany trees rise above the general canopy level, which has itself a rich under-storey of smaller trees and younger mahoganies.

greatest height recorded for a rain forest tree is probably 84 metres, (275 feet) noted by the forest botanist Foxworthy for a specimen of *Koompassia excelsa* growing in Sarawak, East Malaysia, in 1947. The Californian coast redwood exceeds this easily, going on up to 117 metres (384 feet).

Below the canopy grows an *understorey* of shrubs and young trees, of both the emergent and main canopy classes, that are still making their way upwards as fresh recruits.

Beneath this again comes the ground flora consisting of seedling bushes and also of seedling trees of both major and minor size classes. Among them grow the herbs, grasses and bulbous plants that can tolerate the deep shade cast by the three successive layers of trees above them. The ground-level light intensity may amount to no more than 1% of the daylight outside. There are thus four main layers of vegetation – emergent trees, main canopy, understorey and ground flora – in this typical rain forest-structure.

Three other groups of green plants, all less dependent on a particular place in the vertical structure, play a part in the rain forest. Epiphytes, that is plants that grow superficially on tree bark, may find a resting place at any level. Conditions will naturally vary. Those high up on emergent trees enjoy bright light but relatively low humidities. Those low down on the lower trunks of the self-same trees, or else on trees of lesser stature, receive far less light but find it easier to secure ample moisture.

The climbers, mainly woody lianas, range through all the layers. Beginning life as seedlings in the deep shade at ground level they scramble up through the understorey to reach the main canopy where they secure far more light. A few fortunate individuals ascend into the crowns of the emergent trees or possibly get carried up by the latter as they grow taller. The stem length of these top-level climbers must be at least as great as the 60 metres of the trees that support them. Some, because of their wandering growth from one supporting tree to another, are substantially longer, up to 90 metres or more.

A third group of woody plants that move from layer to layer, often without supporting themselves physically, have the curious name of *stranglers*, though they do not always kill their hosts. They are peculiar to the tropics and most belong to the *Ficus* genus of the fig family, *Ficaceae*.

Stranglers begin life as ephiphytic climbers, germinating from seeds stranded in the forks of tall trees. They send climbing shoots upwards and strange descending roots downwards. In this way they avoid the handicap of having to start life in the deep shade of the forest floor. When the aerial roots strike the ground, they take root and begin to function as stems. A group of such roots may eventually encircle the support tree and finally kill it. By then the strangler has usually gained enough rigidity to stay upright, being carried partially by its 'root stems' and partially by the stump of the strangled host.

Parasitic plants may attack rain forest trees at any level. Some thrive in shade since all their photosynthetic nutrition is carried out by their host. The rain forest also holds a wealth of fungi, which live on living or dead tree tissues at all levels and also in the rotting stems on the forest floor.

Each layer of this complex structure has its own microclimate. It is misleading to speak of the 'rain forest environment' because it varies so markedly at different levels. The ground level environment for a plant or an animal is remarkably dark, perpetually humid and almost windless. The tree-top environment is often brilliantly illuminated, subject to rapid changes from wet to dry conditions and exposed to strong winds and frequent thunderstorms.

At this point we must dismiss from our reckoning the 'steaming impenetrable jungle' of amazing science fiction. The rain forest does indeed 'steam' with mist when the sun strikes its wet foliage after a sudden downpour of rain, but so does any highland forest in the cool temperate zone. The impression of impenetrability is given as a rule by the forest edge along a river or track, where foliage comes down to ground level. There are occasional stretches of marshland forest or recent regrowth that man cannot traverse without hacking away with a bush knife such as a Malaysian *parang*, but mature rain forest is fairly easy to walk through. Because it is so dark, undergrowth is sparse and you can pass between the leafless shaded stems of the tall trees and around the occasional shrubs of the understorey.

None of the layers just outlined is static. A process of dynamic change is always under way. When a giant emergent tree eventually dies and falls with a great crash, it cuts a swathe through the layers beneath it and leaves a gap through which light can reach the hitherto overshaded ground. The death of a main canopy tree likewise creates a similar though smaller gap. Once adequate light is available, seedlings of all kinds commence their upward struggle to win their best available place in the complex structure. Eventually a tall emergent tree regains the position held by its predecessor. Meanwhile the storeyed pattern is inevitably uneven.

The total of different species of trees and woody plants found in a typical stretch of rain forest is far higher than that of a comparable temperate woodland. Within one square kilometre there may be 500 different kinds, as compared with only twenty or so in temperate lands. All of these are capable, at least in youth, of growing as seedlings and saplings in the difficult surroundings of the forest floor. Some endure shade, others lie dormant, possibly as seeds, until adequate light arrives during a short-lived break in the dense canopy above. Only a small proportion have the ability to reach the great height and size of the giant emergent trees, and these are not always the fastest starters.

Animal life is stratified in much the same way as plant life. The main canopy is the domain of the monkeys, who use the branches of adjacent trees as a highway, swinging or leaping from tree to tree. From this safe level they descend at intervals to gather nuts and fruits that have fallen to the ground or alternatively climb the trunks of the forest giants to pluck fruit from their high crowns. Here the monkeys compete with large free-flying creatures like flying foxes or fruit bats and big-beaked birds like the hornbills or toucans. The ground level fauna includes large beasts like elephants, buffaloes and tapirs, besides small deer. These find their browse, or tree-leaf fodder, mainly beside gaps in the overhead cover, usually gaps caused by tree-falls, water courses, trails or rock outcrops, though elephants make their own gaps! Predators may be tree-climbers like the leopard or jaguar, or earth-bound like the tiger.

Man appears in the rain forest in several capacities. He may be a primitive hunter stalking prey with blowpipe or bow-and-arrow, seeking at the same time edible fruits or nuts which – though local and seasonal – may be surprisingly large and nutritious. South American Indians gather Brazil nuts while the Malaysian jungle dweller looks out for the huge, delicious durian fruits, *Durio zibethinus*, each the size of a pineapple, that crash down from lofty tree crowns when fully ripe.

Elsewhere man acts as a fairly primitive cultivator, moving from place to place to make clearings to raise his local traditional crops of Asiatic rice, American maize or African millet. Surprisingly, he will tackle the largest trees as readily as the lesser ones. Any he cannot fell can be killed by ring-barking. He abandons each clearing after two or three years, as its store of fertility becomes exhausted. This leaves further gaps for re-colonization by forest trees, fresh points of change in the ever-varying forest.

Man will also exploit the jungle for its timber, winning poles for huts, palm leaves for thatch, logs for dug-out canoes and nowadays enormous baulks of wood for export. Broad clearings may be made and permanently maintained for tropical crops such as rubber, oil palms, tea, coffee or coco-nuts. Sometimes the husbandry may be sound, at others wasteful and disastrous. With the advance of modern communications, tropical rain forest is more likely to be raped than virgin!

Giant Emergent Trees

Interest in the tropical rain forest naturally centres on those trees that attain the largest size and have the greatest utility in world timber markets. These are relatively few in number, both as species and as individuals standing on the ground. Timber men often complain that they can find only four or five marketable stems per hectare though the total stocking runs into hundreds of sturdy close-ranked trees. But the available resources of light and nutrients cannot support more than this stocking. Away up beyond the canopy, each full-grown tree needs a large expanse of ground to expand its broad, deep crown.

Often the mature bole of the tree is clear of branches for a height of 30 metres since all the lower foliage has died through overshading by the canopy trees up to that height and the dead side branches have fallen away. This makes the identification of the species difficult. In practice it is done by characters of bark and 'blaze', that is, the appearance of the underlying wood when a slice of bark has been cut away with a jungle knife. If that does not suffice, fallen leaves, flowers or fruits serve as extra clues. As a rule the timber men are concerned in any one country with only a few valuable species like teak or mahogany, and recognize their 'headmark' characters easily from long experience.

All these trees of the first size must grow in turn through all the layers and microclimates present. Their seedlings must be capable of starting life in the deep shade at ground level and then making rapid growth into the main canopy to keep pace with trees of lesser final stature. Soaring above this, they must next expand their crowns rapidly to exploit the unrestricted light beyond and at the same time develop stout trunks to withstand the wind strains imposed by full exposure.

Many species do not flower and fruit freely until they are approaching full size. Foresters are often concerned about their rate of natural replacement in competition with so many other trees of lower value. Since they alone attract the major timber merchants and the felling of each individual removes a precious source of seed, the position of some valuable species is indeed precarious. The usual practical measure to safeguard the situation is to impose a minimum size for exploitation. If no trees of a lesser diameter than, say, three metres, may legally be felled, there should always be a scattering of trees in the two-to-three metre size class that are shedding seed as they approach commercial maturity. Because the logs must be exported from the forest through check-points manned by forest guards, on roads or rivers, this rule is easily enforced, even under the difficult conditions of remote jungles.

A great deal of time and effort has to be expended by the timber men in locating the scattered merchantable trees. Each concern works through part of its concession in turn. When its scouts return to that section, say, ten years later, a fresh supply of trees will have grown above the initial size for exploitation. Ideally, this simple management plan maintains the forest in perpetuity, always yielding timber and revenue yet always renewing its resources without cost to its owners. A happy balance of this kind has been achieved, though not everywhere, in the national rain forests of India, Burma and certain other tropical Asiatic and African territories. Trees of minor, less valuable species are usually excluded from the minimum size regulations as they are in no particular peril.

Many tropical forest giants appear larger at their base than their con-ventionally-measured diameters suggest because they are usually supported by buttresses. These are remarkable plank-like structures which develop as the tree increases in size. Up to three metres broad at the base, they taper towards the cylindrical trunk against which they end at heights around four metres. Though they appear to prop the tree up on all sides their main physical effect is to resist sway: they act as anchors rather than as struts. Smaller buttresses develop on certain trees, notably beeches (*Fagus*) and spruces (*Picea*) in temperate forests. Their much greater size in the tropics is probably caused by the greater strains that an emergent tree must bear. It carries a larger crown of branches and foliage than its temperate counter-part and is under greater exposure since it is more isolated from its fellows. In the same kind of tree, buttressing is more strongly developed on soft soils than on firm ones, which underlines its support function.

The presence of buttresses poses a real problem for tree fellers. In prac-tice they are obliged to set spring-boards or felling platforms into the side of the trunk at a height of about three metres above ground level. Perched precariously on these boards the fellers wield axes or operate power saws until the great giant is almost cut through and about to fall. As the critical moment of tree fall approaches they drop or lower their tools, then leap clear as the massive trunk heels over and crashes down.

The subsequent transport of the felled timber from the stump where it fell has taken, at different times, varied forms in different regions. The fallen trunk is first cross-cut to carefully selected lengths, nowadays with a power saw but formerly by men using large cross-cut hand saws. A rough track is next cleared leading to the nearest road, railway, or preferably river: water transport is the cheapest method and often the only one available. Certain heavy timbers such as teak must be left to season for several months before they have lost enough moisture, and hence enough weight, to enable them to float. In some circumstances rafts are built or barges employed in preference to letting valuable logs float freely downstream.

Where labour was cheap and plentiful, logs were formerly drawn out by teams of men, being simply slid over other logs used as rollers. Draught animals may include specially trained elephants, domestic buffaloes, ox teams and mules. Today tractors on crawler tracks equipped with winches are the timber hauliers' main motive power.

Where there is no commercial incentive to market the smaller main canopy trees the result of this big timber harvest may only be the creation of long narrow clearings running deep into the forest. The timber men in such surroundings will not fell more lesser trees than they need to clear extraction routes. Such gaps close over quickly, usually within the space of a few years. If middle-aged stems of the desirable kinds remain in the untouched matrix of the forest, they grow still taller to provide the next harvest. The removal of one crop of emergent trees opens the way for another. Light striking into the temporary gaps may at the same time promote active growth of seedlings of the desirable kinds. But many kinds of mismanagement such as overfelling or undue clearing may upset this happy cycle of events.

Trees of the Main Canopy

The smaller trees that make up the bulk of the rain forest stocking yet have little value in world markets commonly play a significant part in the economy of rural people in the forest districts. There is a constant call for firewood because, though dwellers in the tropics never need fires to keep warm, they do use them daily to cook food. Wood is the main (and often the only) material used for building houses, cowsheds, shops and stores. The broad leaves of palms are in many tropical lands the standard material for thatching roofs and constructing side walls. Laid so that one leaf overlaps another, they remain waterproof for years; there is little or no need to conserve heat. Lianas, and particularly the tough rattans of the bamboo group, provide strong ropes. Very little of this valuable harvest from the forest finds its way into the national or international statistics of trade since few records are kept in remote jungles. Often it is collected under long-established local rights rather than as articles of negotiated sale, and no money changes hands. In many countries the work of the administrative foresters is supplemented by that of forest guards, who have the duty of regulating the removal of small material as well as large for local uses. They also have to prevent 'squatting', which implies the illegal use of forest land for cultivation or settlement.

Managing the Rain Forest

The casual visitor often gains the impression that tropical rain forests are left to nature as something far too vast and unexplorable to be subject to human control. Today that is true only in the least developed countries. Elsewhere governments have brought this valuable resource into the scope of national economic plans. The legal situation takes two forms. Either all undeveloped forest is declared to be the property of the state or else its ownership by local tribes or chiefs is conceded but the state undertakes its practical management on their behalf and pays them the proceeds. The areas concerned are defined by proclamations in publications such as the government 'gazette' and the state forest service assumes control.

By the year 1900 most such forests in British India had been brought under official control. The same pattern was followed throughout Britain's tropical colonies and dependencies and also in French, Belgian, Dutch and Portuguese territories. It has been continued by the newly independent states since, and has spread under guidance from experts of the Food and Agriculture Organization (FAO) of the United Nations through tropical America and Asia. Everything is now mapped and planned, even if the execution of the plans is apt to lag far, far behind their first drafting!

Air surveys have proved a tool of inestimable value for the management of tropical rain forests, which are exceptionally difficult to investigate on foot. The aeroplane is independent of roads or rivers, and crosses broad streams and mountain ranges with equal ease. At first the aerial surveyors sought only to map the areas under trees of different types. But the quick development of stereoscopic techniques, whereby two photos are taken of the same area from slightly different angles and then viewed together through a simple stereoscopic viewer, gave the same 'in-depth' impressions as are received by a pair of human eyes. From this it proved a short step to devising estimates of the height and size of tree crowns, and these data were then related, by comparison with known specimens identified on the ground, with the timber volumes of the trees concerned.

Experienced teams can now interpret air photos of enormous areas of rain forest in terms of marketable timber and rate of growth at low cost and in surprisingly short periods of time. The ensuing development of the forest over suitable time spells can be monitored by re-photographing the region concerned. A record of its progress is easily maintained.

The all-seeing eye of the air-borne camera will also reveal any new clearings made in the jungle, whether they have been authorized or not!

Mountain Forests in the Tropics

The characteristic rain forest just described can exist only in lowlands or on relatively low hill ranges where a truly tropical climate prevails. Above an elevation of 1,000 metres, even on the equator, the influence of altitude creates cooler conditions that are reflected in the character of the vegetation. Rainfall induced by the cooling of clouds as the winds rise to cross mountain barriers is often even heavier than on the plains, but temperatures are always lower.

The vigour and particularly the height of forest trees falls off with increasing altitude. Steep slopes make it difficult for deep soils to accumulate and any complete clearance of the forest cover is followed by extremely rapid erosion. In many countries, such as India, the montane rain forests are looked upon as 'protection forests' that must be retained to safeguard the catchments of the great rivers that water the plains. If they were ever removed the silt swept down by torrents would clog the watercourses below and cause widespread flooding and loss of fertility. Timber production becomes secondary to this prime object.

As one ascends the mountains the forests lose their three-storeyed character and become closer to the single canopy type found in temperate lands. There is no clear distinction between emergent trees, main canopy and understorey. With decreasing height each merges into the others. But tropical montane forests are commonly irregular in structure. They hold an exceptionally wide range of species, most being of low value. Broadleaved trees are supplemented by tropical conifers, such as *Podocarpus* species, palms, tree-ferns and cycads. Lianas continue to entwine among their stems, which also support many epiphytes, since moisture is everywhere adequate. The outcome is a paradise for the plant hunter though a poor resource for the economic forester. In commercial terms many trees add up to little wood and the problems of extracting logs from steep slopes in roadless country limit the value of what little there is.

At still higher levels, around 2,000 metres on the equator and proportionately lower as one goes north or south, the cool climate supports only the remarkable 'elfin forest'. This odd tree community, which I have examined on mountain tops in Malaysia and Sumatra, consists of short trees, apparently dwarfed by continuing low temperatures, growing on thin soils impoverished by heavy rainfall. The constant cloudiness and high humidities promote the growth of lichens which cover the low trunks and short branches in loose grey-green masses. This forest is quite valueless in economic terms but plays a critical part in protecting the soil from erosion. Its remoteness is its best protection.

Higher yet, at altitudes of 3,000 metres and over, this dwarf forest gives way to grassland which may be studded with tall herbaceous plants such as the giant lobelias of the East African peaks.

Mangrove Forests in Tropical Estuaries

Few trees tolerate salt water but the muddy estuaries of large tropical rivers often support dense forests composed of trees, collectively called mangroves, that can grow in their brackish water. The character of the coastline governs their existence and they cannot arise on rocky shores fully exposed to the action of storms and strong currents. They are found where the deposit of silt, brought down in great quantities by the rivers that are eroding soil in their hinterlands, starts to build up into banks. These are usually submerged at high tides but exposed twice daily when the tides go out.

Normal plants find it impossible to become established in such situations. The mangroves have a special mechanism called 'vivipary' whereby their seedlings have started to sprout and grow even before they fall from their parent tree. When a mangrove seedling gets stranded on a mud bank it is able to take root at once and will with luck secure an anchorage before tide or current can carry it away. In the favourable surroundings of warmth, moisture and a soil enriched by the siltbearing river it grows rapidly into a small bush. The soft, wet mud is not firm enough to support any normal tree. The mangrove overcomes this problem by sending out from its small trunk a cluster of 'stilt roots' which grip the ground around it. Thus supported on all sides it grows taller and stouter to become a true timber tree, branching widely and bearing flowers and fruit.

At the seaward end of the deltas of great rivers such as the Ganges and the Irrawaddy, vast mangrove forests line the banks of the 'distributary' streams that carry the main waters out to sea. They are impenetrable save by boat but navigable open channels always remain and allow of the forests' exploitation. Mangrove forests form a valuable local resource of firewood, timber and tanbark. They are worked on an orderly plan to ensure regular harvesting and regeneration. As the rivers are always adding silt which gets trapped and fixed between the mangroves' 'stilt roots', the level of the land steadily rises. Eventually it becomes too high and dry for the mangroves, which are then replaced by freshwater swamp forests. Meanwhile the mangroves are advancing on the seaward or downstream side of the estuary. In effect they win land from the sea.

The animal life of the mangrove forests is highly specialized. Remarkable adaptations are needed for survival in this strange environment. The oddest example is a fish that has its fins modified into sucking feet. It can climb the stilt roots and remain out of water unharmed by exposure to air between one high tide and the next.

Forests in Peril

Fears are nowadays widely expressed that the tropical rain forests will vanish within our own time. Some, such as the mangroves and the higher mountain forests, are still protected by their remoteness or inhospitable character. Others now feel the full impact of modern transport and technology. Man can nowadays clear and drain, harvest timber and cultivate crops anywhere in the tropics. Advances in medical science check most of the diseases that once limited his settlement.

The immediate advantages that accrue from forest clearance are obvious. Land-hungry people are also voters in democratic societies. Politicians all too often win popularity by removing the reservation restrictions that protect national forests. This opens the way to quick profits from timber fellings and the cleared land can then be parcelled out to settlers at low prices. But the long-term damage to the country's economy can be devastating. Soil fertility is soon exhausted, erosion sets in, floods follow on the downstream lands and the priceless self-perpetuating resource of the primeval forest has gone for ever. With it disappears the unique wealth of plant life that has taken thousands of years to develop.

In the days of the old colonial empires it was a simple matter for an autocratic government based on a distant European land to decree that certain forests were a national heritage to be preserved forever as reserves of timber, game and wild life, and as protection for soil and water supplies. Today everything rests in the hands of less experienced and certainly less detached local statesmen. However well meaning the new independent governments may be, they are far more likely to regard their forests as a domestic asset rather than as elements of world resources. One can only hope, without much faith, that far-sighted counsels will guide them in the future.

One widely publicized but imaginary threat to the world's wellbeing is the possible destruction of the vast tropical forests of the Amazon basin in South America. These forests obviously remove, by their steady growth, great quantities of carbon dioxide gas from the atmosphere. The argument goes that they have become an essential world 'lung' which absorbs the carbon dioxide produced by the burning-up of the world's fossil fuels, coal and oil. But these same forests also return to the atmosphere, by the steady decay of their substance through fungal life, just about as much carbon dioxide as they absorb. Overall, the jungle is neutral.

Unless a vegetative cover is steadily building up a reserve of coal or peat it exists in a state of carbon balance with its surroundings. Under tropical conditions of year-round high temperature and equal length of day and night, a forest removes carbon dioxide from the air all through the sunlit day but returns an equivalent quantity the following night. There is not even a seasonal gain to the purity of the atmosphere and one must look elsewhere for sound grounds for retaining the Amazonian forests in perpetuity.

Part 4

Trees in the Service of Man

Chapter 14

Raising Trees: The Nurseryman's Tasks

WE saw earlier, in Chapter Four dealing with reproduction, that trees increase their kind in two ways. By far the commonest in nature is *sexual reproduction* by seed, which allows for variation between individuals and between one generation and another, and also permits the offspring to grow at a distance from their parents. Under cultivation the various methods of the alternative way, namely *vegetative reproduction* using cuttings, grafts of various kinds, root suckers or layered shoots, can easily be extended to a mass production scale. They allow of no variation, except by some rare mischance, from the first original parent, which can be an important and indeed over-ruling advantage. Transport of the resulting plants to their new growing site must of course be done artificially.

Both these systems are often employed side by side in the same nursery, but the principles and practices are so different that it is best to describe each separately here. Plate 29 shows the raising of *large* tree seedlings in containers.

Reproduction from Seed

Trees are raised from seed where this is the cheapest acceptable method. Most coniferous trees and a number of broadleaved ones are difficult to propagate by vegetative means. Though none can be considered impossible the special techniques involved are too costly where trees are wanted at low cost, as in afforestation projects.

The first essential is an adequate supply of fertile seed of a desirable strain. In the past seed collections were often made from the cheapest source for any species. This often meant that it was gathered from the shortest and scrubbiest trees in a species' natural range. That was the worst conceivable economy as the costs of all subsequent stages were the same as those for seed of selected strains, while the value of the resulting timber after the crop had been tended for perhaps one hundred years was far less.

Today the parent trees are carefully selected before seed is gathered. Trees that have a wide natural range such as the black pine, *Pinus nigra*, of Europe and the lodgepole pine, *P. contorta*, of western North America, vary considerably in physical form and adaptability to climate from one region to another. Foresters therefore specify the particular *provenance* or region of origin that they require for the plantings they have in view, and in some countries it has become a legal requirement to use appropriate provenances for all timber crops.

Seed can of course be collected from standing trees but this involves climbing and is a slow and costly job, not without its dangers. Certain large seeds such as the acorns of oaks, *Quercus* species, can be gathered commercially from the forest floor. The felling of timber crops provides an opportunity for gathering cones and seeds cheaply because it is done at ground level from parents that have proved their worth by growing to a desirable size. Unfortunately ripe seed is only available with most species for a few weeks, or at the most a few months of each year, whereas felling must proceed continuously to prove economical.

To overcome the problems of ensuring continuous and reliable seed supplies, foresters in several countries have established national *seed orchards*. In these, selected parent trees are grown under ideal conditions to promote seed-bearing in places isolated from others of their kind to minimize the risk of female flowers being pollinated by unselected and possibly undesirable sources of male pollen. The chosen parents are spaced wide apart to ensure ample illumination and they are given ample fertilizers where required. As they are too valuable to be cut down, means such as truckmounted ladders have to be devised for collecting seed from their high crowns, or else from a well-tended grassy surface beneath them.

The higher value of the 'pedigree' seed, and the fact that the crop can be repeated year after year, repay the costs of establishment and management. The species chosen for such treatment are naturally those of high economic value. They include the Para rubber tree, *Hevea brasiliensis*, in Malaysia and Indonesia; the slash pine, *Pinus elliottii*, in the southern United States; teak, *Tectona grandis*, in several tropical countries and hybrid larch, *Larix eurolepis*, in Britain. The last named, being a hybrid tree, requires a seed orchard with alternate rows of its two parents, the European larch, *L. decidua*, and the Japanese larch, *L. kaempferi*. The crossing rate is high since European *male* flowers mature simultaneously with Japanese *females*, ahead of the Japanese *males*.

Long-term planning is essential to ensure adequate supplies of the right kind of viable seed in the right places at the right times. Most national forest authorities run their own forest seed organizations and these are supplemented by international trading companies. Seeds ripen at different times of year in different regions. Some are easily handled, stored and transported. Others are delicate. In consequence, most valuable consignments now travel by air.

The whole business is highly technical as any false move may destroy the seed's germinative power. This is generally tested by placing sample lots of seed, say 100 grains, in an incubator under controlled laboratory conditions to see what percentage will sprout in a given time. Plates 50, 51.

Conifer seeds are extracted from cones by first heating the cones until their scales expand and then tumbling these expanded cones in a wire-mesh drum. The seeds fall out of the cones, then fall through the wire-mesh and are next collected in a hopper. Another machine removes their wings. They are then stored, protected by polythene bags within square tins, in a cool place. A refrigerated store with temperatures kept just above freezing point is ideal and repays its cost by resulting higher yields. Good seed crops occur only once in every few years (see Chapter Four). A well-filled store enables managers to maintain regular planting programmes regardless of good or bad seed crops. Many conifers can be stored successfully for up to six years, but a few such as silver firs, *Abies* species, prove difficult.

The seeds of broadleaved trees vary greatly in size, substance, and surrounding material, and a special technique must be followed for each. As examples, acorns of oaks, *Quercus* species, should be stored through winter under cool, moist conditions, but never heaped up as they then generate enough heat to destroy their own viability. The seeds of ash trees, *Fraxinus* species, and many other common genera including hollies, *Ilex*, and hawthorns, *Crataegus*, require stratification for sixteen months. They have to lie dormant over a whole annual growing season before they will sprout. They are gathered in autumn, mixed with sand and left buried in shallow pits for that period.

Seedbeds

After choosing, collecting, extracting and storing seed with such care the nurseryman naturally aims to give his seedlings the best possible start in life. He chooses the best available place for his nursery, a spot with the right climate and an easily-worked, freely draining, fertile soil. He brings this to the right condition for raising small seedlings by a careful programme of prior cultivation. The area he will need calls for some tricky calculations. One kilogramme of a small conifer seed such as an Oregon Sitka spruce, *Picea sitchensis*, will hold on average around 250,000 grains, with a germination percentage found by test of 80%. With 200,000 tiny seedlings in view the nurserymen must allow a large area of ground, in practice 250 square metres, for this one seed lot. But the same weight, of beech seed, *Fagus* species, holds only 500 separate seeds and requires only four square metres. (Imperial equivalents: Half a pound of spruce seed needs 250 square yards, half a pound of beech seed needs only four square yards.)

The practical problem of spreading these quantities of seed evenly over the surface can be solved in two ways. Either it is broadcast, that is sprinkled by hand, or some ingenious machine is used to set it in drills like the seed of a common vegetable plant in the garden.

It is next covered over with a depth of soil or sand sufficient to keep it moist and to conceal it from its many enemies. Fine white limefree sand is preferred for most conifer seedbeds because it has just the right properties. It holds moisture where it is needed, does not 'cake' and thereby obstruct delicate seedlings as they sprout, and it does not make the soil more alkaline. It reflects heat by day and helps to retain it at night.

Protecting Seedlings

After sowing, a spell of from ten to thirty days may elapse before the tree seedlings emerge and in the meantime weed seedlings may gain a start on them. It is therefore a standard practice to apply *pre-emergence weedkillers* which kill small plants over a limited span of time. The commonest kinds are hydrocarbon oils allied to diesel engine fuel and they are applied as a fine spray by pressure sprayers. Later on, *selective post-emergence* weedkillers may be sprayed on the growing seedlings, provided a formulation is available that is harmless to the tree crop but toxic to the weeds. Conifer seedlings for example are not affected by the 'white spirit' hydrocarbons used as dry-cleaning fluids whereas most of the weeds that infest their seedbeds rapidly succumb to a light dose of these oils.

Whether weedkillers are used or not, hand weeding must be done in greater or less degree to prevent fast growing weeds from over-topping and smothering the little tree seedlings. The soft-tissued weeds grow taller and spread outward much faster than the woody trees can do, and unless the latter are constantly favoured by the poisoning or physical removal of the weeds, they are quickly overcome.

Birds and beasts appear as soon as seedlings emerge above ground and start to take their toll of the little trees. The text book remedies are either to shoot or trap the marauders, or else to set up wire netting screens to keep them out. In practice such precautions are seldom taken owing to the trouble and cost involved. Nurserymen everywhere are inclined to accept a loss of perhaps one-fifth of all their precious stock.

Climatic extremes can do more devastating damage, destroying the crop as a whole, sometimes overnight. The seedlings of many forest trees, which start life naturally under deep shade, cannot tolerate prolonged direct hot sunshine. Screens of various kinds, set at head height or else just above ground level, are therefore found essential in many tropical, and even some temperate zone, forest nurseries. Frost-lift, whereby a succession of frosts and thaws gradually lifts little seedlings out of the soil until they fall over, is a peril in some northern nurseries, and again screens are used to check its effects.

Insect pests and fungal diseases that occasionally afflict young trees out in the forest may be given exceptionally favourable conditions in a nursery where millions of vulnerable host plants are crowded together. But this is one situation in which a forester can economically apply either fungicides or insecticides, as the occasion requires. Serious outbreaks occur from time to time but provided an expert entomologist or plant pathologist gives the right advice, all are quickly checked.

Safeguarded in these ways the seedlings develop at rates peculiar to their kind and the local climate. In their first growing season few conifers grow more than ten centimetres tall, so they are usually left for another year to reach a more manageable height of about twenty centimetres. Broadleaved trees by contrast often grow fifteen to twenty-five centimetres high in their first growing season and are then ready for transplanting from their nursery bed.

Nursery Transplanting

Certain trees in certain surroundings grow large enough at the *seedling* stage for immediate transplanting to their final station in the forest. For example, Douglas fir seedlings are widely used in western North America, and so are seedlings of oak in Europe. But the general experience is that nursery transplanted trees, called for short *transplants*, give better results and repay their extra first cost. Plate 28 shows Douglas fir seedlings.

There are two reasons for this. First, the disturbance of the tree's root system when it is moved to a fresh bed in the nursery causes it to develop a much more bushy set of rootlets which are better equipped than its original root system to take up water and nutrients from untilled forest soil. Second, the same disturbance, shock or check causes shoot growth to slow down for a season. The resulting transplant is 'better balanced' than a seedling of the same age would be. It has a higher proportion of root to shoot and is shorter and sturdier. This fits it better for the first critical year of growth under harsh forest surroundings and lessens the risk of death from drought.

The great majority of small trees destined for forest planting are therefore transplanted from their seedbed to a second nursery bed when they are one or two years old. This is done at a suitable season, usually spring in the temperate zones, when they are still resting but about to re-commence growth. They are set out in straight lines at average spacings of five centimetres (two inches) apart with 15 centimetres (six inches) left between the lines for ease of working and weeding. Traditionally this is done with a garden spade aided by a gardener's line of string to keep the row straight, and hence is known as *lining-out*.

Mechanization is now the general rule. In one method a plough is used to cut a straight trench and the seedlings are set in specially-designed wooden boards so that sixty or so may be planted in the trench at one time; the plough then returns the soil, followed by a roller that makes it firm. Under another system; first developed in the USA, a transplanting machine propelled by its own engine moves slowly across the ground carrying a load of seedlings and a crew of transplanters. Each transplanter puts seedlings into slots on a wheel which revolves and releases the little tree in a slot in the earth already cut by the machine. A pair of rollers follow to close the slot. The work is, of course, monotonous in the extreme, but it is efficient. Each man or girl on the machine can plant over 8,000 trees a day, or 50,000 a day for a six-operator crew! Plate 30.

The nursery transplants, like the younger seedlings, face serious competition from quicker growing weeds. But now that they are established in straight rows at set distances apart, weed control is much easier. The invading weeds can be checked by using hand hoes or alternatively simple hoeing devices drawn by a tractor which treat several rows at a time. Only those few weeds that sprout along the lines of transplants have to be pulled out by hand.

Chemical weedkillers are also used if required. A valuable aid is found in simazine compounds, which are toxic to the newly-emerged seed-leaves or cotyledons of the weeds but harmless to the better established and more substantial transplanted trees.

The transplants are allowed to grow larger for one, or sometimes two or more growing seasons. They are then lifted by either hand tools such as digging forks, or mechanical lifters that free them from the soil with the least possible harm to their roots. They are then counted and examined and any not up to standard are rejected.

To safeguard them during the interval between lifting from the nursery bed and despatching to the forest for planting, one of two methods may be used. The traditional way is to *heel them in* by burying their roots in soil to check water loss. The more modern way is to pack them in polythene bags which are stored either in a cool shed away from sunlight or else in a refrigerated store kept at temperatures just above freezing point. Common coniferous trees can be kept successfully in this way for several months. This enables planting to be done over an extended period, though the later they are planted the less time they have to grow.

The production of forest trees from seed for replenishing the world's forests is a highly specialized mass production business involving a big, long term investment of capital, land and skill. The main concerns involved are national forestry authorities, big timber companies and specialist nursery firms. Despite all the clever techniques now used the actual rate of success achieved is low. On average five seeds are sown to yield a single tree fit for forest planting. The other four either fail to sprout, fall victim to weeds, pests, diseases or bad weather, or get rejected for being misshapen or undersized. Nursery outputs are nevertheless reckoned in thousands, which soon add up to millions. And the cost of individual trees is still very low, only a few pence or cents apiece.

Propagation by Vegetative Means

Whatever process is used, vegetative propagation implies the multiplication of one individual tree. The resulting offspring will simply be branches or even buds that have been persuaded to develop to full size. They repeat the characters of their parent stock precisely, subject only to varying development due to site, weather, and the inevitable randomness of branching. It is therefore very important to start with the right *origin*, *clone*, or *cultivar*, as the foundation stocks are variously known. It is no more costly but far more profitable to multiply a good stock than to increase a bad one.

This foundation stock may be obtained either by selection out of the general population of suitable trees, both wild and cultivated, or else by deliberate breeding. Forest and orchard geneticists are continually making crosses between parents of promising strains of the major crop trees that can be multiplied by vegetative means. This is a long-term business requiring a substantial investment of funds and skill and it is therefore carried on mainly by research stations or the larger nursery firms. There is a very high proportion of failure but if only one hybrid out of a hundred proves to have commercial possibilities the tree-breeder is well rewarded. In many countries he is now able to secure a legal patent on his product and to market it as foundation stocks to other nurserymen at a good price for a fair profit.

Once selected, the clone itself must be safeguarded and increased in quantity until its offshoots are sufficiently numerous to be used in the production of commercially useful stocks. A 'tree bank' must be established and maintained indefinitely solely for the supply of cuttings, or of scions or buds for grafting. With some new strains of fruit trees, for example, several years may elapse before there is enough scion material for substantial orchards to be set up. Other trees such as poplars, *Populus* species, can be multiplied rapidly by establishing *stools* which produce heavy annual 'crops' of branches. These are harvested for planting as cuttings and the stool obligingly sends out a fresh set next year. Provided the land is fertilized at intervals the supply continues indefinitely. Plate 53.

Cuttings

The simplest method of vegetative propagation is the use of cuttings. These are simply lengths of stem severed from a parent tree and thrust, right way up, into the ground. Root initials on the lower, buried portion then develop into active roots, while buds along the exposed top expand in the normal way into leaves and shoots. Rooting is of course the critical factor here, for if it is delayed or fails entirely the cutting dies of drought.

Certain trees *strike* from cuttings with surprising ease. Common examples are poplars, *Populus*, and willows, *Salix*. With most though not all kinds of these trees success is almost automatic. Lengths of stem about 15 centimetres long are simply stuck in the ground during the winter resting season, for about half their length. They sprout in the following spring. As the resulting first shoot tends to be curved and weak, a common practice is to cut it back to a selected bud, placed low down, after one season's growth. This results in an exceptionally vigorous and straight main stem which springs up from the bud and is nourished by a now well-established root system. The sturdy plant, often two metres tall, is then ready for transplanting to its final situation.

Other trees take root far less readily from cuttings, and special techniques must be followed to persuade them to do so. The stems that are to root must be carefully chosen at a particular time of year. The best stem for cypresses of the *Chamaecyparis* genus, for example, is a small one, about seven centimetres long, severed at its base and carrying a *heel* where it joined the larger stem. It may be dipped in a liquid *auxin* or plant *hormone* to encourage rooting before it is thrust into a special medium such as sand or vermiculite mixed with peat. This rooting bed is set within a glass-roofed frame, which may be fitted with wires for underground heating by electricity. The humidity of the surrounding air can be maintained at a high level by mist sprayers, fed by water pipes, which automatically discharge a cloud of fine water droplets whenever the air becomes dry. Under these carefully controlled conditions, nearly any tree can be induced to root. Thousands of individuals can be handled simultaneously in one large propagating frame and transplanted to less refined surroundings once their rooting is accomplished. All the same the method remains too costly and complex for common timber trees, though it is widely used for ornamental garden ones. Plate 8.

Grafting

The craft of inducing a shoot taken from a desirable strain of tree to grow upon the trunk of another, nearly-related one is very old. Traditional skills have been only marginally improved by modern materials and techniques. The basal portion of the union, which remains rooted in the soil, is called the *stock*, and the upper portion, taken from another tree in order to increase it, is known as the *scion*. The two must come from *compatible* sources or their marriage will fail. In broad terms grafts are simple between individuals of the same botanical species, easy between species in the same genus, and possible as a rule between members of different genera in the same botanical family. Trees more remotely related cannot be inter-grafted. See Fig. 19, p. 215.

The critical factor in all grafting is to bring three layers of tissues, each made up of living cells, into intimate contact so that they continue both growth and their living functions as before. Wood layers in both stock and scion must meet at an interface to carry root sap up from rooted stock to scion. So must the bast layers just below the outer bark, to carry leaf sap down from scion to stock. In between these two, the thin cambium layers must link up to enable growth in diameter to go on.

In one method, called a *saddle graft*, the stock is cut across and the scion, which must be a stem of the same diameter, is likewise cut across, except for a tongue of wood that is used to anchor it to a slot in the stock. Wood, cambium and bast in the two shoots can therefore unite as circular bands of like tissues. Alternatively, in various forms of *side grafting* the scion is inserted into the side of the stock in a way that places each tissue adjacent to its related one.

The final preparation, by cutting stock and scion to shape, must be done immediately before the graft is made so that the exposed tissues have no time to get dry. Once the two elements have been brought together they are bound firmly in place with raffia or plastic tape. Wax or a synthetic sealant is then run over the surfaces around the union to keep out air and hold in moisture. If all goes well the two stems quickly unite during the succeeding growing season to form a union almost as firm as that between adjacent parts of any natural stem.

Grafting is usually carried out with dormant material during the trees' resting season. Its success or failure becomes evident as soon as fresh growth begins.

On a commercial scale grafting is widely practised by the growers of fruit trees and also those who market ornamental trees. The basal, rooted, stocks that they use are carefully chosen to suit the varieties represented by the scions. These stocks themselves must be propagated in adequate quantities for each season's work. Plate 54.

Suckers and Layers

Some trees that do not grow freely from seed and are also troublesome to increase by cuttings can easily be propagated by *suckers*. These are shoots that spring up from side roots at varying distances from their parent tree. If the side roots are cut through at suitable distances a sucker can be lifted complete with a root system large enough to sustain it when it is transplanted to a fresh position. This method is generally used for elms, of the genus *Ulmus*, for sumacs, *Rhus* genus, and also for increasing root stocks suitable for plums and cherries in the genus *Prunus*. See Fig. 9, p. 54.

Layers are branches that have been induced to take root by staking them down in firm contact with the ground. They differ from cuttings in that the new tree is not severed from its parent *until roots have formed*. It proves the easiest method of propagation for certain trees that cannot be increased readily by other methods. One example is the snowball tree, *Viburnum opulus* variety *sterilis*, which bears showy white flowers that never set seed.

A variation of layering is used for species of *Cordyline* such as the New Zealand cabbage 'palm', *C. australis*. A length of stem is first severed and then buried horizontally in soil with parts exposed; buds then develop from these exposed positions, supported by young rootlets.

Air layering involves the fastening of a pack of rooting compost to a length of exposed stem and keeping it suitably moist. This induces the branches of certain trees, such as beech, to put forth roots to tap an unlikely source of moisture and nutrients. Once this has occurred the branch can be sawn through at a point on its main-stem side and a viable, rooted, young tree can be removed for planting in the real ground, where it soon assumes an upright growth habit.

The work of a tree nurseryman is a remarkable blend of old traditional skills, modern science and commercial expertise. It is essential to raise regular supplies to meet varying demands. A balance is often achieved by interchanges of stocks between growers, on trade terms. Standards are high. Good trees last long and form a constant advertisement for the ability of the men who raise them.

Chapter 15

Trees for Ornament: The Arboriculturist's Approach

AN arboriculturist, sometimes called an 'arborist' or even an 'arboricultur-alist', is a man who tends trees because they are beautiful. These decorative trees may be called 'shade trees', 'shelter trees' or 'wind-breakers', but the basic reason why people spare land for them and spend money on their cultivation is that they improve the quality of life. Plate 55.

What Trees are Worth

A tree's contribution to man's sensuous enjoyment of his surroundings is not easy to assess in positive, that is, financial terms. Arnold Grayson, a leading British forest economist, has described it as a 'non-market benefit'. In other words it is not a product, like a log of timber or a crop of apples, that you can load on a truck and cart to the market place to barter for the best price you can get.

But people will readily make a pilgrimage to look at splendid trees and even pay to enter an *arboretum*, which means a collection of them. Experts in outdoor recreation studies have sought to evaluate ornamental trees in terms of the expense that people will incur to visit them. But they have met with little success since people usually have more than one motive when making a recreational journey. Often they are more concerned with getting away from a place they *don't* like than with getting to one that they *do*!

In America more definite financial results are claimed. The pres-ence of a desirable shade tree is reckoned to add an assessable sum or proportion of a valuation to the market price of the property on which it stands. Without a tree, a house of a certain character in a certain district is worth so many thousand dollars. If an acceptable, healthy tree is growing on the front lawn it is worth so many thousand dollars more, always provided an astute realtor or estate agent is negotiating the sale!

Firm assessments of a tree's worth in hard cash also arise under the Tree Preservation Orders that local public planning authorities are empowered by the Town Planning Acts to make anywhere within Great Britain. In a representative situation, developers seeking to build houses on a wooded site may aim to put, say, ten houses worth £10,000 each on a certain plot. But the planning authority may and frequently does insist on the preservation of, for example, four specimen trees that lend a wooded character not only to the new development but also to surrounding houses and the district as a whole. To allow enough land for these the developers may be obliged to re-shape their plans and build only eight houses instead of ten. The omission of two houses reduces the total potential value of the project by £20,000, equivalent here to £5,000 per tree! But in practice the developers will try to offset this loss by stressing to purchasers the advantages of a 'well-wooded' site. With luck, they may get £12,500 instead of £10,000 for each of the eight houses they are allowed to build, so the four trees on this calculation add £2,500 to the market value of each house, while the developers themselves suffer no loss.

By whatever means the assessments are made, the arboriculturist is generally concerned with trees of high value. He can and does give them close and costly care in ways that are out of the question, in economic terms, for a forester or even a fruit grower. In the past arboriculturists worked for wealthy landowners since only the rich could afford to grow trees for fun. Today their main employers or customers are the public authorities who maintain street trees, parks, and avenues, and the developers of both industrial and residential properties who desire, or are told they must have, ornamental trees on privately-owned sites. A landscape architect who may or may not be an arboriculturist himself usually directs such schemes.

History of Arboriculture

Though trees were grown for ornament in the gardens of the wealthy during the great oriental and classical civilizations, they usually had a utilitarian value as well. Date palms in Assyria shed fruit as well as shade, while the Romans preferred to cultivate the walnut, the sweet chestnut and the mulberry in their villa grounds, rather than unfruitful beech or oak.

During the Middle Ages the need for defence left little scope for cultivating decorative trees save perhaps in monastery grounds immune from strife. Noblemen lived in grim fortified castles and dare not tolerate trees standing near them which might hide or shelter attackers, particularly archers. Townspeople dwelt in walled cities, crowded too closely together to allow any space for a tree to thrive.

Opportunities to develop arboriculture came only with the Renaissance movement of the fifteenth century and a fresh appreciation of natural beauties. But what really mattered in practical terms was the perfection of cannon and gunpowder. Noblemen began to build comfortable houses with wide windows instead of gaunt castles with only slits in their outer walls, because the latter were no longer defensible. They could at last risk planting trees to ornament the views from their mansions. Gradually too, the towns expanded beyond their walls and gained space enough for trees to figure in their layouts.

By the year 1600, specimen trees and avenues had begun to feature in the rather formal sketches of towns and great houses made by contemporary artists throughout most of western Europe. In England the Restoration politician and diarist John Evelyn published his classic work *Silva, or a Discourse of Forest Trees and the Propagation of Timber within His Majesty's Dominions* in 1664. Straying a little from his purpose, he recorded the practice, already widespread, of planting trees to ornament the surroundings of great houses. From his descriptions it is clear that much work had been accomplished quite early in the seventeenth century and that an able body of professional gardeners was already well established.

The expansion of trade and industry together with improvements in agriculture enriched landowners throughout Europe to an astonishing degree. As rents and incomes rose, the fashion of laying out great parks and ornamental grounds flourished exceedingly and on very fertile soil! Happily for all concerned, the typical park, once made and fenced in, proved an asset rather than a liability. It provided handy protected grazing to its proud owner for his horses – his main means of transport and travel – and it sustained cattle from the home farm to provide him with milk and meat, and possibly a flock of woolly sheep and a herd of deer, yielding tasty venison, as well.

Every respectable park had to be landscaped and it was here that the great outdoor planners like the famous 'Capability' Brown (John Lancelot Brown, 1716–83) came into their own. Trees were essential elements in their pictorial compositions and they worked with rewarding skill. The foresight of both owners and planners deserves our admiration today, for the trees when set out were relatively small. Imagination was needed to visualize how each grand scheme would look when its trees reached full stature – to delight generations of country lovers still to come.

The fashion for ornamental grounds was readily transplanted across the Atlantic. In America land was available more readily than in Europe, and a greater range of trees could be grown. All the European species were soon introduced and many native kinds were adapted in Colonial times to garden and park cultivation.

The reverse traffic, from the New World to the old, was at first less successful. Relatively few trees from the eastern United States proved at home in Europe. Noteworthy exceptions are the robinia, false acacia or black locust tree, *Robinia pseudoacacia*, and the tulip tree or yellow poplar, *Liriodendron tulipifera*.

But when botanists reached the forests of America's western seaboard early in the nineteenth century, a whole treasure-house of new trees was released for European, as well as American cultivators. In particular the Lawson cypress, *Chamaecyparis lawsoniana*; the Monterey cypress, *Cupressus macrocarpa*; the Douglas fir, *Pseudotsuga menziesii*; the Californian coast redwood, *Sequoia sempervirens* and the giant sequoia, *Sequoiadendron giganteum*; these all proved to be reliable growers, immensely popular in Europe. They were quickly spread by imports of seed throughout the British Isles and the Continent.

At the same time explorers finding new trees elsewhere enriched both American and European gardens. The deodar or Indian cedar, *Cedrus deodara*, was brought from the Himalayas, and its handsome ally the blue Atlas Cedar, *C. atlantica*, variety *glauca*, from Morocco. The monkey puzzle or Chile pine, *Araucaria araucana*, came from the snowy southern Andes of South America, while a number of nearly-hardy *Eucalyptus* species were introduced from Australia. For over a century a great encouraging factor in arboriculture was the excitement of raising trees previously unknown in one's own land. Hundreds of kinds failed through climatic differences but scores survived and became the mainstays of ornamental tree growing today.

The aims of a typical aristocratic tree planter in a rural region were simple if somewhat selfish. Tall trees beautified the surroundings amidst which he and his family spent most of their daily lives. They were something that he could pass on to his heirs as an enhancement of his property's value. And, significantly in an age of marked social distinctions, they proclaimed his wealth and station to the world at large. His park and its tall trees stood second only to his imposing mansion house as a status symbol declaring wealth, rank and worth. It stood out in the countryside as something that set him apart on a plane above the working populace of farmers, farm servants and assorted peasantry.

This pattern is recognizable in all the western European countries, and also in the eastern states of the USA. England has the largest parks and the finest arboreta, but only because, as a legacy of the Norman Conquest and its resultant well-ordered feudal system, the English landowners were the most successful at keeping good rural land under their own direct control, rather than sharing control with others.

The pattern set by the greater landlords was faithfully copied by the lesser owners. A gentleman's residence, whether in France or England, is distinguishable anywhere in the countryside by its clump or row of ornamental trees. Today most suburban gardens, if big enough, repeat the same time-honoured plan. They may even stress the association with such apt names as 'Two Trees' or just 'One Oak'.

Collective as contrasted with individual ownership of ornamental trees takes two forms. They may be used to beautify highways or to decorate open spaces like squares, parks and sports grounds.

Urban avenues first came into their own as parts of grandiose town planning schemes in the late eighteenth and early nineteenth centuries. They gained impetus with the 'garden city' movement at the start of the twentieth century and feature in countless schemes of expansive town planning today.

Rural avenues are widespread throughout France but exceptional elsewhere. They consist of striking double rows of trees – poplars, planes and beech being the most frequent kinds – that continue for mile after mile of national highway and provide welcome summer shade for travellers. A recent development in many countries has been motorway or freeway planting, in which plantations are established, rather than single lines of trees, in order to relieve the monotony of driving along scenically featureless highways.

The planting of town squares apparently originated in continental Europe as a measure of securing shade below which the townsfolk could sit in summer. In southern France the spacing is exceptionally close and the trees are often lopped like a hedge, but they thrive nevertheless and give a welcome cool ambience on the hottest of days. Elsewhere the specimens – usually limes, *Tilia* species, or plane or sycamore trees, varieties of *Platanus* – are allowed to spread more freely, to shed a lighter, more dappled shade.

The area of land owned collectively by local authorities or other communal bodies in the form of parks, school grounds, public sports grounds or golf courses, etc., continues to increase under modern social and political trends. This brings in the constraints peculiar to public control. For example, no one man may be able to decide what tree to plant without the help of a committee! On the other hand it ensures continuity and a sense of purpose for the public good.

Nowadays in most countries a large proportion of arboriculturists work for public bodies, either carrying out tree planting and care directly or dealing with planning matters on independently-owned properties. Other arboriculturists are engaged on planting and maintenance schemes, often on a contract basis for independent concerns, usually landowners, property developers or industrial firms that hold land.

Free-growing and Restricted Trees

Arboriculturists grow trees in two ways, with and without restriction of growing space. Both of these contrast with the work of a timber-growing forester. The latter expects that the outward expansion of each tree's crown will be constrained throughout most of its career *by its neighbours*, and he plans accordingly, as we noted in Chapter Five. But the arboriculturist is usually tending single specimen trees, either free-growing or restricted, that stand apart from others of their kind. Plate 34.

Ideally a *free-growing tree* can expand its crown of branches wider and raise its leading shoot higher, than a forest-grown one, since it has no physical limitations of available space and sunlight. It should therefore assume the perfect shape peculiar to its kind and this may prove a valuable indication of what other trees of the same kind can achieve when grown for timber or shelter on a similar site. In practice, the rate of growth, ultimate size and life-span of each specimen tree will be restricted by the physical factors and hazards to which all trees are subject.

To achieve its maximum size and grace of form, the tree must root in a deep fertile soil, well-drained but with a water supply adequate at all seasons. It must grow in a favourably mild climate with no unseasonable frosts and escape damage by weeds, rabbits and other sharp-toothed beasts, insects and the fungi that cause disease. Even then its tall crown remains liable, when it has outgrown surrounding shelter, to be distorted and blown sideways by strong prevailing winds.

A specimen tree that grows in this fortunate way is indeed sure to be a thing of beauty and a joy, if not forever, at least for a life span of possibly 200 years. It will have a symmetry that is denied to its fellows growing in crowded plantations for each bud will be free to expand in the direction that provides most light. The branch pattern will therefore reflect the bud pattern all round the trunk and such a tree is described in simple terms as 'perfectly balanced'. Because no browsing cattle, sheep or deer are present, this decorative specimen will be able to expand its lower branches sideways to their fullest extent, for nothing will bite or cut them back. It will therefore merit the description of being 'fully furnished' with foliage right down to ground level.

Such splendid trees are most likely to be found in privately-owned parks and arboreta, which are particularly frequent in the British Isles. Alan Mitchell, in the Forestry Commission publication *Conifers in the British Isles*, lists over 500 that he has personally visited and explored, recording the heights and girths of the outstanding trees in each. Records of the private estates on which these trees stand show how each was carefully tended by a diligent forester or gardener to give it a good start in life. Naturally they were planted near the mansion on the best available land.

More often than not, however, the arboriculturist today is required to grow trees *in a restricted space* where the surroundings do not allow the free growth of any large tree to its normal size. Well-known circumstances are the small garden, the highway verge and the courtyard or shopping centre where private residents or public planners demand trees but welcome them only if they can be kept in their proper place!

There are two basic solutions to this problem. You can either choose a tree that is inherently limited in its ultimate size, or you can choose a tree that *could* grow bigger than your available space and then restrain it by pruning. In practice the two methods are often combined by using a tree of a fairly vigorous kind, though not one of the forest giants, and trimming it to only a moderate degree. The drawback in using an inherently small tree is that it may also be slow-growing while the owners of the property always want early results.

Choosing, Planting and Caring for Ornamental Trees

The ideal but so far undiscovered tree for street or garden planting would grow quickly to a foreseen size and then stop! It would have pretty foliage, bright green in spring and vivid orange in the autumn, or alternatively be evergreen. Its attractive flowers in early spring would be followed by brilliant berries that would attract birds but not small boys, as the boys would stand in the roadway and create risks by throwing sticks to bring the fruit down. Alternatively it might have no fruits at all; this actually happens with sterile strains of cherries.

The closest approach to this desirable tree is usually found in temperate climates to be one of the rose-tribe trees in the family Rosaceae. Most are unimportant in the forest, where few grow large enough to yield commercial timbers. Hence in a garden or street location little pruning need be done. There are a large number of genera, most with many species and some with a quite bewildering range of varieties to choose from. All are easily increased by grafting. The outstanding genus is *Prunus*, which includes all the delightful ornamental cherries, many being of Japanese origin, and also plums, peaches and almonds. Decorative species and strains of crab-apples, some with handsome flowers, others with crimson foliage and all with attractive fruits, are found in the genus *Malus*. The large genus *Sorbus* contributes the widely planted mountain ash or rowan tree, *S. aucuparia*;

the lovely whitebeam, *S. aria*; and the pretty feathery-foliaged service tree, *S. domestica*.

The full range of 'well-behaved' trees of medium size includes the golden-blossomed laburnums, which are species and hybrids in the genus *Laburnum* of the sweet pea family or Leguminosae. For a bolder display the horse chestnuts or buckeyes, of the genus *Aesculus* in the family Hippocastanaceae, have no rivals in temperate climates. In the tropics the jacarandas, *Jacaranda acutifolia*, give a marvellous show of deep purplish-blue blossoms over feathery foliage.

People who have to plant on restricted sites usually demand trees between two and five metres (six to fifteen feet) tall at planting time. There are sound reasons for this. First, such trees give quick value for money. Next, they have survived the early perils of life which might endanger seedlings or small transplants used on the same sites. Third, they are large and robust enough to stand staking to hold them erect. Finally, a large tree that has clearly cost money and effort is less likely to be damaged by vandals than a smaller one placed more casually; even so, it will need in most places open to the public a stout wire-mesh tree guard.

Such trees are relatively costly to raise. But as we have seen, this is of little consequence in relation to each project as a whole – whether it be a highway, a courtyard surrounded by high-value shops or offices or a cherished private garden. In each of these places the total sum laid out by any individual on trees will be small though they will give pleasure to a great many.

Trees of the desired upright character, known as *standards*, are raised in one of two ways. For many kinds, particularly selected varieties of cherries and similar rose-tribe flowering trees, a stock of some common but tough and hardy species is grown to the required size and then, a year or two before the tree is needed, a scion of the required variety is grafted on to the tall, upright stem. Other trees are grown from seeds or cuttings 'on their own roots' in large country nurseries that allow adequate expansion of both crown and root system.

Trees of these dimensions can be safely transported from the nursery to the planting site over a period of days or even weeks in suitable cold, moist weather provided their roots are protected against drying out. The traditional way of doing this is to enclose the root ball within straw or peat, and to bind it up with hessian or sacking. Plastic sheeting or bags which are impervious to water are widely used today instead. Most broadleaved trees show surprising resistance to disturbance provided it occurs during a resting season when they are transpiring little water. This is the cold winter in temperate zones but precedes the onset of the rains in tropical countries.

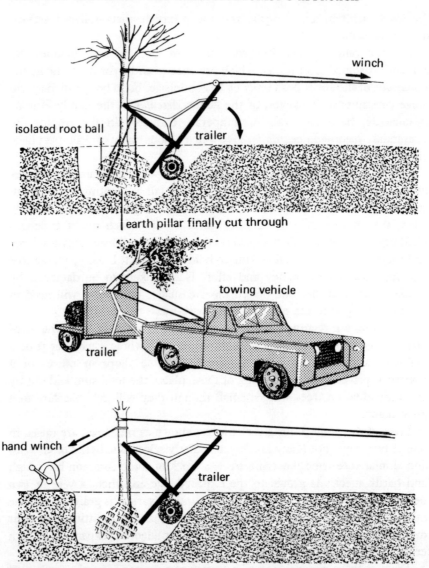

Figure 17   Moving a semi-mature tree. *Top*, the tree, with root ball isolated all round, is drawn on to a trailer by a winch on the towing vehicle. *Centre*, the tree can now be transported any distance by road, with root ball, bound in hessian, intact. *Foot*, at the new site, the tree is lowered into a prepared hole, then drawn upright and staked.

Conifers, in contrast, can only tolerate a minor degree of disturbance and for a more limited time. It is not a practical proposition to transplant them once they have grown more than a few metres high unless a large mass of earth can be taken with them, and the whole parcel, tree plus earth ball, put into its new position right away.

As long ago as the early 1800s ambitious planters started to move large well-established broadleaved trees up to ten metres tall complete with large, heavy roots and associated soil. This was done to give immediate effect to the landscape plans of wealthy landowners. The equipment used was a very strong trolley equipped with winches to raise the tree, usually in an upright position, clear of the ground. A gang of strong labourers was needed to dig its root ball free first and also to excavate the new hole to receive it. A team of sturdy horses gave motive power for transport.

Nowadays all this has been mechanized. The simplest machine excavates a cone of earth around the roots of the tree, using a giant semi-circular power spade. The tree is then tilted horizontally on to a trailer which can be towed along highways for any distance to the new planting site. Here a new cone-shaped hole is excavated, and the tree is lowered from the trailer to fit into it, made firm and if necessary staked and guyed.

A practical problem here is getting suitable open-grown specimens. Owners are reluctant to part with prominent ones while those taken from forests tend to have restricted crowns and diffuse root systems. The ideal is to raise them in an extensive nursery, but this takes time and costs money.

Planting sites on which arboriculturists have to work are often beset by physical restrictions. Some of these snags stand above ground and are obvious to the eye. For example trees even after they have grown tall must stand clear of buildings and overhead wires and must not obstruct views from windows or the sight of car drivers. Less obvious restraints lie underground in the shape of sewers, pipes for water and gas supplies, electric cables and rock-hard foundations for buildings. On clay soils those trees such as poplars that transpire large amounts of water in dry summers must be set well clear of buildings because they intensify the movement of the soft earth caused by shrinkage as it dries, and may cause the downfall of whole buildings. In practice every tree must be planned for its site.

Pruning

Slow-growing trees and those like Lombardy poplars and certain cypresses with narrow crowns may never need pruning. But others have to be restrained within set limits of height and branch spread by cutting back every few years. Sometimes root pruning is also necessary.

The old, primitive and ugly way of doing this was to 'lop and top' large branches and the main trunk, leaving an ugly tree that always remains unsightly. The sprouts that sprang out vigorously from around the cut surfaces never look natural. Modern pruning methods remove a careful selection of smaller branches well out amid the crown, holding the tree within limits without wrecking the natural symmetry and delicate tracery of limbs and twigs. There are books about pruning shrubs and trees for amateurs.

Tree Surgery

Tree surgery is a highly specialized art directed at prolonging the effective and rewarding life of valuable specimen trees that are constantly in view. It is far too costly to be worth practising anywhere else. Its typical 'operation' is the arrest of decay caused by a fungus attacking the heartwood of a standing tree, as described in Chapter One. This is followed by disinfection to prevent a fresh attack and some form of strengthening of the weakened trunk and branches to enable them to resist strains despite the loss of solid woody substance.

A competent tree surgeon will first diagnose the extent and character of decay in the affected tree before deciding whether it is worth saving at any acceptable cost. If so, he will excavate the pockets of rot that have developed, removing all unsound and affected timber. If necessary, he will provide drainage channels to keep the cavity dry. Next he will treat the whole surface of exposed wood with a disinfectant, usually a tar-based substance such as creosote, so that the last threads of the fungus are killed and re-invasion by air-borne spores is halted. He may then fill in the cavity with a plastic foam or a mixture of sawdust and bitumen or even a concrete mix, depending on circumstances. Finally he will cover over the surface with a neutral-coloured waterproof paint. If all goes well the *callus* tissues living on healthy wood around the edges of the former hole may gradually grow out over the new surface, and hide the repair work almost completely below new bark and sapwood. This will ensure a further lease of life for a tree that would otherwise die on its feet or else suffer breakages in its crown of branches.

Other treatments involve the bracing of weak limbs to stronger limbs or to a sturdy main trunk, using strong wire cables, and the rejuvenation of failing specimens by giving their roots massive doses of chemical fertilizers, applied through holes dug at intervals in the ground wherever the tree's roots are found to range. Such treatments are often combined with skilful pruning to lessen the weight of the crown or to remove ailing limbs completely. Tree surgery may often prevent a hazard developing to neighbour-ing property or passers-by.

The cost of all this can be weighed against the amenity that the safe-guarded specimen tree may offer over the longer span of years that it will, in all probability, survive. This is a unique value for if a mature tree falls it will never be possible to replace it within the lifetime of one single owner. It may accordingly be rated very high, especially if it ornaments a well-loved home.

This brings us round to the key belief that prompts all the activities of arboriculturists, namely that a tree has aesthetic qualities that cannot be assessed in the hard cash transactions of the market place. It enriches life for all who behold it and sit and dream in its shade.

Chapter 16

Trees and Agriculture

THE relationships between man the farmer cultivating crops and tending livestock, and man the forester looking after trees as the source of timber for his industries and fuel for his fire vary markedly from place to place and from one period of time to another.

The same individual often plays both parts. In Scandinavia and New England, for example, the traditional story-book farmer-forester grows grain through the summer and cuts logs through the winter. His property, owned outright, is divided according to the quality of the land into farm land and wood-lot. On the former he raises enough cattle and sheep to meet the immediate needs of his family, for milk, meat, leather and wool, plus a surplus for exports to local markets to get cash. From the wood-lot he wins firewood, timber for building and repairs on home and farm, and again a surplus for cash trade with a timber merchant. The system is self-perpetuating and there may be a balance between land under crops and animals, and land under trees, that persists for centuries. Plates 26, 27.

Freehold ownership of farm and forest combined is, however, unusual over the world as a whole. It is important to recognize this because it is fundamental to any understanding of local relationships between forestry and agriculture, that is, between trees, crops and stock. Human civilization is basically a matter of group co-operation and development and even the near-independent Scandinavian farmer or New England settler would be found on examination to have close links with a community through church and village council. Over great areas of the globe the concern of the community runs much deeper than this. The land itself is held to belong not to individuals but to the community *per se*. This belief reaches its modern climax under Communist ideologies in which the all-powerful state is the sole landowner.

Communal Claims on the Forests

Under less extreme political regimes the theory of land tenure is that the ground belongs to an identifiable local group which may be a tribe or simply the accredited residents of a particular parish. It is easy to see how this viewpoint arose. When all men were hunter-gatherers, like the Australian aborigines today, it was vital for each group to own territory. The area over which a tribe hunted game and gathered fruits was defined by tradition and landmarks, and defended against intruders by warfare. One outcome of this is that even today large expanses of tropical forests with immense value as timber may belong in legal theory to some primitive poverty-stricken tribe. Quite unable to develop its wealth of wood these people may gain a bare living from hunting, trapping, fishing and gathering fruits and nuts. In this harsh world they generally fall victims to some form of exploitation even though it takes the respectable shape of transferring the forest to the state!

When agriculture developed it was a group procedure and the cultivators naturally claimed territories in just the same way as the hunter-gatherers. Even when they were derived from the same ancestral stock the cultivators formed themselves into separate tribes from the hunter-gatherers, and usually pushed them out into the wilderness. In every encounter the farmers eventually won because they were better fed, better equipped, bred quicker and could sustain a larger population on any given area of land. This conflict, begun in the Stone Age, has not yet been concluded in many of the remoter forested regions of the world.

In forested regions most early farmers developed systems of shifting cultivation which have already been outlined in Chapter Five. It became customary to work on a cycle within a defined area of forest. In this way the group might return to the patch that they had first cleared and tilled after allowing it an interval of twenty years or more to regain its lost fertility. This meant that they did not have to trespass on the lands of any neighbouring group and hence they could live peacefully among their neighbours. Under such systems, which are still widespread in tropical Asia and Africa and occurred in the past in Europe and the Americas too, no one individual has any lasting claim to any piece of land. The head of each family has an immediate entitlement to a patch in the communal clearing and a stake in the surrounding forest which his group is entitled, by established custom, to clear on the rotating basis.

Under shifting cultivation the forest is complementary to the communal farm. When the farmers need poles for fencing or house building or firewood, they turn to the forest that surrounds their clearings and claim such produce by traditional right. But trespassers from other group areas are not welcomed any more than they would be allowed to take part in the cultivation of the group's own grain plot.

A development from complete communal ownership is widespread in central Europe and also in many parts of Asia where 'fixed' farming has replaced shifting cultivation. In a typical Swiss commune, for example, the forests remain under joint public ownership. Each member of the commune has the right to cut timber and firewood within set limits, or to share in the profits of the woods if they are managed as one unit. But he does not own any forest land or growing timber directly; he only acquires possession of wood when he cuts it within his set quota. By contrast, his farm is his own.

Most farming communities own cattle, sheep and horses, and possibly goats, donkeys and camels too, all of which need pasture. In many rural societies there is a village herd, or herds, comprised of beasts owned by various families, which is looked after by a communal cowherd or shepherd. Its grazing ground is naturally the communally-owned waste land, either mountain, waste or woodland. Wherever forests are involved they suffer because the livestock destroy seedlings by grazing and browsing and so prevent the replacement of the older trees by younger successors. Group grazing is the worst enemy of the forest. It has worked havoc with the forests of the Mediterranean region and many countries in North Africa and the Middle East, where goats have proved particularly destructive. In Britain the joint-grazing or common-right pasture procedures found on the Welsh hills, the Pennine uplands of northern England and the crofting counties of north and west Scotland have destroyed all tree cover over vast areas. Sheep are the main culprits here.

Today the best organized group grazings in the British Isles are those of the New Forest, which began as custom and are now stabilized by local laws. Common rights belong to defined farms in and around the Forest and the owners can *depasture* cattle and ponies on its open wastes. As a result these unfenced areas are largely treeless, though woods can and do survive in a few favoured places. By contrast timber crops flourish in the fenced-off enclosures under modern management.

Allied to these grazing rights, called *common of pasture*, certain commoners can claim other necessities from the Forest. *Common of estovers* (Norman French *estover* – to stoke a fire or stove) gives them firewood. Alternatively they can cut turves under *common of turbary*. They may dig fertile clay for their farms by *common of marl*, cut bracken for bedding stock and rushes for thatching houses, barns or corn ricks. In the exercise of these rights they can and do destroy seedling trees, checking the re-establishment of the woods after felling. On other commons, though not nowadays in the New Forest, right-holders can claim timber as *housebote* for building and repairing houses and barns, *fencebote* or *haybote* for making and patching fences, *ploughbote* for constructing and repairing ploughs or other tools. *Firebote* is the right to take firewood. The Middle English word *bote* here means 'privilege' or 'advantage'. It survives in modern English in the expression, 'to boot'.

Such practices, preserved on rather a large scale in the Royal New Forest, were repeated on a small scale in most parishes or manors throughout lowland England and less tidily in the English uplands, Scotland, Ireland and Wales. Each village had its jointly-worked agricultural land and its communally-owned woodland and open grassland. The stake of each manor in forests was neatly recorded by William the Conqueror in his masterly taxation roll, the *Domesday Book*, circa 1086 AD. The woodland of each manor was measured by the number of swine that it could support. These animals fed on the acorns and beech nuts that fell from the branches in autumn.

Alas, communal herding, swine keeping and timber cutting made dire inroads into the woods of Britain, once fairly evenly spread across the land. Gradually but inevitably they became treeless wastes, still grazed by sheep and cattle but yielding no timber and sheltering no deer.

Landowners Controlling Fields and Forests

As the social structure of European nations evolved during the Middle Ages, individual landowners became increasingly important as arbiters of land use. Similar devolvement of control from the community to an individual who directed the work of others occurred in Eastern countries also, but it had no place in the individualist philosophy of the new settlements of North America and Australasia.

The shift from communal to personal control of the land and all that goes with it is best studied in England where the Norman Conquest of 1066 introduced an alien aristocracy. The socio-economic structure of English rural life, at least in the lowlands, was ideally suited to a take-over by foreign adventurers. All the land was neatly parcelled into manors, which typically held so much tilled ground, so much grazing land and so much woodland spread around a village with its parish church. These units were survivals of the group settlement unit of the Anglian and Saxon invasions some 500 years earlier and often bore the name of the leader of each group. As an instance, Edlingham in Northumberland is named for a certain Edla or Edlin who led his clan, the Anglian Edlings, from either southern Denmark or northern Germany to make their new homestead or 'ham' in a fresh land.

Each Anglo-Saxon manor was controlled by its lord or thane but he was limited in his actions by the weight of traditional practices, being little more than the 'first among equals'. The boundaries between woodland and farm, for example, became fixed through centuries of practical usage, with the trees relegated to the poorer land and the crops, naturally enough, grown on the better soil.

The feudal system brought in by William changed all this at a single stroke. Claiming the whole country by right of conquest, he parcelled the manors out among his Norman followers in return for an annual tax or *feu* and the liability to support him in war. Each lesser landowner owed allegiance to a greater baron, earl or duke, who in turn supported – except in times of rebellion or disorder – the ruling king.

The effect on land use was gradual but fundamental. Title to the land had passed from communities to individuals. With the land went all the timber, for each tree was regarded in law as a 'fixed asset'. Yet the farming and woodcutting continued with little change. Life had to go on and the new lord of the manor had to continue the old system even if only to raise the rent due to the king.

Changes came gradually, through the *enclosure movement*, which did not reach its peak until the eighteenth century, that is, seven hundred years after the Conquest. This process draws its name from the fact that early crop-growing was carried out on open, unfenced fields, from which farm animals were excluded either by herding or some temporary barrier. It was far more efficient to make *permanent* enclosures using either stone walls or else fixed hedges. This implied a permanent allocation of each enclosed field to an owner or to a tenant farmer. English landlords usually preferred tenancy arrangements, which enabled them to keep a permanent stake in their property, rather than to sell land outright to farmers.

In a characteristic manor enclosure of the eighteenth century, over half the land – say, 70% – would be apportioned between about seven substantial tenant farmers who undertook to pay annual cash rents to the landowner. The landowner would retain 10% of the very best land as his own farm, worked by himself or his bailiff. The remaining 20%, comprising the poorest land, or that least suited to sustained agriculture, would be managed as the landowner's woodland.

In this neat subdivision nothing has been left under communal ownership and that was in fact a common outcome. Locally commons were preserved as part grazing land, part woodland, to meet the needs of surviving peasant farmers. But over areas as large as whole counties all such common-right property vanished from the map. The displaced peasantry became hired labourers on the farms or in the landlord's forest. They lived in cottages *tied* to the land they worked with little prospect of movement or advancement. A man who changed jobs without approval lost his house.

The English landowners of this great enclosure period were enthusiastic tree planters and they found a way of linking timber growing to farming at low cost for high eventual profit. They controlled the enclosures, although the farmers carried them out. A common requirement was that each farmer in addition to establishing a sound hedge of hawthorn, *Crataegus monogyna*, must plant along it at regular intervals young trees of oak, ash, sycamore or elm. The landlord provided the trees but they remained his property. They occupied land for which the farmer paid rent but in return his crops and livestock gained those benefits that will be described presently. As the landlord was in a monopoly position, intending farmers had to accept his terms or else get no land. When the timber matured perhaps a hundred years after planting, the then landlord kept all the proceeds. As a rule he provided fresh young trees as replacements for those felled and the farmer of the day had to accept these like his predecessor. He could not opt out of tree growing.

The landscape values that resulted were superb. Growing on fertile land, regularly cultivated and enriched by the dung of farm beasts, in full exposure to sunlight, the hedgerow trees grew quickly to a majesty seldom attained by others of their kind amidst the competition of the forest. The placement of these specimens along the neat hedges that bounded fields of fairly constant size, but with varied outlines adapted to the rise and fall of the land between streams and hillocks, was ideal.

A succession of gifted landscape painters, among whom the most famous was Constable (1776–1837) found inspiration from the unrivalled play of sunshine on the tall towers of foliage broken by varied shadows and matched by an ever-changing pageant of moving clouds.

But all this glory was linked to agricultural procedures and a system of land-holding that have undergone radical change during the present century. The replacement of horses and small agricultural machines by tractors and larger equipment has meant that the small field of five hectares or so has become uneconomic. An expanse of twenty hectares is a more satisfactory unit and thus four fields have often been thrown into one with the resultant loss of half the hedges. The associated hedgerow trees are naturally felled at the same time.

Under pressure of taxation, particularly capital transfer taxes paid on the death of each landowner, the great estates have been gradually but steadily broken up. Whereas in 1900 around 80% of the farms belonged to land-lords, less than 50% do so today. The new owners are the farmers them-selves, formerly tenants but now in full control of the land. Most of them see few advantages in the retention of hedgerow trees and are apt to fell and sell them as soon as they can to help meet the purchase price of their farms.

In some counties, notably the eastern ones of Lincolnshire, Norfolk and Suffolk, they have been allowed to do so, and the outcome is an almost treeless countryside like an American prairie. Elsewhere active county councils have clamped legal Tree Preservation Orders on the hedgerow trees, particularly in Kent and Buckinghamshire, in a heroic effort to preserve precious regional landscapes.

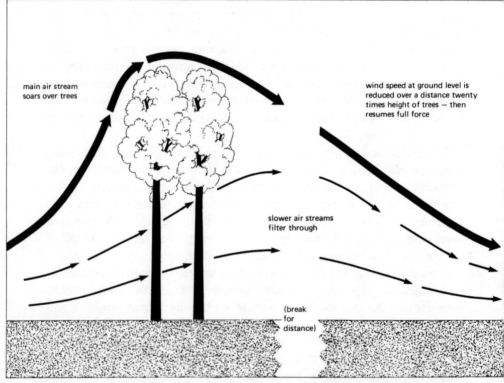

main air stream
soars over trees

wind speed at ground level is
reduced over a distance twenty
times height of trees — then
resumes full force

slower air streams
filter through

(break
for
distance)

Figure 18 How shelterbelts work. When an airstream strikes a belt of trees, its main current is diverted upwards. A slower current filters through trees and prevents downward eddies. On flat land, wind speeds are reduced, at ground level, for a distance twenty times the tree height.

Shelterbelts

The value or otherwise of trees to farming rests so much on local climates and systems of husbandry that it is difficult to say just where a pattern of tree shelter is justified or else unnecessary. Most of the crops man cultivates, such as wheat or sugar beet, are natives of open steppes, prairies or sea-shores. They can withstand high degrees of exposure to sunlight and fierce winds. In selecting and breeding strains for cultivation man has naturally favoured varieties that need little shelter for good growth.

Nevertheless, higher yields of grain and root crops are in practice secured by giving protection from drying winds. The increase may be of the order of 20% as compared with unsheltered crops. The physiological explanation of this is probably that the crop plants grow under lower transpiration stress and use less energy in replacing water needlessly lost. They are also better placed to resist drought.

Similar environmental considerations affect livestock. Ideally a cow should live in an air-conditioned stall, never too hot nor too cold. If it is required to live on an exposed pasture its surroundings will be too cold for it during the winter and to stay alive it must divert much of its total intake of food to maintaining its body heat. This means slower rates of growth for young stock, a slower rate of fattening for beef beasts and a lower yield of milk from cows. Cattlemen overcome these drawbacks in many regions by housing the animals through the winter and carting food to them. There is an obvious economic advantage in leaving them out of doors to find their own fodder. Tree shelter can often secure longer periods of outdoor grazing. It should be remembered here that cattle are originally woodland beasts, not creatures of open plains.

A less obvious loss to cattle output arises through overheating in summer. Here the need is to hold body temperature down to the most efficient level and cattle naturally seek out the shade of trees or even buildings.

Sheep husbandry in upland regions with severe snowy winters benefits from tree shelter in two ways. In or beside woodland there are nearly always patches of ground that escape being covered by snow. There the sheep can find sustenance from the sparse herbage at times when all the grass on open ground is deeply buried under snow. Second, the wind slowed down by the tree cover sheds its load of snow unevenly. Snow-free or lightly covered patches of ground remain. Here, even during the worst blizzards the sheep can huddle and survive whilst their unfortunate fellows out on open ground perish through exposure.

Over lowland Britain the needs of both cattle and crops for shelter have been met over the past two centuries by the marvellous interlinked pattern of hedges which make each field, close to ground level, a pool of slowly-moving air. Scattered hedgerow trees contribute further shelter from wind, sun and snow alike. In the uplands, particularly in the Scottish Highlands, woods of scrubby birch and oak, useless for timber, provide winter refuges for sheep flocks. They enable the sheep to be kept on much larger areas of otherwise exposed hill land, adjacent to the scrub woods.

Other shelterbelts are deliberately planted. This is only done on a modest scale in the British Isles but on both the American prairies and the Russian steppes vast schemes have been put into operation. The physical laws governing their effectiveness have been closely examined and are now well understood. If a current of air, that is, a wind strikes a solid barrier rising above ground level, it generates fierce eddies but soon resumes its accustomed speed. But if it meets a *permeable* barrier, such as a screen of trees, a curious thing happens. The lower zone of the air current divides, in effect, into two streams. One stream accelerates and rises over the top of the barrier. The other stream remains near the ground, filters through the barrier and is slowed down by friction to a small proportion, possibly only one-fifth, of the prevailing wind speed. This gives a moving 'cushion' of slow-moving air that increases in speed only slowly, through interaction with the faster-moving current passing above it. On flat land with a wind blowing at right angles to the barrier, an appreciable slowing down of the air at ground level can be measured over a distance to leeward equal to twenty times the height of the barrier.

In practical terms this means that a screen of trees 20 metres tall will give effective shelter over a distance of 400 metres in its lee. In Imperial measures these dimensions approximate to 66 feet and 440 yards, or roughly a quarter of a mile. The best width for the shelterbelt is only 20 metres (or 66 feet) so that little land need be taken out of agricultural production to support the trees. Ideally, a network of belts intersecting in two directions needs 10% of the available area. If as experiments show it results in an increase of output of some 20% every year, it proves an excellent investment.

Nevertheless, the theoretical gain to farm production from shelterbelts is seldom considered enough, on its own, to justify their establishment. The investment of land and capital is commonly justified by associated advantages. Wherever they occur these tree belts provide good roosting, nesting or hiding places for game. Landowners and farmers cheerfully give up land to grow strips of woodlands that will harbour pheasants, wood pigeons, roe deer, hares or rabbits, even though these animals will eat a fair share of their crops! The return, of course, comes in the form of sport. The shooting may either be enjoyed by the occupier or let at a high rent. In England, in fact, the conventional method of pheasant shooting demands the presence of long high belts over which the birds, flushed out by the beaters, must fly. This obliges them to present difficult high targets to the sportsmen positioned below.

In other situations shelterbelts are planted for their landscape value. They either look good themselves, or else screen a less desirable feature such as a factory or a quarry. In Russia, a new, immense shelterbelt system across the steppes is held to have a strategic defence value. Invaders who could advance unchecked across open treeless plains can be resisted by defenders concealed and sheltered below the bands of trees. In a land that has known repeated invasions from the horse-borne Huns led by Attila to the German tanks of the 1939–45 war, this makes sound sense.

Scottish practice has been to use shelterbelts to push the limits of farming higher into the hills. A well-sited protective screen placed all round a sloping field may give it a local climate many degrees warmer than the neighbouring exposed uplands. Cultivated pastures can then replace poor heather and rough grasses.

Various trees are chosen for shelterbelt planting, in the light of local experience of their hardihood. Evergreens have the great advantage of providing year-round shelter, unbroken by any leafless period. On the western uplands of the British Isles, exposed to violent salt-laden winds off the Atlantic Ocean, the most satisfactory tree is the Sitka spruce, *Picea sitchensis*, from Alaska and British Columbia. In the drier east hardy pines such as the rugged Austrian pine, *Pinus nigra* variety *nigra*, are preferred. In tropical countries like Rhodesia the most effective year-round shelter is provided by quick-growing *Eucalyptus* trees introduced from Australia. In South Africa the Californian Monterey pine, *Pinus radiata*, has proved well adapted to the local climate.

Farmstead Shelter

Trees make the most efficient practical year-round screen for farm houses and their associated barns, cowsheds, stables and pigsties. Here the farmer, his family and his staff must move continually, whatever the weather, to tend their livestock, even though in winter the beasts may be housed indoors. In the exposed uplands of England, Scotland and Wales there is a well-established tradition of planting European sycamore, *Acer pseudoplatanus*, as the hardiest and most wind-resistant shelter tree. Its vigorous growth in such places is largely due to the abundance of nutritious dung from the farm livestock to which it responds more rapidly than most species. Farther south on the chalk downs, beech, *Fagus sylvatica*, plays a similar role.

The 'crown' of trees over each farmstead proves effective even on a hilltop because there is plenty of space all round it through which diverted air currents can flow. The trees, even when leafless in winter, create a local

cushion of slow-moving air over the buildings which provide an impermeable barrier below them. Plate 62.

In Kent, southeast England, single lines of trees are planted around hop
gardens in order to protect a crop that is peculiarly vulnerable to wind. The
hop is a climbing plant that has to be trained up thin strands of twine,
supported by overhead wires, to a height of some three metres. If one gale
blows unchecked through this soft-stemmed crop it will be irretrievably
damaged. Single rows of a quick-growing tree, usually a poplar, *Populus*, are
therefore established along the exposed sides of the gardens, topped at a
height of about four metres, and then pruned to maintain their size and
shape. The hop fruits that develop along the climbers are used to flavour
beer and in consequence command high prices that justify intensive shelter.
As hops are only a summer crop, broadleaved trees that lose their leaves in
winter prove adequate.

Yet another use of trees as agricultural shelter is found in the tropics,
where certain crops need shade from hot tropical sun. Suitable small trees
are therefore planted at intervals amid the crop, which benefits from their
dappled shade effect. They lessen water loss through transpiration and
reduce wind speeds. An example is cocoa, *Theobroma cacao*, itself borne on
a low tree which may be sheltered by kapok, *Ceiba pentandra*.

Chapter 17

Fruit and Nut Trees

THE harvesting of sweet juicy fruits and hard nutritious nuts for food is the oldest activity of man. He inherited it from his ape-like ancestors and for many thousands of years he did not elaborate it at all. Primitive tribes of food-gatherers still resort, as their forefathers have done, to groves of wild fruit or nut trees at the appropriate harvesting season. As a typical example certain Malaysian peoples visit stands of the tall durian tree, *Durio zibethinus*, which ripens a huge, strong-smelling but delicious pineapple-shaped fruit deep in the jungle. In Chile the Araucanian Indians have as their tribal property groves of the Chile pine or monkey puzzle tree, *Araucaria araucana*, a bizarre evergreen conifer that grows on the cold Andes and sheds remarkably large, nutritious seeds.

Trees bear seeds so abundantly, over repeated seasons, that this human harvest rarely has any harmful effect on any particular tree's spread or abundance. On the contrary, man's roving and untidy habits tend to favour the spreading of fruit and nut trees at the expense of those that bear other types of seeding structures. The odd cherry or apple tree arising from a discarded stone or pip is quite a common sight along the hedgerows. From the standpoint of the tree, man is just another agent, like a monkey or a squirrel, for the dispersal of its potential offspring.

Orchards

Collection from wild stands, even where some kind of ownership is claimed by a group of people, is obviously a chancy and unsatisfactory way of securing a food supply. So from the earliest times of agricultural development men began to cultivate fruitful trees in planned orchards. The word 'orchard', incidentally, is of Anglo-Saxon derivation and was originally *ort yeard*, meaning the yard or enclosure, safe from grazing animals, in which *worts* or *orts*, meaning roots or vegetables, were raised. Fruit trees needed protection too, especially in their younger stages, and somehow the name got transferred to their area of cultivation.

Orchard husbandry had become well established by biblical and classical times and has since developed into the most elaborate and scientific form of tree culture, requiring the most intensive care and highest investment of capital. Here only an outline can be given, and rather than digress over a surprisingly wide range of temperate and tropical crops, we will take as an example an apple orchard run commercially in the county of Kent in south-east England.

At one time orchards to supply local needs were a common feature of farms and county estates in most parts of Europe and North America. But the increasing elaboration of the fruit-growing industry led to the concentration of commercial establishments in a few regions favoured by high quality soils and warm climates. In England most fruit-growing is carried out in two zones with notably sunny summers, namely Kent and the Severn valley around Hereford in the west Midlands. In America the predominant position of California is well known.

Even within a favoured fruit growing centre such as Kent a careful choice is always made for a site for a new orchard. The land must be fertile with free-draining light soil, and preferably with a slope towards the south so that it benefits to the full from the sun's rays. Hollows and the bottoms of valleys are always avoided because experience shows that cold air, being denser than warm air, flows down into them on cold, clear, windless and cloudless nights. During spring or even early summer, the resulting localized frost can destroy tender shoots, flower buds and developing fruits, and ruin the crop.

Because of the long-term character of their crop the land must either be owned or held for a long term of years by the fruit growers. They will make a very large investment in it with a yield inevitably delayed for several years. Under conventional management the trees will be spaced about five metres apart in both directions. Closer spacings aiming at smaller fruiting trees but a higher overall yield from the same area of land are also adopted today. The gaps between the trees are usually, in Kent, kept under grass. This is grazed by sheep which provide an additional profit. Alternatively the soil may be cultivated, either overall or in strips. Ground vegetation is always controlled to allow free movement below the trees, and to ensure that trees, and not weeds, benefit from any fertilizers that may be applied.

Fruit trees are nearly always grafted individuals. The base of each one consists of a *stock* of a selected, known strain, chosen as the result of research to find the kind best suited to nourish the fruiting scion that actually bears the flowers and fruits.

The *scion* will belong to a variety chosen, from among scores of possible named cultivars, as being well suited to bear heavy crops of attractive apples in demand for the commercial market. Scion wood is drawn from mature or *adult* trees and is therefore ready to bear fruit within a few years of its grafting. It does not have to pass through a long *juvenile* phase, lasting several years, as the shoots of seedling apples normally do. The trees are usually raised by specialist nurserymen rather than by the orchardist himself. New kinds are deliberately bred by enterprising nurserymen or at research stations and the most promising of them are then propagated for general use.

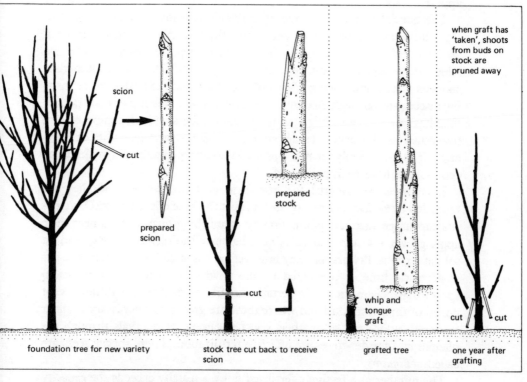

Figure 19   Fruit trees of desirable kinds are increased by grafting a living *scion* on to a *stock* of another, selected variety.

Once established the young trees require three to four years to develop to their fruit-bearing stage. After only one season of growth the orchardist starts the process of pruning that will persuade the branches to dispose themselves to the best advantage for fruit bearing. There are many pruning patterns but in a typical one the tree is encouraged to form a framework of sturdy branches that radiate outwards and upwards from its trunk. Side shoots that do not conform to this pattern are clipped off at an early stage with pruning shears or secateurs. The aim is to secure a basket-like structure that allows light and air to reach all parts of the tree's crown.

Apples, in common with a number of other fruit trees, do not bear flowers or fruits on their main branches but only on short shoots called *spurs*. The pruner controls the speed of growth of the main shoots by clipping them short and this promotes the formation of spurs situated some way back from the branch tips. Once formed these spurs elongate only slowly but in most years they develop flower buds. They must, of course, be left intact at each winter pruning. If they are removed no fruit will appear.

The normal annual life cycle of the apple tree involves an outburst of fresh leaves, accompanied by shoot growth, each April. About one week after the leaf-burst flower buds open and green sepals expand to reveal five white petals tinged with pink on their outer surface. Within these, numerous stamens extend and open golden anthers which make available to the visiting insects, that are attracted by the petals, an ample dusting of male pollen. Within these stamens again stands the central female pistil, composed of a five-celled basal ovary, a slender style and a receptive stigma at its tip. The apple fruit, technically termed a *pome*, will only ripen after the ovules in its central cells have been pollinated.

It is therefore essential for insects to visit the flowers and they are rewarded by nectar secreted by nectaries at the base of the petals. Orchardists encourage adequate pollination by establishing hives of bees near their apple groves – a step that costs nothing since the resulting honey can be sold at a profit. Pollination may however be hindered by cold, wet weather at a critical time or prevented by the unwise application of insecticidal sprays that poison the bees. Certain varieties of fruit trees will not accept pollen of their own kind and where these are grown it is necessary to plant scattered individuals of another, selected variety, at intervals through the plantation, in order to secure effective fertilization. These special trees are called *pollinators*.

The number of effectively fertilized flowers usually exceeds the capacity of the tree to sustain them all to the fruiting stage and a proportion are usually shed when the petals and stamens wither. The remainder develop and ripen steadily. The base of the flower, now united to and enclosing the ovary, swells and its tissues become firm and hard below a green skin. As growth slackens off when autumn approaches, the flesh softens and the juice, formerly acid, becomes sweet to the taste. At the same time the outer skin may change colour from green to red or yellow, or a blend of these colours with green or brown, depending on the variety concerned. Ample sunshine is needed to effect these changes of colour, texture and internal chemistry, and this explains the concentration of fruit growing in sunny districts with hot summers.

The crop is harvested at a stage judged right by experience rather than by any simple critical factor. The flesh of the fruit must be ready to mature to the tasty state that the buyer demands yet still be firm enough to stand handling on its way to the shops, possibly hundreds of miles away, and maybe to endure a long spell of storage.

The apple fruit itself is still a living organism that must breathe to remain sound. It cannot be safely stored like an inert dead object, but needs controlled conditions of temperature and ventilation. Varieties vary in the length of their commercial storage life, from a few weeks to several months. Technical aids to storage include refrigeration, artificial ventilation and carbon dioxide gas which inhibits the growth of fungi.

After the crop has been harvested, the orchardist prunes his trees during the ensuing winter, aiming as before to maintain an open framework of branches carrying numerous fruit-bearing side shoots or spurs. He also tends the ground beneath it, possibly cultivating strips, applying fertilizers or grazing a flock of sheep which keep the grass short and also contribute manure. The annual cycle of pruning, harvesting and tending is repeated over scores of years until with advancing age the trees cease to yield liberally. They are then felled and replaced with a fresh young plantation.

Despite all this care the yield of fruit is sure to fluctuate from one year to another. This is simply a continuation of what goes on among wild apple trees, where it is seldom noticed. Variations range from the abundance of a bumper crop to total failure. This is a serious economic drawback for the fruit grower, for in a year of failure he gets no income and in a bumper year only a small one because prices fall. Only an 'average' year ensures both a fair quantity to market and a fair price.

The rhythm of light and heavy cropping depends largely on seasonal weather. During a good, hot, sunny summer a tree builds up large reserves of carbohydrates. Some are used to nourish the fruits of the current year but most are retained to promote abundant flower bud formation in the *year following*. If everything else proves favourable a heavy crop results but the nutrition of this at the fruit-ripening stage exhausts the tree's reserves for the succeeding year – the third in this cycle. Hence a pattern of normality, abundance and scarcity results, which is apt to continue for a long span of years. It may however be disrupted by poor summers or by exceptional late spring frosts that halt the progress of promising crops. Hence long-term prophesies are never reliable!

Protecting the Crop

Orchard fruits and nut crops differ from timber trees in giving substantial cash yields in most though not all successive years. Because of this speedy and regular return it is possible in economic terms to spend large sums of money annually to stop losses from insect attacks or fungal diseases. The timber grower, by contrast, cannot afford this because he would incur repeated annual outlays for long-deferred financial returns.

In fruit-growing, protection usually takes the form of spraying the crop at a critical stage of its growth to halt the spread of either a harmful insect or a serious fungal disease. The presence of an abundant crop of fruit provides an exceptionally favourable opportunity for such organisms to multiply and spread. Given a favourable season the insects may multiply far more rapidly than the predators, such as parasitic and predatory insects and insectivorous birds, that normally control them. Likewise damp, mild weather may favour an abnormal outbreak of a fungal disease that is normally a minor trouble.

The formulation and application of sprays has become an elaborate scientific business. The chemicals used nowadays are so potent that only a minute amount of the *active ingredient* of each is needed to render a large surface of tree leaves and buds unsuitable and possibly toxic to the insect or fungus concerned. The problem of applying this small amount is overcome by diluting it in a larger volume of a *carrier* material, which in turn is dissolved in water and then sprayed. Alternatively a powder may be dispersed through the air of the orchard. A recent development is *ultra-low-volume spraying*, in which the chemical is rendered into an aerosol form and spread by a small powered atomizer; this obviates the handling, transport and spraying of large volumes of water.

Whatever method is used, the fruit-grower takes out his equipment each growing season and systematically covers the whole of his crop to render it resistant to all foreseen forms of attack. A problem can arise in the form of *toxic residues*, which are the remains of the chemical adhering to, say, the skin of an apple. They may persist there until the fruit is eventually harvested and eaten and so present a risk of poisoning to the purchaser. Many otherwise effective insecticides and fungicides cannot be applied to fruit crops because of this risk.

The ideal protective chemical is *non-persistent*. It should kill the insect or fungus against which it is designed and then disintegrate leaving no trace. In practice only a *persistent* or at least partially persistent chemical is both effective and economical. Many insects and fungi have stages in their life history that resist chemicals, and any substance that failed to remain toxic for several days, weeks or months would need repeated, costly applications to achieve results.

Varieties of Fruit Trees

Since fruit trees are propagated by grafting it is a simple matter to increase the numbers of any desired kind indefinitely and to do so quite rapidly. The actual characters of the apple fruit vary enormously. One of the wild ancestors of most cultivated kinds is the crab apple, *Malus pumila*, whose odd name is derived from the old Norse word *skrab*, meaning a scrubby tree. It bears spines on its twigs, though its cultivated descendants are thornless. Its yellow fruits are small, hard, round and bitterly acid in taste. They become just sweet enough to be eaten raw after maturing through the winter, but most are used, if at all, for making crab apple jelly. This is prepared by sweetening crab apple pulp with ample sugar. The jelly is eaten like jam or else used to enhance the piquant flavour of game or venison. Other kinds of crab apple are grown in gardens simply for the beauty of their flowers and fruits, one attractive example being the red Siberian crab, *Malus prunifolia*.

A third breed of hard, rather acid apples are those used for making cider, a refreshing alcoholic drink. It is produced by crushing the fruit mechanically and then squeezing out the juice, which ferments under the action of yeasts. A strong spirit can be obtained by distilling cider, and this is marketed in Normandy under the name of *Calvados*.

The bulk of the world's apple crops, however, falls into two groups, the 'cookers' and the dessert apples or 'eaters'. The cookers, usually green in colour, keep well for several months but are too sour for eating until cooked. Sugar is often added to sweeten them.

The eaters, which are more difficult to store, develop natural sugars as they ripen and become sweet enough to be eaten uncooked. A well-known example is the delicately flavoured Cox's Orange Pippin.

Decay of apples is the work of fungi like *Venturia chlorospora* which find their soft tissues an ideal medium for rapid growth. Infection is spread by myriads of microscopic spores which are released by inconspicuous sporophores on the surface of the rotten fruit. Apples are also attacked by weevils, which lay eggs in the soft tissues of developing fruit. The grubs that hatch out concentrate their feeding on the nutritious seeds but ruin much of the flesh in the process. After pupating they eventually emerge as adults through small round holes in the apple's skin.

Irrigated Orchards

The sunshine that is so important both for nourishing the fruit trees and ripening their crop falls most abundantly on regions with hot dry summers. But since their skies are cloudless at that time, such places then receive little or no rain. Rain is needed to maintain active growth and provide the moisture needed to fill out the succulent fruit. If water can be provided by man by planned irrigation it becomes possible and profitable to carry out fruit-growing in sun-drenched regions where natural summer rainfall is too low. Plate 33.

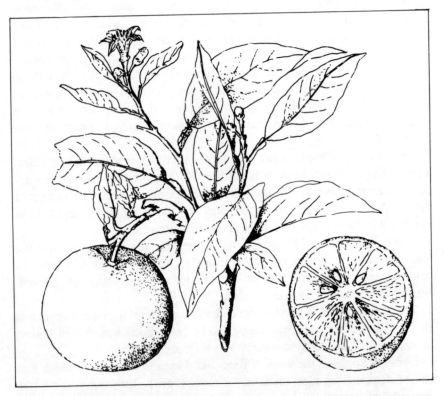

Figure 20   Foliage, flowers, fruits, and seeds of orange, *Citrus auriantiaca*, from an early French botanical illustration.

A large-scale enterprise of this kind has been developed in France in the valleys of the great River Rhone and its tributaries. These are fed all summer through by the melting glaciers and high level rainfall of the Alps, where they rise. They flow first west, then south through a region of

Mediterranean climate where hot sun shines all through the summer. The irrigation scheme involves the control of river flow by dams in the mountains, and these dams also provide a valuable source of hydro-electric power. As the rivers approach the hot plains part of their flow is diverted into huge *feeder channels* on one or both sides of the main stream. These feeders carry a large share of the available water parallel to the main river bed, at a convenient distance from it and at a slightly higher level.

At intervals along the course of each feeder channel, part of the water is directed through sluicegates to smaller feeder channels called *distributaries* that run at right angles to the main watercourses. These pass through the orchards, supplying the parched soil with the vital water that the trees need. Any excess, and the drainage water that arises during winter rains, run down to the main stream through a linked series of outlets. This drainage keeps the soil free of any accumulation of harmful salts.

Similar orchard irrigation schemes are found in California where water from the rainstorms and snowfields of the Rocky Mountain chain is harnessed to irrigate sun-drenched valleys. Others have been established in Israel using the flow of the River Jordan on its way towards the inland Dead Sea. Rhodesia has extensive orange groves watered by channels from a high dam in the Mazoe District, otherwise too arid for their growth.

Leading Fruit Crops

Apples are overall the world's major orchard crop owing to their varied character and adaptability to a wide range of climates. Grown all over Europe and North America they have also been promoted as commercial crops in South America, South Africa and New Zealand. The closely allied pears, which are domesticated forms of the wild species, *Pyrus communis*, are grown in the same regions on a lesser scale, and provide fruit for dessert eating, for cooking or for the fermentation of an alcoholic drink called *perry*.

The 'stone fruits' which belong to the genus *Prunus* in the same family, the Rosaceae, as the apples and pears, are distinguished by a single hard seed or 'stone' set at the heart of a sweet fleshy mass of soft pulp. They include the cherries, which are cultivated strains of the wild *Prunus avium*, and the many sorts of plums derived from the wild blackthorn or sloe tree, *P. spinosa*, and allied species. The same genus holds the luscious peach, *P. persica*, native to the Near East, which is now grown in most lands with a sufficiently warm climate. The almond, *P. amygdalus*, is remarkable in being a 'fruit' tree that is cultivated for its nuts. Below the tough leathery skin of the fruit comes a thin zone of unattractive pulp and then a hard pale brown stone with a pitted husk. This husk is cracked to release its tasty and nutritious kernel, the commercial almond, which is eaten raw or used as an ingredient of almond paste, or marzipan. Plate 32.

The citrus fruits, members of the genus *Citrus* in the family Rutaceae, are the leading orchard trees in sub-tropical regions. They include oranges, lemons, limes and grapefruits, along with such curiosities as the ugli, which lives up to its name. All are evergreen with lustrous dark green, shiny foliage and they bear pretty small white flowers with waxy petals united at their base to form a tube. Their fruits are encased within a tough green, yellow or orange skin which conserves moisture and proves an excellent protection against handling damage when they are exported, by the million, to distant markets in countries of temperate climate. Each juicy fruit is divided into segments and in the wild races and some cultivated varieties each segment holds one or more hard-shelled seeds or pips. Other varieties, particularly certain grapefruits, are sterile: they ripen large fruits but set no seeds. Plate 33.

Leading Nut Trees

Walnuts, of the genus *Juglans* in the family Juglandaceae, are the most highly prized of nut-yielding trees. Native to the Mediterranean zone, they were introduced by the Romans to countries north of the Alps. This accounts for their English name of 'wal-nut' – in dialect form also 'welsh-nut' – and their German name *Welchnuss*, which all mean 'foreign nut'. In more recent times they have been taken to the Americas, Australasia and South Africa, and there are large commercial groves in California as well as in southern Europe.

Walnuts, which are large, sturdy trees with a strong and valuable timber, bear their flowers in separate male and female catkins. The latter, after pollination, ripen curious green fruits resembling plums. These are sometimes plucked in their half-ripe stage to make pickled walnuts. As they ripen more fully, their green skin and soft pulp wither away. This reveals a hard-shelled nut holding a remarkable wrinkled kernel. The kernels are rich in fat and protein as well as being deliciously flavoured and are widely used in confectionery as well as for dessert. High-yielding varieties are grafted on stocks of the common species to increase output.

Hazel, *Corylus avellana*, which is a tall woody shrub rather than a real tree, provides abundant crops of small round cob nuts or oval filberts, according to the strain. These nuts ripen each autumn from tiny female catkins that have received pollen from the males in the spring. Hazel nuts are a popular ingredient of nut chocolate. The main crop is grown commercially in southern Europe and southwestern Asia, which enjoy favourable sunny summers.

Figure 21   Foliage and ripening fruit of walnut, *Juglens regia*, a leading orchard nut tree. Detail includes male flowers (*bottom left*); female flowers (*top left*) and ripe seed (shown also in cross-section). From the French botanical book, *Les Arbres Fruitiers*, by Duhamel de Monceau, 1835.

The coconut palm, *Cocos nucifera*, flourishes along the seashores of most tropical countries. The familiar large, hard, brown seed ripens within a much larger husk which is composed of pale brown fibres within an outer smooth, tough skin. This structure serves as a float that carries the seed on ocean currents for hundreds or even thousands of miles until it gets stranded on some sandbank where the seed can take root. Most tropical peoples who live near the sea or along rivers cultivate coconuts in small groves as a reliable, long-lasting food source.

There are also large commercial plantations that meet the needs of distant markets. Within its hard shell the coconut holds a small quantity of refreshing white liquid 'milk', and a greater weight of nutritious white 'flesh'. The main commercial use for this is in its dried form, called 'copra', which is an important source of vegetable oil used in margarine and other commodities based on vegetable oils.

Throughout the world there is an enormous range of other fruit and nut yielding trees, many of which are cultivated locally. The majority serve only regional markets.

Chapter 18

Trees for Timber:
The Forester's Profession

Foresters are men who control large areas of land carrying crops of trees intended for timber. Nowadays this is seldom the only object of management because, as described in Chapter Eight, the owners of forests and the administrators who lay down policy on a national level usually require some form of dual or multiple use for the land. But even where sport, scenery, water supply or soil conservation play a large part in the purpose of a particular forest, the timber output remains the central objective. Without the need for wood there would be no trees.

The term 'forester' includes both the university-trained scientist-executive who manages several scattered forests or perhaps one very large one, and also the men trained to technical college level who carry out the daily work in each forest. The former, who may work either for a private individual or more likely for the state as a 'Forest Officer' or 'Chief Forester', often has a hand in formulating national forest policies and works from an office located conveniently for visits to the forests for which he is responsible. The foresters who work for him usually live in or very near the woods they tend.

In national forests the staff structure naturally resembles that of the civil service of the country concerned; private owners have a less rigid system of ranks and spheres of control.

In both cases, like farmers, the foresters are responsible for the woods in their care at all times and these areas are immense by farming standards. A 'Chief Forester' may control 100 square kilometres (40 square miles) of woodland and the men he supervises around 20 square kilometres (eight square miles) each. These figures apply to intensively managed woods in developed countries. Far larger areas are involved in northern wildwoods or tropical jungles. Nevertheless a good forester cares for every sapling as if it were his own personal property. His major, continuing concern is of course safeguarding the forest from fire. He has to be on call at any hour since he alone knows the ground well enough to direct firefighting

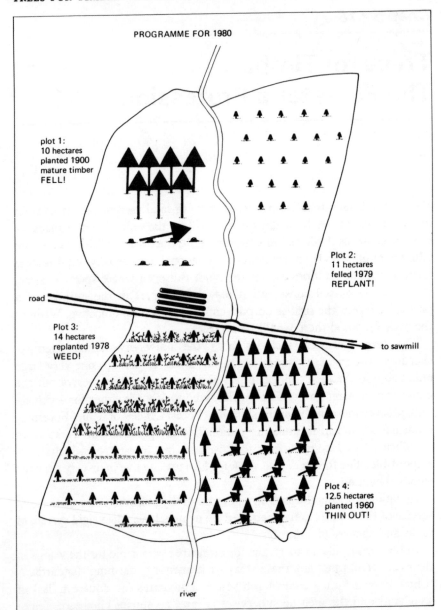

Figure 22 Management plan for a section of a forest. Each year an area of mature timber is felled, and an equivalent area replanted. Plantations of intermediate ages are weeded, or thinned out to yield small logs.

operations, however willing and well-equipped outside helpers may be.

Because trees live longer than men, foresters are trained to look after crops of all ages and control the output of timber so that a fresh supply is always coming forward for future generations. In the ideal situation, rarely found in practice, a young man trained in forestry is appointed to take over a well-balanced national forest or woodland estate holding due proportions of young, middle-aged and maturing trees. As the years go by he fells the mature trees for timber, gaining substantial monetary returns for the forest's owners. Meanwhile the middle-aged trees are maturing and our forester secures further income by thinning out each stand at the appropriate time. Their place in turn is taken by the youngest crops which grow in stature as the years roll by. These too need replenishment so our forester replants the land left vacant by the fellings of mature crops. This starts what is called a new *rotation*, being the age to which a crop is grown, e.g. a rotation of, say, 80 years.

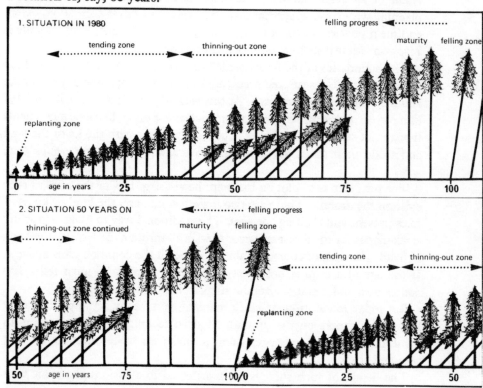

Figure 23 Conventional profiles of a forest, showing treatment of successive tree crops of differing sizes and ages, following a management plan, at two different times.

When at length our forester retires, all the land that carried maturing trees at the outset will have been worked over by the timber merchants and will now be carrying young crops instead. Similar changes will have occurred elsewhere but the forest as a whole will present the same balanced composition as it did, say, forty years earlier. A timber yield has been steadily harvested but the lost volume has been restored by equally steady regrowth.

Maps and Plans

In order to control the orderly progression, or *cycle*, of work through his woods, and in fact to know where he is going physically as well as metaphorically, the forester's first need is a map. In the better-developed countries the starting point is naturally a topographical map prepared by ground surveys, but in the wilder regions of the world it will more likely be the result of an aerial survey. Whatever the source, the forester starts his planning with a topographical map that shows his forest's situation, extent and main physical features such as hills, rivers and roads. A usual scale is 1:10,000, equivalent to about six inches to one mile.

The boundaries of the forest, which may consist of a single block of land or include smaller, scattered areas, are drawn on to this topographical map and the total area is calculated. At this stage the ground is usually divided into *compartments*, which are small management units, like a farmer's fields though not separated by fences. Their shapes vary with the lie of the land and so do their sizes, but a common average is 10 hectares, roughly 25 acres.

The next step is to plot on the map the *growing stock* of the trees as they exist on the ground. There are two main factors here, the kind or kinds of trees present and their age or ages. The traditional way to make a growing stock map is for the forest surveyor to walk all through the woods, notebook in hand. He must of course be able to name all the common trees at sight. If the age of a crop is not known from past records he must fell a few *sample trees* and count the annual rings at the base of each.

But today much growing stock mapping is done by aerial photography backed by checks on the ground. Modern techniques enable experts to name the leading forest species and to make workable estimates of their ages and sizes.

The details of such surveys are transferred to a basic topographic map using symbols such as initial letters for names of trees and figures for ages of crops. Brightly coloured inks may be added to give a quicker visual impression. For example, the notation 'Cpt 7, 12 ha, S.P. 25', will signify:

'compartment 7, 12 hectares, Scots pine, 25 years old', and the plot may be coloured pink to indicate a conifer.

Two more important factors need to be determined before serious planning can be done. One is the volume of timber present, by kind of tree, age and size-class of logs that can be cut, since this size-class controls their sale price. The other is rate at which the trees are increasing in volume as this will determine the rate at which fellings can reasonably be made, that is, the *allowable cut*. These factors are assessed by taking samples at appropriate points, measuring selected trees and discovering how fast they have grown in recent years. Modern statistical methods are applied to get trustworthy results. Fortunately the rate of height growth supplies a clue to the rate of volume increment, except in the older stands.

The whole business of mapping and measuring adds up to a *forest inventory*, a complex physical stocktaking that includes forecasts for future growth and timber yield. Armed with this inventory, the forester can now draw up a *working plan* showing how this forest can best be managed. Usually he does this in detail for five years or even longer. He has to allow for many factors besides simple timber growth. For example, a new road may be needed to enable timber lorries to reach a distant sector of the woods where valuable timber is maturing, or clear felling may be ruled out from certain areas because it could lead to the silting up of a reservoir, while other areas must be left undisturbed each spring to allow game birds to breed. After considering, he hopes, all interests, the planner prepares a document showing what work should be done each year and where it should take place. This takes the form of schedules for, say, planting, weeding, thinning-out and felling.

He will add to this a forecast of labour requirements, possibly allowing for a share of the work to be done by timber merchants who fell the trees, they have purchased. He will also make estimates of expenditure on wages, materials and the salaries of the supervisors. These outgoings will be offset by estimates of returns from the sale of timber and of any other sources of income, like shooting licences or camping permits. For an old established forest in normal times there should be a substantial surplus each year of income over expenditure. Trees cost little to grow but timber is a valuable commodity.

Today practically every forest of any value has such a plan intended to guide its destiny. The wilderness may look trackless but you may depend upon it that somewhere in some forester's office there is a map or an air photo of it, while some diligent economist is working out its significance, if any, for his country's overall economic plan. Even if its timber is worthless it can figure in the national budget as a tourist attraction!

Putting Plans into Practice

The day-to-day business of most foresters consists of putting plans into action to meet prescribed targets. Like other managers they manipulate men, machinery and money, but unlike most they do so over large tracts of land at all seasons and in all weathers all the time. Their stock-in-trade is the growing tree that, after being nurtured from a seed for perhaps a century, yielding no intermediate returns, suddenly becomes a marketable asset, being transformed by a few minutes work with axe or saw into a log of timber.

In the popular imagination the forester stalks through the woods on foot as a stalwart but lonely figure, his only companion being his hound. In fact he speeds from office to woodland work-site by car or cross-country truck, constantly meeting people in various capacities. He finds, supervises, trains and pays his forest workers, who often give their best outputs when encouraged by complex systems of piecework or cash bonuses. He is an expert in handling a varied range of machinery including ploughs, road construction plant, power saws for timber felling and tractors and winches for hauling logs out. He deals with the timber merchants who have bought timber in his woods and knows the details of every contract.

The forester also deals with the surprisingly varied visitors who – for one reason or another quite unconnected with the actual business of raising timber – turn up on forest highways or byways at any hour of the day and through much of the night. These include neighbouring farmers who have rights of way for tractors, carts or cattle; sportsmen with shooting rights or licences; tourists who come simply to gain fresh air and exercise, with or without horses or dogs; and eager groups of students seeking the benefits of nature and the open air. Forests in fine weather become a magnet for a remarkable cross-section of the community from courting couples to poachers, pilgrims and even escaped convicts. Only in foul weather when snow lies thickly on the boughs is he likely to walk alone!

Planting and Replanting

Planting is a comprehensive term covering any operation that involves establishing trees; while replanting, also called *reforestation*, implies the planting of trees on land that has recently carried a previous timber crop. A parallel process, called *afforestation*, covers the planting of fresh land that has not within recent times been used for timber growing. Plate 35.

There are many fortunate forests where the natural regeneration of the trees by their own seeding suffices to replace those trees that are removed. Here all the forester need do is to plan his individual tree fellings or small clearings so that ample seed reaches the right places at the right time, and then regulate the regrowth. But in most reforestation situations he must replant, while planting is always essential for schemes involving the first afforestation of bare land.

At this point we must ask why plants are used, rather than seed. The technique called *direct sowing* is in fact found in every forestry textbook, though it is rarely seen practised in the woods. The reason is that both seed and seedlings face so many enemies that enormous quantities must be used to secure a crop, and this proves unduly expensive in labour. Pine seed has been broadcast from airplanes only to be eaten by hungry wood mice scouring the ground below. If it is sown in patches on moorland grouse quickly learn to find each prepared patch and gobble up every seed. Acorns sown in woods, quite lavishly, attract flocks of immigrant wood pigeons as well as local pheasants. The few seedlings that survive face immediate competition from vigorous weeds and the labour involved in finding and weeding them is unduly expensive.

The practical forester, therefore, imports his young trees from a nursery where they have been artificially raised as has been described in Chapter Fourteen. This of course involves advance planning for he must place his orders months or years ahead to ensure that the nurseryman can supply just what he wants when it is needed. He specifies the kind of tree, its age, size and general character – for example, short, sturdy and robust rather than tall and slender.

In some regions the *seedlings*, taken directly from the seedbed, can be planted successfully. But as a rule successful establishment can only be secured by using *transplants*, which, as we have noted, are trees that have been transplanted at least once within the nursery, and have as a result developed extensive bushy root systems accompanied by relatively short shoots. Experience shows that this kind of early growth fits them to survive the shock of a second transplanting to the harsher conditions of the forest far better than seedlings can do, hence losses are lower.

Before planting is done the ground is often prepared to receive the new crop. In former woodland the soil is usually left undisturbed except for the clearing of brushwood and the cleaning of watercourses to drain wet patches. New land for afforestation is usually ploughed with various objects in view according to its character. On peaty, wet moorlands the plough furrows, spaced about two metres apart, serve as effective open drains and are linked at suitable points to a deeper drainage system. The *slices* of peat that the plough turns up are left as long ribbons and provide planting

231

positions for the young trees. A step may be cut in the side of the turf ribbon or alternatively the roots may be spread out below the turf, a position that always remains moist.

On hard ground, often dominated by heather, the purpose of the ploughing is to break through the *podzol* or *hard-pan* structure described in Chapter Six. This allows air and water to penetrate through infertile, compacted layers and the tree roots soon follow them to gain anchorage, water and nutrients. Giant tractor-drawn ploughs can penetrate half-a-metre deep. The young trees are usually planted on the side of the upturned slice of soil. On dry sandy soils shallower furrows are cut so that rainwater collects in their depressions and the young trees are planted there.

The spacing of the furrows is naturally linked to the spacing planned for the trees, which is nowadays on average two metres apart in each direction. This is the outcome of practical experience rather than clever theory. If trees are spaced more closely, costs rise sharply. For a spacing of one metre you need four times as many trees at nearly four times the cost, and many of the extra individuals will be crowded out or thinned out before they have any sale value. If trees are spaced farther apart than two metres any casualty leaves a wide gap and lowers the profitability of the crop.

In a similar way the size of tree selected reflects the forester's economic objectives. Common sizes range from fifteen centimetres to one metre tall, depending on the kind of tree, the nature of the soil and the vigour of the surrounding vegetation. Trees smaller than the accepted normal for the site concerned lack the reserves needed to see them through, say, a spell of drought or unseasonable frost, and are easily smothered by vigorous weed growth. Bigger trees have better reserves and withstand stronger competition but become very expensive to raise and plant.

The regular spacing of even-sized trees is often attacked by critics who say that it imposes too rigid and artificial a pattern upon the scenery of the countryside. But it is, quite simply, the only sensible way to establish a forest crop. As the years go by, the ranked appearance of the trees is sure to lessen through chance losses, deliberate thinning out and the inevitably random differences in the growth of individual specimens. Plate 48.

In most parts of the world planting is a seasonal operation. It is not possible to plant into frozen soil and this rules out the winter in the mountains and northern latitudes generally. In regions with marked dry seasons success can only be achieved by planting during the rains. Spring is therefore favoured in Europe, northern Asia and North America, and the onset of rainy weather elsewhere.

Machines are rarely employed for planting because they can only work effectively and cheaply on flat land free from obstacles. Their use is therefore limited to American prairies, Russian steppes and similar exceptional territories. Usually the forester has to place his trees on steep slopes, between tree stumps, on plough slices, in packets of soft earth between rocks or similar tricky situations that only a man on his two feet can find and fill. Hand tools are therefore the rule and most of these are modified spades or mattocks. The young trees are normally carried in bags slung from the worker's shoulders, leaving both his hands free for action.

In contrast to the care applied to specimen trees those intended for timber are put into the ground by methods so crude that they appear almost cruel! In the commonest methods a notch is hacked into the ground or alternatively two notches meeting at an angle. A little soil is then levered upwards to open the notch or angular gap. The tree's roots are threaded into this, and the tree is drawn to the level at which it previously grew in the nursery. Then the ground is pushed down or allowed to fall back, and stamped firm around the buried roots.

This stamping firm is very important as it ensures effective contact between the roots and the moisture-holding soil. With firm planting losses are low, only a few per cent, but loose planting is followed as a rule by many deaths. The young trees must of course be brought to the site with moist roots. This is usually achieved by transporting them in polythene bags which have to be kept out of the sun to prevent the trees within from heating up. Alternatively the trees may be *heeled-in*, which implies setting them with their roots buried in soft earth until they are actually needed for planting.

A skilled operator can plant as many as 1,000 small trees in the course of a single working day, taking no more than half a minute for each one.

Protecting the Crop

Once a tree crop has been established the main concern of the forester is to protect it from a wide range of perils. Most of these are only serious in its youth and diminish as it grows taller. Even fire risk is lower for a mature crop than for a young one. In a typical forest, therefore, the forester concentrates his main protective measures on the newly-planted crops while maintaining constant vigilance over the whole woodland.

Weeding

Weeding, which implies keeping the trees safe from competition by other plants, varies greatly in necessity and intensity. On ploughed moorlands, at one extreme, the reviving vegetation may never compete seriously with the young trees and no weeding whatsoever is then required. The same situation can occur in arid sandy country. But amid more fertile forests the growth of unwanted grasses, herbs, ferns like bracken, briars, brambles and woody climbers can be fierce and furious. It continues for several years before the trees become tall enough to outgrow their competitors.

Most weeding is done by hand with metal cutting tools that vary in character from curved reap-hooks, relatively thin, to stout bill-hooks or jungle knives. The weeds are slashed back during the active growing season to allow the young trees to maintain their lead over the competing growth. This may have to be repeated for anything up to five years, until the increasing height of the trees and the shade that they cast, which checks their competitors, puts them out of danger.

On suitable ground a variety of machines may be used to cut back the weeds more cheaply than hand tools can do. Provided there is space enough for them to proceed between the rows of trees, grass-mowers, rotary flails and even heavy rollers can do effective damage to the weed plants whilst leaving the crop unharmed.

Another approach is to spray the crop with *selective weedkillers* or herbicides, so called because they appear to pick out the weeds for destruction whilst leaving the crop trees unharmed. Naturally there must be some major difference in character between crop and weed-species, and the commonest situation involves conifer crops amid weeds that are common herbs and grasses plus the regrowth of broadleaved trees. The synthetic brushwood killer (SBK) called 2,4-D fills this need when applied in the right amounts at the right season.

In theory chemical weedkilling appears an ideal solution but there are many snags. The chemicals involved are intrinsically expensive and most are poisonous to some degree. They can only be applied by specially trained men wearing protective clothing and using purpose-designed machinery, at favourable times of the year. Early methods called for the transport of large volumes of water or other diluents for the active chemicals; recently ultra-low-volume techniques needing far less material have been developed. Despite the drawbacks and cost chemical weedkilling is gaining a place as a weapon against varied types of vegetation from heather to hazel coppice and a variety of tropical and sub-tropical weed plants.

Harmful Birds and Beasts

Few birds threaten young tree crops, the only common European exceptions being the capercaillie, *Tetrao urogallus*, and the black grouse, *Lyrurus tetrix*, which consume the buds of pines in northern European forests. But four-footed beasts that eat plants, birds and bark are another matter and many diverse species, from mice to elephants, can devastate young plantations, sometimes overnight. Against these potential perils the forester can oppose three solutions: 'Fence out, kill out, or thin out.'

Fencing is the usual, and usually effective, method of keeping out domestic livestock of all kinds – cattle, horses, sheep, goats and pigs – all being creatures that have lost their original wild roving traits. Against truly wild four-footed creatures it is far less reliable, though effective barriers can be built and maintained for a limited time against anything from a rabbit to an elephant. (The rabbit fence must of course check burrowing – in practice it is bent out at the base towards the rabbit, instead of going straight down.) But just as a chain can only be as strong as its weakest link, a fence can only be as effective as its poorest section. The American poet Robert Frost wrote:

'Something there is that does not love a wall,'

and every forester soon learns that there are many and varied 'things' that do not love his fences. A falling tree may make a gap that allows a group of deer or just two rabbits, male and female, to cross his carefully built barrier; after that it may just as well not be there! People leave gates open, landslides or floods create gaps. A six-foot fence will not delay deer for long once a hard snow-drift, five feet deep, piles up against it! All this means that the 'fence-out' approach can have only limited application for wild animals, though it is locally and temporarily useful. Every fence must be patrolled and repaired.

'Kill out' is generally and rightly ruled out by conservationist opinion. Life would certainly become easier for foresters if every deer, antelope, elephant, mad March hare or what-have-you were exterminated from all regions where they may threaten trees, which means just about everywhere. But a priceless heritage of wild life would be sadly diminished or lost.

This leaves 'thin out' as the most practical measure of control for all four-footed beasts, and over most of the world's forests the forester is also the effective game warden. His aim is to keep the population of wild animals, particularly the large herbivores such as deer and the many races of antelopes, at a level where only 'tolerable' damage is suffered by tree crops. What 'tolerable' means is a subject of constant assessment, discussion and dispute. Sportsmen cannot have too many beasts to shoot, while many foresters hate to lose a single tree.

The United States provides a curious exception to the control of game by forest managers, for there the licencing of shooting is reserved by the national constitution to the authorities of each state. But the local zeal for hunting is so marked that few problems arise except to safeguard fewer and fewer deer from more and more marksmen by shorter and shorter open seasons!

The protection of trees against other common, though fortunately occasional and local perils, such as fungi, invertebrates such as insects, and extremes of weather, demands specialised knowledge. Foresters seek the aid of plant pathologists, entomologists and experts in meteorology.

Fire Danger

Fire presents exceptional risks and every well-run forest has its fire plan aimed to cover all contingencies. The degree of danger varies from negligible in tropical rain forests and many temperate deciduous broadleaved woodlands to very high in most conifer forests and among certain evergreen broadleaved trees such as those of Mediterranean climatic zones. It also fluctuates markedly with the seasons of the year, the resulting character of the vegetation and the humidity of the atmosphere.

The well-equipped forester combats fire in three well-defined stages. His *advance planning* provides for fire-breaks and access routes. His *detection procedures* ensure a constant watch over the whole area at risk by men in fire towers, ground patrols or patrolling aircraft, and this is linked to meteorological assessments of fire hazard in terms of wind and humidity. Finally, his *fire-fighting activities* mobilize men and machines to tackle each reported blaze promptly on the actual spot when and where it occurs.

When all these perils are considered together, it may seem surprising that any tree crops can run their full course from planting to maturity. But good management and the odds against minor disasters becoming major ones usually ensure that only a small proportion of each year's planting is lost, even over the long span of years needed to grow trees to the right ages for felling.

Fertilizing

Artificial fertilizers may be applied, at planting time or later, to promote the rapid growth of the crop. Most real forest soils, however, already hold adequate nutrients and nothing is gained by adding more. On poorer land, particularly new afforestation areas where soil fertility has been exhausted by extractive cropping or over-grazing, the addition of certain elements can make a dramatic difference to the crop's progress. Phosphorus is usually the critical element but locally potassium or nitrogen may be needed. Deficiencies are assessed by experiments or by chemical analysis of the foliage of growing trees.

The quantities applied are remarkably low, only a few tonnes per hectare. Scattering such small amounts over large areas of land, often carrying trees, poses technical problems. Aircraft often prove cheaper than application by hand or machine.

The vital elements are returned to the soil by the tree's annual leaf-fall and re-cycled through the roots. Thus they have a very long-term effect, especially as only trifling amounts are removed in the timber that eventually leaves the forest. This contrasts with the situation in agriculture in which substantial quantities of critical elements leave the land in food crops or the carcasses of animals, or their milk or wool, and hence must be repeatedly replenished.

Controlling the Harvest

Each year in a well-planned forest the trees in certain compartments will require thinning-out while others elsewhere will reach the age and stage at which a final felling falls due.

Thinning implies selection for removal and this is done with varying degrees of care depending on the value of the crop. In the earlier thinnings whole lines of trees may be removed, say, one line in every five. This opens the way for the easier extraction of the poles that are felled either by allowing a tractor or horse to enter between the close-ranked trees or the cable of a powerful winch to be used to haul the harvested timber out.

Later thinnings demand the skill of the forester or his assistants to choose for retention the right proportion of the better trees, having the best prospects as large and valuable timber, yet standing at the right spacing. Similar skilled selection is needed for certain kinds of fellings where the maturing trees are taken out gradually rather than cut down *en masse*. This may be desirable, for example, to promote natural regeneration by leaving a proportion of 'seed trees'.

The workers who cut down the selected trees and haul them out may or may not work directly for the forester. But in either circumstance he remains responsible for the orderly progress of their work. He must ensure that the right roads are used and left unobstructed and that the land is finally left in a fit state for his next crop. After the big logs have been hauled away and the smaller ones taken for firewood or pulpwood the remaining branches are either burned or left to decay. Only the stumps and roots, too costly and awkward to remove, remain in the soil as relics of the tall timber crop, and these too eventually decay.

In a planted forest the young trees are set about two metres apart, which means that 2,500 trees start their growth on each hectare of ground. Forests that arise by natural seeding show far higher densities, often carrying as many as 25,000 seedlings on one hectare. Losses through mutual competition soon reduce these numbers sharply. The forester thins out both planted and seeded stands at intervals of a few years to allow adequate growing space for the survivors. By the time the timber crop is mature the stocking may have fallen to only 250 trees per hectare, only one tenth by number of a planted crop, or one per cent of a naturally seeded crop.

These 'final crop' trees, relatively few in number, will nevertheless hold about half of the commercially useful timber produced by the crop, for they are naturally the largest specimens. All their fellows, though at least nine times as numerous, have been cut out at younger ages and smaller stages of growth, and collectively they only contribute a volume equal to that of the final crop.

Chapter 19

The Wood from Trees

Felling, Transporting and Measuring Timber

Trees are felled by cutting through the trunk as close to ground level as possible so as to make use of all or nearly all the available timber. Only the smallest individuals are felled by axe or hand saw alone. Traditional methods require both tools for larger stems. The axe is used first to cut off any projecting buttresses and then to make an *undercut* on that side of the tree, called the *face*, towards which the feller intends the trunk to fall. The saw is then inserted on the opposite side, called the *back*, at a slightly higher level than the base of the undercut. Its blade is drawn swiftly to and fro by one or more often two workers until it nears the gap made by the undercut. Just before the last fragment of wood is sawn through, the whole tree leans towards the face since support has already been removed there. Then it heels over and falls with a crash to the forest floor. Plate 36.

The loggers next cut away the branches, setting aside the larger ones for use as small timber, firewood or pulpwood. The smaller ones may be burnt to clear the ground or simply left to rot on the forest floor. The bark is usually left attached to the logs but is removed later at the sawmill, paper mill or wood-preserving plant.

The log that now remains in its trimmed-out state is one of the most fascinating raw materials available to man, with complex technical properties that can be put to a bewildering range of end uses. It may range in size from a small pole, that can be carried out by one man and is suitable only for fencing, to a huge trunk perhaps 60 metres long by 2 metres in diameter at its mid-point, that weighs around 180 tonnes! The larger logs are cut across to reduce the weight and size of each piece for transport, at intervals carefully measured to fit the intended final use for each one.

Whatever the kind of tree or the situation of the forest the log is sure to be exceptionally heavy when first cut down, for it is saturated with the sap that is the life-blood of the tree. It has on average a specific gravity of 1.0, which means that each cubic metre weighs 1,000 kilogrammes or one metric tonne. This means too that it will barely float in water, and in some situations the logs are left to season, that is, to partially dry out in the forest to lessen their weight for haulage or floating down rivers.

An amazing range of transport methods is applied to different kinds of timber in various parts of the world. Every kind of draught animal has been used including horses, mules, oxen, buffaloes, camels and elephants. To an ever-increasing degree these are being replaced by either wheeled or track-laying 'crawler' tractors which can nowadays move up to the actual tree stumps in most forests, save those on very steep slopes or soft marshlands.

Tree trunks by reason of their slender shape and handy size are exceptionally well suited to movement by cables, and winches have long been used to transport them up or down steep slopes. From simple hand devices these developed through powered winches, driven first by steam engines and later by stationary tractors, to elaborate overhead cable systems. The cableway, suitably engineered, can reach far out from a road or railway into the depths of an otherwise inaccessible forest, crossing rivers or ravines in its stride. A range of 400 metres is possible for small tractor-powered systems, while in the Alps and similar mountainous regions the cableways may extend for several kilometres, using gravity as their main motive force.

In North America fantastic 'yarding' or cableway systems are used to haul the huge logs of spruces, Douglas fir, and Californian redwood (*Sequoia sempervirens*) to the stack-yards or 'landings' where they are transhipped to road, rail or river transport. At one time selected standing trees were used as 'spars' to carry the rigging, but this required an exceptionally skilled and daring logger to top the tree and fix cables at heights around forty metres above the ground. Today portable steel towers which can be dismantled and re-erected speedily wherever required, are used instead. A curious alternative sometimes used in the remarkably wind-free Pacific Coast zone is a captive balloon, used to support the cables at an adequate height. In other parts of the world it would soon be blown away!

During the nineteenth century, and earlier in *this* century, railways played a large part in timber transport and remarkable lines were built often crossing high timber trestle viaducts to reach timber-rich though remote nooks of the woods. Today the road truck or lorry has nearly everywhere taken over since it proves more flexible in all respects. Roads are easier to build and one truck with a single driver can carry enormous loads, up to fifty tonnes, piled high on an immensely strong frame, borne on enormous tyres. Cranes of some kind are needed for loading but all save the biggest logs can be lifted by a hydraulic hoist carried on the lorry itself and powered by its own engine.

In the past the felling of trees and extraction of the resulting timber were in many countries usually seasonal occupations. In Scandinavia, for example, the farmer who could not tend crops in the frozen winter took his horse to the woods and harnessed it to a sledge, on which he carried logs to a frozen lake or riverside so that they could be floated when the spring thaw came. In tropical jungles the rainy seasons, which make transport difficult over soft ground, were avoided. But nowadays the increasing cost and complexity of the machinery engaged and the high wages paid to skilled operatives have made lumbering an all-the-year round business practically everywhere.

Most jobs are done on a piece-work basis keyed to the volume or occasionally the weight of lumber handled. The amount of timber in each log is calculated, under metric measurement systems, by multiplying its length in metres by its cross-sectional area at its mid-point, an assumed average figure. This cross-sectional area is obtained by multiplying the square of the log's radius by the mathematical constant π. In practice the diameter is measured in centimetres and divided by two to get the radius. Since one square metre equals 10,000 square centimetres, the formula for a log's volume becomes:

$$\frac{\pi \left(\frac{diameter}{2}\right)^2}{10,000} \times \text{length} = \text{volume in cubic metres}$$

In the United States and Canada however, a traditional unit called the *board foot* is used to measure the volume of trees and logs. Its basis is the number of 'foot-run' or length of planks, each one foot wide and one inch thick, that a sawyer could cut from a log using inefficient, out-dated machinery. There is a big and variable allowance for wastage. For international calculations one cubic metre of round timber is considered equivalent to 250 board feet.

Converting the Felled Log

The process of changing the log into a form suitable for its final use is called *conversion*. Timber is so versatile that this change takes many forms. Sometimes it is done in the forest where the tree falls but more usually it is carried out in a distant sawmill, workshop or factory.

Throughout the world an enormous number of logs are used 'in the round' without further alteration in shape. They are selected for diameter, crosscut to the desired length, barked, and for many purposes, pointed. If they are to be used in contact with the ground they may be treated in whole or part with preservatives to check fungal decay, as will be explained later.

241

The main uses of round timber are in fencing, building, poles for telephone wires and electrical transmission lines and supports for the roofs of mines.

Where smaller pieces of wood will meet a similar purpose, especially in fencing, round logs are often *cleft*. This is done by driving a wedge down them lengthwise so that they split into semi-circular or triangular segments. This operation is difficult to mechanize and remains a hand craft.

Sawing is the major method for converting round logs to planks, beams and smaller members with square or oblong cross-sections. The earliest saws were worked by hand, being drawn through logs set over wooden frames or saw-pits that is, brick-lined holes in the ground. One man stood on top and another less fortunate one below, where all the sawdust fell! This method is still used in some tropical countries where labour is cheap and ready to accept hardship. During the Middle Ages ingenious craftsmen discovered how to use the power of windmills and watermills to move saw-blades up and down. By setting several reciprocating blades in a single frame they were able to cut several planks at one time from one large log, which was propelled slowly towards them on a moving bench. This method is still used, though nowadays the saw is powered by steam or oil engines, or by electricity. Plate 40.

Circular saws came much later, being patented in the year 1777 by Samuel Miller, of Southampton in England, who intended them to cut stone as well as wood. In 1808 William Newberry of London thought up the band saw, in which an endless belt of metal carrying sharp teeth travels round two large wheels, one of which provides power. But it was not until 1855 that improvements in the quality of steel made band saws a practical proposition.

Saws of circular and band patterns revolving at fantastic speeds nowadays convert enormous quantities of round timber in sawmills built in every forested region, and even in industrial cities far from any woods. The sawing process can be the simple one of cutting through the logs just as they come forward, to get planks or beams of the desired dimensions by 'through-and-through sawing', or it may be a highly specialized technique that isolates the best part of each log for some particular purpose. For example, the heartwood of the tree may be isolated from the surrounding sapwood or the central core that holds knots can be eliminated to obtain 'clear', that is, knot-free timber.

The direction of the saw-cut relative to the pattern of annual rings or rays will influence the quality of the manufactured timber. For example, saw cuts that follow the radius of an oak log instead of running at right angles to it (i.e., tangentially) give planks that are less prone to change shape later. Such sawing also exposes the beautiful 'silver grain' of the ray tissues.

Timber required for everyday use, as in fencing, building or boxmaking, is sawn to its final dimensions at the outset. That needed for exacting work, for example, in furniture-making or fine joinery, is first cut to convenient sizes then seasoned as described later and finally resawn to its final outline.

Allied to the saws come a number of powerful machines based originally on the craft tools of the carpenter. Planing machines give smooth surfaces wherever they are needed and machines for cutting tongues-and-grooves, mortises, tenons or dovetails prepare the wood cheaply for joining one piece to another. Moulding machines quickly provide curved outlines wherever they are needed.

In *turning*, another basic process of conversion, a piece of timber is *spun*, that is, whirled rapidly round in a lathe powered by foot-power or else by some kind of engine or electric motor. A chisel or similar cutting tool is applied to the whirling wood to sculpt it into a round shape, perhaps a bowl, a platter or a chair leg. But turners rarely use a round log to start with, as if they did the end-product would split as it dried. Instead they start with a sawn 'blank' already cut out 'off-centre'. This is placed in such a way that shrinkage causes no cracks.

Seasoning Timber

The seasoning of wood is one of the transformations that mystifies the layman and most professional handlers of timber prefer to see him left puzzled! In Germany where the allied word *törren* simply means 'drying', matters are more straightforward!

In the growing tree each trunk and limb is saturated with water whether the season be winter or summer. Once a tree is cut down no more water comes into its wood from the roots and the water that was present at the time of felling is slowly lost to the atmosphere until a state of equilibrium is reached. Consequently the wood gets lighter. It also becomes somewhat stiffer and better able to withstand heavy strains. At the same time it shrinks in a peculiar way.

A round log diminishes by only a minute amount in length, and this change is in practice ignored. It shrinks slightly from its outside towards its centre, that is, *radially*. But it shrinks markedly around its circumference, that is, *tangentially*. This difference in shrinkage directionally causes the log to split here and there along one or more radii, for the mechanical forces are too strong for the connecting cells to resist. Cracks open up along its length from the outside towards the centre.

In rough-and-ready work such as fence posts or telegraph poles, this splitting is accepted. But for all finer work special techniques are employed to minimize the changes in shape that the drying of wood invariably brings. Oak planks intended for furniture, for example, are first sawn to fairly large sizes and then stacked exposed to the open air, but under overhead cover, with *stickers*, that is, small pieces of wood between each plank so that air can circulate. After a year's exposure to the weather, which explains the term 'seasoning', the oak has lost most of its free water and has completed most of its shrinkage and change in shape. It can then be sawn and shaped to smaller sizes for final uses, with little fear of further change of character. If, however, it is to be used in a centrally-heated building, it requires further artificial seasoning in a heated drying kiln to reduce its water content to a safe level.

The amount of water remaining in any piece of wood can be conveniently expressed as a percentage of its oven-dry weight. This latter figure is readily obtained by drying a sample of the wood in an oven until it can lose no more water, and therefore no more weight. When a log is first felled its moisture content is often as high as 100% of its oven-dry weight, which means that it holds by weight as much sap as solid matter. For use in joinery or furniture in houses heated by open fire, a moisture content of only 20% is appropriate, but the figure for centrally-heated buildings is only 15%. At such low moisture contents neither wood-destroying fungi nor wood-boring insects can survive. This explains why wood kept continually dry lasts indefinitely, though it may decay rapidly once it is allowed to get moist again.

Timber used commercially in building, packaging, and ordinary furniture-making, joinery, and so forth, is nowadays seasoned artificially in kilns. This is cheaper because the same degree of moisture removal is secured in days, rather than the months needed for slow natural seasoning in the open air.

Preserving Timber

The fibres of wood are suprisingly resistant to attack by any kind of chemical, strong or weak. Teak, for example, is commonly used for laboratory benches on which chemists spill acids, alkalis and other substances that quickly corrode metals, yet it survives unharmed. Anyone who has tried to destroy an unwanted tree stump soon realizes that nothing short of fire makes any impression on it. Yet this astonishingly tough material can be broken down completely by biological agencies, namely, certain specially-adapted fungi and insects. In the modern jargon it is *biodegradable*.

Forests hold simple plants and specialized insects that can feed and breed on wood, though only when conditions are suitable for them. Both these groups of organisms need both oxygen and water for life. Hence timber can be preserved indefinitely by sinking it in deep water or deeply in wet peaty soil where there is little free oxygen. This explains why sunken warships, such as the Viking long ships found buried in Norway and the famous Swedish vessel *Wasa* found sunk below water near Stockholm, have remained more or less intact for centuries. At the other extreme wood kept perpetually dry, as in a well-constructed building, lasts indefinitely, and so do the building's constructional timbers themselves. Even the so-called 'dry-rot' caused by the fungus *Merulius lacrymans* can only develop where water is available from leaking roofs or pipes, or from damp earth.

Where both water and air are freely and continuously available, however, decay can be rapid. This occurs most commonly at and near ground level where untreated fence posts or building poles quickly rot. This also means that they give way at the point where maximum strain occurs.

The folklore surrounding timber decay is even more faulty than that concerning seasoning. People are easily misled into the belief that certain timbers are inherently durable through-and-through while others are naturally perishable. In fact the sapwood of *any* timber is readily attacked by the organisms that cause rot provided conditions are suitable for them. But the chemical changes that occur when sapwood becomes heartwood result in *certain timbers only* acquiring resistance, though only so far as their heartwood is concerned. Outstanding examples are oak, teak and yew.

In the past this situation was accepted by users, and if timber was needed for long service in places where it could not be kept dry, as in posts or the foundations of buildings, only heartwood of well-proven species was used. To avoid the waste of sapwood involved, and also to enable practically any timber to be used anywhere, technologists invented preservatives. These are of two main kinds – the creosotes or tar-oils, derived by distilling coal tar, and the poisonous mineral salts. The latter usually involve three elements, namely, copper, chromium and arsenic. One or the other of these preservatives is applied to the timber, after it has been shaped to its final form in one of several ingenious ways. The timber may be steeped in a preservative fluid or first heated and then allowed to cool in it, causing the preservative to be drawn into its cells. Alternatively, elaborate machinery may be used to force it in by a combination of heat and both vacuum and pressure devices. The outcome is always the same. Wherever the preservative penetrates, no wood-rotting fungi or wood-eating animals can develop. The treated timber thus acquires a very long endurance wherever it may be used, often resisting decay even at ground level for forty years or more.

The Merits of Timber

Timber like all basic materials faces competition from other substances. Little more than a century ago it was the main medium for building houses, ships, bridges and vehicles as well as being a major fuel. Today metals, concrete and plastics have taken the place of wood for many purposes needing great strength, or at the other extreme, ease of manipulation. Yet world demand for timber still keeps pace with advancing civilization. One reason is the development of new technical means of using wood as man-made board or in paper-based products. But solid wood is still needed in increasing amounts. Plates 39, 65.

Qualities that ensure its continued employment are its high strength proportionate to its weight, its ready availability in handy sizes and the ease with which it can be cut, shaped and fixed with simple hand or powered tools. Wood is also a good insulator against heat loss. Like many natural products it is attractive in appearance and can be made more so by many processes of special cutting to expose attractive grain or figure. It is easily treated with stains or polishes or painted in pleasing colours. It can also be obtained in varied kinds, some adapted to cheap everyday work like board-ing and packaging, others specially suited to take strains as in tool handles or ladders and others that simply look good. Even where alternatives prove cheaper, people still prefer wood because it is a homely, friendly, tradi-tional material. It is adaptable to all man's needs from his cradle onwards through his active life. He works with wooden-handled tools, lives as like as not in a timber-framed dwelling, sits on wooden chairs before a wooden table and sleeps on a wooden bed. Eventually, his labours over, he will be borne to the churchyard in a wooden coffin!

Wood is able to play these many parts because it is an organic substance built up of myriads of varied cells. It is unique in consisting of *flexible* fibres that combine to make a *rigid* substance able to bear weights and resist strains. This explains why it can hold screws and nails and withstands bending strains without breaking. It is also a fundamental characteristic that enables man to use wood in reconstituted forms, including the bonded fabric that we call paper.

Man-made and Reconstructed Wood

The so-called man-made woods are created by breaking down logs into components of varied shapes and sizes and then reconstructing a woody material by gluing them together. The invention of plastic resins, in effective industrial use from 1940 onwards, has made this a practical large-scale commercial activity.

To make *plywood* large logs are peeled to yield *veneers*. Each log is spun in a huge, powered lathe. As it turns, a large fixed knife cuts into its surface like a great pencil sharpener and skims off a thin continuous layer of timber. This sheet is called a *rotary cut veneer*. If it is highly decorative it may be used as an ornamental finish to a piece of furniture actually built of cheaper and coarser timbers.

The next stage in forming plywood is to glue three or more veneers together so that adjacent sheets have their grain running at right angles to that of their neighbours. This produces a thin, light, strong and flexible material, which – thanks to the differing directions of its components' grains – is virtually impossible to split.

Laminated boards and *block-boards* are built up on the same principle, using thicker and more rigid timbers, for use where greater strength and more firmness are required. All three types of reconstructed timber have practical advantages over sawn planks. They can be made in wider sizes, are less prone to warp or split, and can be finished off with a variety of surfaces – smooth, decorative or resistant to heavy wear.

Chipboards, also called *particle boards*, are made by chipping wood into small pieces – around one centimetre long – with powerful machines. The chips are then mixed with a powdered plastic glue called a *binder* and spread out in a thin layer between metal plates. The whole set-up is then placed in a powerful press and subjected to strong heat and high pressure. This process liquidizes the glue and causes it to bind the chips together into a firm sheet of 'man-made wood' which remains intact after removal from the machines.

Many technical refinements can be applied to give sheets of various thicknesses or strength properties and they can be finished off with a great range of surfaces such as decorative wood veneers, metal plates or hardwearing laminated plastics. For some purposes chipboards have better properties than sawn timber for they do not readily warp or split and today they have become a leading material for making furniture; but they are unsuited to out-door use. Originally this process was invented about 1940 for using up waste material from sawmills. Today whole trees or tree-tops too small for profitable sawing are regularly chipped. The process proves very economic because no wood is wasted.

Hardboards, used for lighter work, are made by taking the disintegration process a stage further. The wood is broken down into its actual fibres which are then bonded together to form very thin yet tough and consistent sheets, strengthened by plastic binders. Similar processes are used to make *insulation boards,* sometimes called *softboards,* which are much thicker and lighter. They are used in interior trim, joinery and light building construction to deaden sound or check heat loss. Further refinements of such processes produce packaging boards used in box-making or cartons for holding foodstuffs.

Paper

Wood is nowadays the only raw material used on any effective scale for making paper in any of its multitudinous forms. The basic process is to break the wood down by mechanical means, with or without the aid of strong chemicals, into its component fibres or clusters of fibres. This *pulping* is done in water or chemical solutions and the resulting mass of wet *pulp,* around 99% of water to only 1% of wood fibre, is poured over some form of wire sieve. As the water drains away the fibres, crossing one another at many points, meet and form *bonds* that strengthen as the material dries, forming a *web* of paper.

This remarkable restructuring of a fibrous material takes place so quickly that it can be carried out on very high-speed machines. In ancient China the first paper makers shook their pulp on hand-held sieves. Today in a modern paper mill a continuous stream of wet pulp is poured onto an endless belt of wire mesh, travelling at high speed. In a matter of seconds the web is strong enough to be automatically transferred to a second belt, this time made of felt, where further draining occurs. The web now moves on to heated metal rollers where it is dried. It then passes between further rollers that gives smooth surfaces to its two sides to emerge as a great roll of finished paper wound onto a cylinder.

To provide paper in the many grades that people need it today a wide range of technical processes, all of them needing elaborate plant, have been developed. Basically there are two classes of paper. In the *mechanical* ones all the wood is reduced to fibres usually by forcing short logs against grindstones under a constant stream of water. The resulting pulp contains both the main chemical constituents of the fibres. One, called cellulose, is the valuable pliant component. The other, called lignin, is little more than an impurity that leads to the gradual discoloration and decomposition of the resultant paper. But since nothing is spent on removing it a cheap paper results, perfectly satisfactory for newsprint and other materials that are not required to have a long life or exceptional strength.

To make *chemical papers* the wood is first broken into small chips and then 'cooked' or 'digested' in vats holding strong chemicals that separate the lignin from the cellulose. The lignin is then discarded as a waste product in the spent liquor and only the cellulose goes forward to the paper-making machines.

Contrasting types of chemical paper are the strong brown wrapping papers, thick and tough, made by the *sulphate* process, and the very fine papers used for small bags, which are light yet strong for their thickness, made by the *sulphite* method. The same raw material may be used for either. Other common chemical papers and paper products are those used for writing, the printing of books, cartons to hold milk and refrigerated food, and tissues of all kinds. Technical wizardry treats the basic raw material with bleaches or dyes to match every colour of the rainbow or gives it special surfaces to resist water, take ink or show a high gloss to add lustre to packages and displays.

Modern technology enables paper makers to use *any* kind of wood but some prove more satisfactory than others. The softwoods of coniferous trees hold longer and more homogeneous fibres than do the hardwoods of broadleaved trees and are therefore universally preferred. Among these coniferous trees the spruces, in the genus *Picea*, yield soft-walled fibres that collapse from relatively large tubes to form flat ribbons during the pulping process. This characteristic results in a surprisingly tough paper, derived from a relatively weak timber. Because spruce wood is pale in colour this paper needs little bleaching and is therefore cheap to produce. Hence many of the biggest paper mills are built close to major sources of spruce logs in the vast conifer forests of North America, Scandinavia and Russia. Plate 64.

The world demand for paper and allied products is now so great that in these countries around 40% of all the forests' output is used for them and only 60% as solid timber. But over the world as a whole, after allowing for the many other purposes that wood serves as fuel, fencing, simple building and other products that do not figure in international trade statistics, the proportion utilized as paper may be no more than 25%.

By further chemical treatment cellulose can be isolated for many purposes that utilize wood in virtually unrecognizable forms. One of these is rayon, that is, artificial silk, used for fibres and fabrics. Another is cellophane for light, cheap transparent wrappers. Cellulose can also become a constituent of nitro-cellulose explosives or even the basis of synthetic foods for livestock.

Chapter 20

Trees as Sources of Sugar, Rubber, Resin, Cork and Chemicals

The intricate internal chemistry of tree metabolism results in a number of exceptional products becoming available for man's use in commercial quantities. These were especially valuable in the days before the modern science of organic chemistry had developed. Though most of the substances concerned can now be manufactured synthetically, tree-based production still continues for some of them because an exact match is rarely possible or costs too much. Many of the materials can be found in small amounts in a wide variety of trees but harvesting is naturally concentrated on the most productive species. As a rule these occur in natural forests which also yield timber. Para rubber, *Hevea brasiliensis*, is a noteworthy exception. Because it is a rare tree in its jungle home, vast plantations of this South American tree have been planted in Indonesia, Malaysia and other tropical countries with rubber production as their main objective; the timber, of low value, serves only as firewood.

Tree Sugars

Maple sugar is won from the root sap of the North American sugar maple, *Acer saccharum*, by tapping the trunk during the spring sap-flow. It provides a striking demonstration of the storage of a tree's nutrients in its trunk and roots during the winter resting season. All broadleaved trees that shed their leaves are obliged to do this, having no other place to hold their reserves, but only a few justify sugar tapping. In Europe species of birch, *Betula*, and maples, *Acer*, were occasionally tapped in the past.

Effective production is limited to the time of spring thaw, around March. If maples are wounded at this time their sap flows freely under pressures generated in their root system. Tapping is done by making a small hole with a round chisel or gouge that penetrates both bark and bast to reach the sapwood. A steady flow of sugar-rich root sap then emerges and is directed by a metal spout into a cup fixed below the hole. This sap must be collected and concentrated the same day or it will ferment and turn sour. The New England or Canadian sugar tapper therefore works busily during the short season collecting the yield in buckets and carrying it, often by horse-drawn sledge, over the snow or the soft ground to his boiling shed. There the liquid is concentrated in a large metal pan, set over a wood fire, until it becomes maple syrup. It may be bottled in this form or else concentrated further until it crystallizes out as solid maple sugar, generally eaten as candy.

This seasonal trade can only be run economically as a side-line to a farm that includes a 'sugar bush' among its assets. Even so, the high cost of labour and the competition from other sources of sugar make maple sugar and syrup a luxury sweetmeat today. Harvesting is now helped by the use of plastic tubing but remains a laborious task. The Indians knew about maple sugar long before the European colonists arrived but were unable to concentrate and preserve it because they had no iron pans.

In the tropics certain palm trees yield sugar commercially in the same way. In southeast Asia the nipah palm, *Nipa fruticans*, can be tapped by incisions in its stem made near ground level and renewed daily.

The common coconut palm, *Cocos nucifera*, is a major source of a sugar-rich sap in India and the neighbouring lands. Agile tappers climb high into the crowns of tall coconuts to tap the main flower spike. This yields a copious flow of sweet liquid which is directed into an earthenware pot and carried down to the ground. After a few hours in the tropic heat this liquid has fermented to an alcoholic drink called palm wine or toddy, which is the cheap and potent daily drink of low-paid Indian workmen. Each day's harvest must be consumed that day. Any residue quickly ferments further to become a sour vinegar. A more potent spirituous liquor known as arrak can however be obtained by the prompt distillation of palm wine. So long as they are tapped for wine-making the coconut palms never ripen fruit because all their reserves are side-tracked on their way to the flower-heads.

Resins, Latex and Wound-Gums

Several curiously diverse products arise as natural protective substances that the tree makes in order to seal off wounds.

Resin

Resins are found in most coniferous trees. They occur in a wide range of tissues including wood, bast, bark, cones, seeds and leaves. They are secreted by special cells that make up continuous resin canals. If a tree is wounded or attacked by an insect the resin flows through this canal system and covers the wound, possibly engulfing the insect. The resin itself is a combination of a waxy solid called *rosin* and a volatile liquid solvent called *turpentine*. Once exposed to air the turpentine quickly evaporates leaving a hard coating of white or yellow rosin. This protects the cut surface against further attack by insects, invasion by fungal spores and water loss.

The main resin tapping regions are the southeastern United States and southwest France, along with neighbouring zones of Spain and Portugal. In America a variety of pines, such as the longleaf pine, *Pinus palustris*, are tapped, while in Europe production is concentrated on one species, the maritime pine, *P. pinaster*. Tapping is carried out in spring and early summer when the resin flows most freely under the stimulus of active growth. The tapper, armed with a very sharp chisel-like tool, cuts a slanting groove on one side of the tree, penetrating both bark and bast to slice into the sapwood beneath. Resin oozes out of resin canals in the exposed wood, flows down the groove and drips into a little pot placed beneath it. It is collected daily before it has time to solidify and each day the cut is freshened by shaving off a fresh sliver of wood. This results in a *blaze* or cut face that is gradually extended up one side of the tree. Plate 38. Sulphuric acid is sometimes applied to the cut to check congealing and stimulate resin flow.

The same tree may be tapped each season for many years by opening up fresh faces at different points. Though growth is slowed down the tree is rarely killed by this persistent wounding, and when it is finally felled it still yields sound timber.

The resin is collected in buckets and taken to a distillery where it is heated under controlled conditions. The volatile turpentine evaporates and is condensed as a separate clear liquid which is used as a solvent mainly in high-grade paints and varnishes. The waxy, amber-coloured rosin that remains is most often seen in the hands of violinists, who use it to wax their bows. But its largest commercial use is in printing inks or as a surface treatment for paper since it promotes the quick drying needed by modern high-speed printing machines.

Despite the high cost of hand collection and the dirty character of work with a sticky material, resin tapping continues because the natural products remain superior to synthetics. In America resin and its derivatives are called *naval stores*, a reminder of the days when resin and tar were used to caulk the planks of wooden ships to make them waterproof.

Para Rubber

Para rubber, the wound gum of a Brazilian tree, *Hevea brasiliensis*, is by far the most important of tree by-products today. Though rubber can be synthesized, the natural product remains competitive in price and is superior in some respects to man-made substitutes. It is secreted as a white milk-like fluid from canals that run through all parts of the tree *except* the wood. In practice tapping is carried out in the bast tissues between wood and bark where this fluid, called *latex*, exudes freely. The tapper, using a curved or straight grooved chisel, opens a slanting cut running towards a spout that leads to a cup. As with resin, he freshens the cut, in practice every two days and so extends the tapping face downwards. After a spell of alternate-day tapping, the trees are 'rested' to enable them to replenish their latex reserves, so on average they are tapped on one day in three.

Rubber tapping differs from resin tapping in that the tool must never be allowed to penetrate into the wood as that would cause awkward calloused wounds. Instead the skilled tapper stops just short of the important but wafer-thin zone of cambium cells. These obligingly start to grow a fresh layer of bast, protected by outer bark, and this enables tapping to be repeated over the same surface several years later. Tapping is never extended over more than half the tree's circumference at any one time. The trees, which grow steadily stouter, can be tapped four years after planting; after about twenty-five years in production they are felled to make way for a more vigorous fresh crop.

Tapping commences at dawn in the cool of the morning and by mid-day all the cuts have been freshened. The workers then collect the milk-like latex by pouring it from the cups into buckets and carry it to the factory. Here the latex, which consists of an emulsion of about one-third pure rubber substance in two-thirds of water, is coagulated by a surprisingly simple process. It is placed in a big acid-resistant aluminium tank and a cupful of a weak organic acid, such as tartaric acid, is added. This is stirred around and then slats of aluminium are set across the tank to split it into many thin sections. Within an hour each section of latex has solidified into a slab of white, soft material that resembles junket. The slabs are then taken out and pushed between the metal rollers of a powerful mangle. This squeezes out the water, leaving thin squashed sheets of white solid rubber. To check the growth of moulds these sheets are next smoked over a wooden fire, fuelled by logs of over-aged rubber trees, in a specially built smoke-house. After a few days smoking they become quite dry and a rich brown in colour; they are then packed in plywood chests for shipment to processing factories, usually overseas.

This *sheet rubber* is only one of several forms manufactured commercially. Another, called *crepe*, is obtained by milling larger slabs of coagulated latex into thin layers that knit together. Much latex is also concentrated in vacuum evaporators, after being made alkaline to stop coagulation, and then shipped in liquid form. These raw materials are the foundation of a large and elaborate processing industry in which rubber is compounded with sulphur, carbon and other chemicals, and possibly allied to textiles or steel mesh to make an almost endless range of products. The major world-wide use of rubber is in pneumatic tyres, a surprisingly recent invention. Less than one hundred years ago my great-uncle Robert William Edlin, constructed the world's first pneumatic tyre for its inventor, John Boyd Dunlop. Since 1888 countless millions of tyres have rolled on every kind of vehicle, including aircraft, all made possible by this remarkable exudation from a tropical jungle tree.

When first discovered in Brazil, rubber was a curiosity used for making balls and toys by the Amazon Indians. Growing world demand led to low-yield collections from scattered trees at high cost, while the Brazilians maintained a monopoly but did little to cultivate the tree. Then in 1870 an English botanist, Henry Alexander Wickham, smuggled a few plants out by steamship, cultivated them at Kew Gardens near London and then tran-shipped some to Ceylon and Malaysia. There they throve under climates like that of Brazil, were easily propagated by seed and gave rise to the enormous plantation industry that now supplies the world. Great areas of jungles were cleared to make way for the plantations. The greatest asset of this Asiatic region, however, was the presence of large numbers of skilled labourers – Indians, Chinese and Indonesians – who were ready to work for relatively low wages.

I once worked as a manager on a large Malaysian rubber estate where a thousand immigrant Tamil Indians were profitably engaged on tending some fifty square kilometres (twenty square miles) of rubber trees and harvesting their product every day of the year.

Gum Arabic

Gum arabic is a remarkable wound gum that arises from cuts made in the bark of a small leguminous tree, *Acacia senegal*, which grows in the arid regions of Arabia and northeast Africa. This tree has feathery foliage, yellow flowers like mimosa and hard flat seed pods. It bears spines on its twigs to discourage grazing beasts. The gum is gathered by nomad tribes-men, such as the Somalis, who make incisions in the bark and return to collect the gum a few weeks later. It consists of clear, white or pale yellow lumps of a crystalline substance which is readily soluble in water, so it can only be harvested in an almost rainless desert region. Gum arabic is widely used as an adhesive, for example, on stamps and envelopes, as an ingredient in many chemical formulations and also as a glaze on confectionery since it is harmless and perfectly edible.

Tanbark and Cork

Leather is made by steeping the hides of animals in a solution of tannins, which are complex organic compounds found in the wood, bark, leaves and seed pods of a wide variety of trees. The tannins form chemical bonds with the skin tissues and halt their decay. They also maintain their flexibility. Leathers range from delicate tissues used to make purses or clothing to tough ones used as footwear or belting, but all must be tanned during their manufacture.

Many sources of vegetable tannins have been exploited and pure chemicals are nowadays extensively used. But the inner bark of trees was for long the most useful practical source and it still remains a major one. Leading tanbark trees include eastern hemlock, *Tsuga canadensis*, in North America, and wattle, *Acacia mearnsii*, introduced from Australia to South Africa, where it is grown in plantations to yield both bark and mine props. Oaks, of the genus *Quercus*, are the main traditional sources over most of Europe, Asia and North America.

Tanbark is always harvested from trees that have been felled or ones that will be cut down in the near future as its removal around the whole circumference of a stem kills that stem through the removal of the bast and the exposure of the cambium. A traditional practice was the peeling of large pieces of bark, from standing oaks due for felling, in the spring when rapid sap-flow and cambial division made separation easy. The trees were then cut down and bark removed from the branches with the aid of simple tools called *barking spades*. Because the tannins are soluble the slabs of bark were always stacked with their outer surface uppermost. This kept each inner surface, rich in tannin, dry during rainstorms until the bark could be carted to the tanneries.

Tanbark was so valuable in the economic terms of the period that large landowners maintained big oak coppices. They cut, say, one-twentieth of the area every year and allowed the cut-over stumps twenty years to grow again. This gave the owners steady yearly incomes.

The evergreen cork oak, *Quercus suber*, which grows in Spain, Portugal, southern France and North Africa, develops an exceptionally thick bark that restricts the loss of water from its trunk, during hot dry summers, to the absolute minimum. On every other kind of tree, any artificial separation of bark takes place at the main or *wood cambium*. Any all-round cut therefore kills the tree because the conductive channels through the bast, which lies between bark and wood cambium, are broken.

The cork oak is unique in that, if the separation is made in the summer, the bark breaks away at its *bark cambium*. This leaves the bast tissues below unharmed and moreover the cork cambium continues active and produces a fresh protective coating of bark. This makes possible the repeated harvesting of cork from the same trees every twelve years or so throughout the oak's life span of a century or more.

The first harvest consists of a rough, open-textured material called *virgin cork*, which is suitable only for such rough uses as insulation in refrigerators, floats for fishing nets, packing material for grapes or the coarser forms of flooring. Subsequent harvests give the smooth, fine-textured high-quality mature cork that is used for bottle stoppers and high-grade floor tiles. The harvesting is done with long curved knives that split off large curved slabs of cork which are then transported to factories. It exposes bright orange-brown faces on the tree trunks that make a stark contrast with the blackish-grey outer bark elsewhere.

Because the living tissues of the tree trunk must breathe, cork holds numerous pores or lenticels with dark brown margins which allow through passage of air from the outside of the bark to the bast and wood. In order to make an effective bottle stopper the cork must be cut in such a way that these pores run *across* the neck of the bottle and not up and down it. Look at any bottle cork and you will find that this is so. The pores run from one glass face to another. The escape of water vapour and also of highly volatile alcoholic spirits is stopped by the main body of impermeable tissue that extends, without any through passage, from the top to the bottom of the cork.

Yet because this tissue is made up of air-filled cells with waterproof walls it is possible to compress the cork and so ensure a tight fit all round. The compressed, trapped air ensures a tight fit that persists indefinitely until the cork is withdrawn and automatically expands. The presence of enclosed air also accounts for cork's low density, which enables it to be used for net floats and life jackets, and also for its low heat conductivity, which makes it an excellent insulator against either heat or cold. It is also waterproof and remains undamaged by long immersion in sea water.

Other Bark Products

The inner layers of the barks of certain trees, and their associated bast tissues, are rich in potent chemicals. Before the synthetic industry developed many of them featured in the doctor's medicine chest and a few survive today. The most important is the drug quinine, an invaluable antidote to malaria which is obtained from the bark of a small tree called *Cinchona ledgeriana*, native to the highlands of Peru and Ecuador. Its value was realized by the Indians from earliest times and its employment by

Christian missionaries under the name of 'Jesuits' bark' dates back to the seventeenth century. But it was not until 1854 that a British trader, Charles Ledger, was able to smuggle out seeds for propagation. Subsequently quinine was grown as a commercial plantation crop in Indonesia and became available world-wide as a dependable treatment for malaria, a mosquito-borne disease prevalent in all tropical countries.

Some barks are used as spices, the most familiar example being cinnamon, obtained from the small tree *Cinnamonum zeylanicum*, cultivated in Sri Lanka.

Bark itself has no nutritive value and the bast layers beneath it only occasionally attract animals, such as squirrels which are equipped with teeth sharp enough to reach it. But it has been used as a last resource in times of famine. Aeneas Sylvius, who travelled through Scotland in about 1430 AD, recorded that 'the Scots of the wooded region sometimes eat the bark of trees (probably pines) for food.'

A few barks are toxic, a common example being those of yew trees, *Taxus baccata*, *T. brevifolia* and allied species. Others yield dyes: for instance, the inner bark of common alder, *Alnus glandulosa*, will dye wool tawny red, but the juice pressed out of its catkins dyes cloth green. Finally, much pulverised bark from trees of many kinds, is nowadays used as a mulch or rooting medium in horticulture.

Leaf Products

The leaves of a few trees are important locally and even in international trade as sources of materials or drugs not readily manufactured by other means. One common though little recorded use is as food wrappers. Peasants in most tropical lands commonly take their merchandise to market in large tree leaves, which cost nothing, rather than expensive paper bags.

Large tough leaves such as those of broadleaved palms provide a useful constructional material under hot climates. When fixed in an overlapping pattern over a wooden framework they make adequate walls or surprisingly waterproof roofs, known in Malaysia as *attap*.

The carnauba palm, *Copernicia cerifera*, native to Brazil, is the source of the valuable carnauba wax used in shoe polishes, furniture polishes and other waterproof surface coatings that provide a high gloss. This palm, which lives in an arid climate, develops a thick waxy leaf coating that resists water loss whilst still allowing the leaf to breathe. This wax is harvested by cutting off the leaves and then scraping the waxy coating from their surfaces.

Eucalyptus oil, an effective remedy against coughs and colds, is obtained

257

by distilling large quantities of eucalyptus leaves. The heat of the still causes the volatile oil to escape from the cells that secrete it and the resulting vapour is then condensed as a clear liquid. Though all species of *Eucalyptus* originate in Australia the industry is concentrated in India where labour costs are lower.

Leaves of certain trees provide fodder for livestock and form an important element of some peasant farming economies. Elm leaves, *Ulmus* species, are used to nourish goats in temperate countries, as are the leaves of certain *Acacia* species in the tropics.

The fallen leaves of deciduous broadleaved trees are a major source of litter for bedding livestock under farming economies that yield little straw. A classic example is the use of beech, *Fagus sylvatica*, in central Europe. Diligent peasants gathered this free bedding material so assiduously that, over the centuries, the fertility of the beechwood soil diminished. Nutrients removed in the leaves stayed on the farm and never found their way back to the forest.

Timber for Fuel and Charcoal

The use of wood as fuel for heating and cooking dates back to the earliest days of man's conquest of his environment. It remains a main benefit from the forest in all the less developed countries even today. The steam engine readily converts firewood into the energy of motion and in the past many railways and even steamboats ran cheaply on local supplies of wood fuel. Wood was also widely used for firing pottery and bricks in simple kilns.

Charcoal, though little used today, was historically the key substance that enabled man to master metals. If an ore of copper, tin or iron is heated by a fire of wood or coal, the temperatures reached are too low for any chemical change to result. This is due to the presence of volatile hydro-carbons in the fuel as well as the element carbon. If however the volatile carbons are first removed, an almost pure carbon fuel is obtained which will only burn at a much higher temperature. If burning carbon comes into contact with a metallic ore it removes oxygen from that ore, so that the pure metal remains.

Today this process is usually effected by using coke, obtained by heating coal in a closed metal vessel until its volatile gases have been driven off. But this is a recent method that only became practical in the eighteenth century. Before that all metals were smelted with wood charcoal.

The main problem in charring wood to get charcoal is to prevent it all burning away completely. In the age-old traditional method this is achieved in an ingenious way. Short billets of wood are piled around a central upright stake until a domed structure, about five metres (15 feet) across and two metres (six feet) high, results. The wood is then covered with straw, as a clean separation layer, and finally with earth, usually in the form of square-cut blocks or sods. This seals off the wood from free air access, and permits control of the burning.

When all is ready the fire is started by removing the central stake and dropping burning wood down the resulting hole, to reach the base of the stack at its centre. This burning wood ignites the central mass of logs but as air is limited they char instead of burning freely. The smouldering fire gradually spreads through the whole mass of wood until it has all been converted into black charcoal. The burner then halts the process by sealing off the air channel at the top of the stack with a sod of turf or a tile. The stack must then be left for two days to cool down before it can be safely opened. If opened too soon it will burst into flame and everything will be lost.

In practice each burner works a set of at least three stacks. Whilst he is building one he is watching another 'burn' and waiting for a third to cool down. All the time he must live beside these stacks, out in the woods, as any mishap – such as a strong wind fanning his controlled fire in the middle of the night – will lead to the loss of a whole stack. A modern, simpler method employs a large round metal cylinder, with a lid and stove-pipes to control air flow, in place of the earth-covered kiln.

Charcoal is almost pure carbon, holding only a small proportion of mineral ash. It preserves in a remarkable way the cellular pattern of the original wood. It is possible to identify the tree species that produced it from a small fragment of charcoal that escaped burning, for example, on the hearth of a prehistoric settlement, possibly 3,000 years ago.

Besides its value as a reducing agent for metals, charcoal has many applications in chemical industry. It is used as a purifying agent for liquids and gases, in paints and pigments and as an aid to digestion in dog biscuits! It is an essential constituent, along with sulphur and saltpetre, in traditional gunpowder. This was essential to warfare over several centuries and is still employed for mine blasting.

Wood Distillates

Under the simple methods of charcoal production just described all the volatile constituents of the wood are lost to the atmosphere. But if charcoal is made by heating wood in an enclosed kiln at a wood distillation factory these substances can be collected in a still by cooling the vapours that are driven off. They include creosote, a useful wood preservative, and acetone, which is a valuable chemical employed in dyes, paints and solvents. The industry flourished for over a century from 1850 onwards and numerous plants were set up near cheap sources of wood in many countries. But competition from cheaper and more plentiful sources of hydrocarbon-based chemicals, namely coal and oil, have caused its decline.

Index

Where appropriate, the first entry shows each text figure number, linked to the page on which it appears. Main text references follow. Numbers *in italics* refer to photographs on the plates.